Roster of War of 1812 Southside Virginia

James L. Douthat

Heritage Books
2024

HERITAGE BOOKS

AN IMPRINT OF HERITAGE BOOKS, INC.

Books, CDs, and more—Worldwide

For our listing of thousands of titles see our website
at
www.HeritageBooks.com

A Facsimile Reprint
Published 2024 by
HERITAGE BOOKS, INC.
Publishing Division
5810 Ruatan Street
Berwyn Heights, MD 20740

Originally published c1814, 2007

International Standard Book Number
Paperbound: 978-0-7884-7774-4

MUSTER ROLL

Of the Field and Staff Officers of the First Regiment and First Brigade, Virginia Militia, commanded by General William Chamberlayne, in the Service of the United States during the year 1814.

NAMES.	RANK.	TIME OF SERVICE.		REMARKS.
		Months.	Days.	
Wm. Chamberlayne,	General,	3	3	
James Byrne,	Colonel,	3		
James Scott,	Lt. Colonel,	3		
Philemon Holcombe,	"	–	10	
Harwood Jones,	Major,	3		
Joseph G. Wilder,	"	3		
Saml. T. Winston,	Brig. Major,	3	3	
Wm. Armistead,	Aid de Camp,	3	3	
Timothy Thorp,	Adjutant,	3		
John Nicholas,	"	–	10	
Edmond C. Goodwin,	"	–	27	
Henry Curtis,	Surgeon,	–	11	
David Walker,	"	3		
James Henderson,	"	–	10	
——— Morgan,	Surg. Mate,	–	7	
John Bragg,	"	3		
Nicholas Scherer,	"	–	11	
John H. Brown,	Qr. Master,	3		
Nicholas Mills,	B. Q. Master,	3	3	
John Holcombe,	Qr. Master,	–	9	
Spencer Wooldridge,	For. Master,	3	3	
Andrew Moore,	B. W. Master,	2	22	
Peter F. Barrow,	"	3	3	
Archibald Baugh,	Pay Master,	3		
Thomas G. Tinsley,	"	–	–	Under arrest.
James Whitelaw,	"			
Ralph Wingfield,	Serg. Major,	–	5	
Joseph Caldwell,	"	3		
Henry Ligon,	"	–	6	
Armistead T. Townes,	Q. M. Serg't,	–	9	
Benjamin Walker,	"	3		

PAY ROLL

Of the Field and Staff Officers of the First Regiment, First Brigade of Virginia, in the Service of the United States, commanded by Col. Wm. Trueheart, at Camp Bottom's Bridge, under the command of Brigadier-General William Chamberlayne, from 22d August to 16th November 1814.

NAMES.	RANK.	*Time of Service.*		REMARKS.
		Months.	Days.	
William Trueheart,	Lieut. Col.,	2	25	
Christopher Tompkins,	Major,	2	25	
Henry Tabb,	Major,	2	18	
Hudson M. Wingfield,	Adjutant,	1	28	
Charles Morris,	Surgeon,	2	14	
Henry Curtis,	S. Mate,	1	28	
Wm. R. McCaw,	"	2	14	
James P. Ragland,	Q. Master,	1	1	
Ralph Wingfield,	"	1	21	
Reuben Austin,	Q. M. Serg't,	1	21	
Ralph Wingfield,	"	1	21	
James Muse,	Serg't Major,	1	21	

PAY ROLL

Of Captain Samuel V. Allen's Company, of the First Regiment of Virginia Militia, Amelia County, of the "Flying Camp," commanded by Col. James McDowell, (Camp Holly,) from 29th June to 4th October 1813.

NAMES.	RANK.	Time of Service.		REMARKS.
		Months.	Days.	
Samuel V. Allen,	Captain,	3	5	
William S. Venable,	Lieutenant,	3		
Henry E. Watkins,	"	3		
Sam'l L. Lockett,	Cornet,	3		
Archer Fuqua,	1st Sergeant,	3		
Pugh W. Price,	2d "	3		
Peyton Randolph,	3d "	3		
Booker Foster,	4th "	3		
James J. Foster,	1st Corporal,	3		
Henry N. Watkins,	2d "	3		
Lewis Farley,	3d "	3	–	Or Lewellyn.
Wm. B. Booker,	4th "	1	13	
Obediah Morton,	4th "	3	5	
Peter Grigg,	–	3	5	
Edward Dillon,	Trumpeter,	3	5	
Francis Walthall,	Saddler,	3	5	
Leonard Anderson,	Private,	1	5	
Merit B. Allen,	"	3	5	
Thomas Anderson,	"	3	5	
James R. Allen,	"	1	7	
Archer Borum,	"	3	5	
Jonathan Christian,	"	2		
John Deshayer,	"	3	5	
James Deshayer,	"	3	5	
Thomas Ellington,	"	3	5	
Stith Farley,	"	3	5	
George Foster,	"	3	5	
William Fleming,	"	3	5	
Paschal Foulkes,	"	3	5	
Joseph Goode,	"	3	5	
John Holcombe,	"	3	5	
Thomas E. Haskins,	"	3	5	
Benjamin Haskins,	"	3	5	
Simon Hughes,	"	3	5	
Joel W. Jones,	"	3	5	
John Nash,	"	3	5	
Thomas L. Nicholas,	"	1	23	
Ben. H. Price,	"	3	5	
William Price,	"	3	5	
Houston Poe,	"	3	5	Or Austin.
Hugh Ritchie,	"	3	5	
Josiah M. Rice,	"	3	5	
William Scott,	"	3	5	
Wm. B. Smith,	"	1	25	
Henry H. Vaughan,	"	3	5	
Samuel Venable,	"	3	5	
John H. Venable,	"	3	5	
Geo. B. Woodson,	"	3	5	
Blake W. Woodson,	"	3	5	Or Blake B.
Thomas Wilburne,	"	3	5	
Samuel Watson,	"	3	5	
Sam'l J. Wortham,	"	3	5	
James D. Wood,	"	3	5	

PAY ROLL

Of a Company of Light Infantry and Infantry of the Line, commanded by Capt. Green Blanton, of the First Regiment of Virginia Militia, in the Service of the United States, from the 30th August to the 30th November 1814, both days inclusive.

NAMES.	RANK.	Time of Service. Months.	Days.	REMARKS.
Green Blanton,	Captain,	3	6	
William Evans,	Lieutenant,	3	6	
William Harwell,	"	2		
George Rogers,	Ensign,	3	6	
Abner Newman,	"	3	6	
Martin Puckett,	Sergeant,	3	6	
William Blanton,	"	3	6	
William King,	"	3	6	
Robertson Ezell,	"	3	6	
Thomas Ryland,	"	3	6	
Thomas Walker,	Corporal,	3	6	
Edward Walker,	"	3	6	
John Barron,	"	3	6	
William Johnson,	"	3	6	
Daniel Pegram,	Q. M. Serg't,	3	2	
John Rottenbury,	Drummer,	3	6	
John Allgood,	Private,	1	26	
Joseph Alfin,	"	3	6	
Sylv. Blankinship,	"	3	6	
John Burnett,	"	3	6	
Edmund Burton,	"	3	6	
Thomas Bennett,	"	3	6	
Jones Burton,	"	3	6	
James H. Berry,	"	3	6	
Thomas Brame,	"	3	6	
Samuel Bennett,	"	1	10	
William Bailey,	"	3	6	
Abner Bates,	"	3	6	
Abraham Bailey,	"	2	3	
Jeremiah Brown,	"	3	6	
Grief Carrol,	"	3	6	
Isaac Carrol,	"	3	6	
Bartlett Crowder,	"	3	6	
John Curtis,	"	3	6	
Thomas Cleaton,	"	3	6	
William Cleaton,	"	1	6	
Peter Coleman,	"	3	6	
Bartlet Cheatham,	"	3	6	
William Cook,	"	3	6	
Thomas Crafton, jr.,	"	3	6	
Orren Davis,	"	3	6	
Peter Davis,	"	3	6	
Abraham Dunnivant,	"	3	6	
Francis Dedman,	"	3	6	
Tilman Elder,	"	3	6	
Elijah Ellington,	"	2	26	
Matthew Evans,	"	3	6	
Robt. S. Edmunson,	"	3	6	
John Fowler,	"	3	6	
Berry Fergusson,	"	3	6	
Sterling Fowler,	"	3	6	
Asa George,	"	3	6	
William Gualtney,	"	3	6	
Benja. Gualtney,	"	3	6	

NAMES.	RANK.	Time of Service.		REMARKS.
		Months.	Days.	
Wm. Gallivan, - -	Private,	3	6	
George Hudson, - -	"	3	6	
Richard Hudson, - -	"	3	6	
James Hargrove, - -	"	3	6	
Leonard Hardwick, - -	"	3	6	
Samuel Insio, - -	"	3	6	
Collin Jarvis, - -	"	3	6	
Thomas Johnson, - -	"	3	6	
Benj'n Jackson, - -	"	3	6	
Jacob Johnson, - -	"	3	6	
John King, - -	"	3	6	
John Lambert, - -	"	3	6	
Edmund Lambert, - -	"	3	6	
James Lambert, - -	"	3	6	
James Mekenny, - -	"	3	8	
Daniel Morris, - -	"	3	6	
Joel Mabry, - -	"	3	6	
Joshua Mabry, - -	"	3	6	
John Marshall, - -	"	2	26	
William Morgan, - -	"	3	6	
Washington McCaulin, -	"	3	6	
Pleasant Moon, - -	"	3	6	
James S. Nance, - -	"	3	6	
Sterling Nicholson, - -	"	3	6	
Daniel Nanny, - -	"	2	9	
Walter Pennington, - -	"	3	6	
William Pulley, - -	"	3	6	
James Palmor, - -	"	3	6	
Allan Raney, - -	"	3	6	
Hunley Ryland, - -	"	3	6	
Daniel Rottenbury, - -	"	3	6	
Harrison M. Ryland, - -	"	3	6	
Robt. Singleton, - -	"	3	6	
Green Stephens, - -	"	3	6	
Sterling Smith, - -	"	1	25	
Jesse Saunders, - -	"	3	6	
James Smith, - -	"	3	6	
William Thompson, - -	"	3	6	
Goodwin Taylor, sen., -	"	3	6	
Goodwin Taylor, jr., - -	"	3	6	
Thomas Tucker, - -	"	3	6	
David Towns, - -	"	3	6	
Joseph Taylor, - -	"	3	6	
Manoah Vincent, - -	"	3	6	
Green Worsham, - -	"	3	6	
Reuben Wright, - -	"	3	6	
Daniel Wall, - -	"	3	6	
Henry Wall, - -	"	3	6	
Archibald Wilson, - -	"	1	29	
Joshua Wright, - -	"	3	6	
Jonathan Williams, - -	"	1	21	
Thomas Wall, - -	"	3	6	
William Young, - -	"	3	6	

MUSTER ROLL

Of Captain Charles H. Braxton's Company of Cavalry, attached to the First Regiment, commanded by Lieutenant Colonel Phil. Holcomb, in the Service of the State of Virginia, from 3rd to 13th September, 1814.

NAMES.	RANK.	TIME OF SERVICE.		REMARKS.
		Months.	Days.	
Charles H. Braxton,	Captain,	–	11	
William H. Spiller,	1st Lieutenant,	–	11	
Lodwick Slaughter,	2d "	–	11	
John Skyim,	Cornet,	–	11	
Herbert A. Clairborne,	Sergeant,	–	11	
John Crafton,	"	–	11	
Richard S. Taylor,	"	–	11	
Collin C. Spiller,	"	–	11	
William Newman,	Corporal,	–	11	
Warner L. Womley,	"	–	11	
Reubin Crouch,	"	–	11	
Edward Pollard,	"	–	11	
Dudly Armstrong,	Private,	–	7	
Thos. Anchews,	"	–	11	
Samuel Banass,	"	–	11	
John W. Baylor,	"	–	3	
Isaac Cock,	"	–	11	
John Castlen,	"	–	11	
Drewby Dugen,	"	–	11	
John B. Foster,	"	–	11	
Larkin Garrett,	"	–	11	
Robert Johnson,	"	–	11	
Warren Lipscomb,	"	–	11	
Christopher Lipscomb,	"	–	4	
John C. Pollard,	"	–	7	
William Powell,	"	–	6	
Thomas J. Powell,	"	–	6	
John B. Richardson,	"	–	11	
Joseph Row,	"	–	11	
Geo. Simpkins,	"	–	11	
Benjamin C. Spiller,	"	–	11	
Robert Simpkins,	"	–	11	
Warner Shackelford,	"	–	11	
John B. Stuart,	"	–	11	
John H. Taliafero,	"	–	11	
Robert Taliafero,	"	–	11	
W. W. F. Tompkins,	"	–	11	
William W. Timberlake,	"	–	11	
Nathaniel Trumucr,	"	–	4	Appointed wagon master on 6th.
John Woody,	"	–	11	
John H. Walker,	"	–	11	

Captain William Grigg's Company—First Regiment.

NAMES.	RANK.	TIME OF SERVICE.		REMARKS.
		Months.	Days.	
Benjamin Walker,	Sergeant,	–	16	
Delbridge Dennison,	Private,	–	15	

(For rest of this company, see publication of Pay Rolls.)

MUSTER ROLL

Of Captain Charles Betts' Troop of Cavalry, from the First Regiment, in the Service of the United States, under the orders of the Deputy Adjutant General of the State of Virginia, from the 31st August to the 12th September, 1814.

NAMES.	RANK.	TIME OF SERVICE.		REMARKS.
		Months.	Days.	
Charles Betts, - -	Captain,	–	13	
John Bigger, - -	1st Lieutenant,	–	13	
Edmund Hardy, - -	2d "	–	13	
John W. Scott, - -	Cornet,	–	13	
John Buford, - -	1st Sergeant,	–	13	
Joseph A. Watson, - -	2d "	–	13	
Gillie M. Bacon, - -	3d "	–	13	
Benjamin Oliver, - -	4th "	–	13	
John L. Williams, - -	1st Corporal,	–	13	
Joseph Williamson, - -	2d "	–	13	
John Riggins, - -	3d "	–	13	
John Norvell, - -	4th "	–	13	
Edward M. Jones, - -	R. Master,	–	13	
George Hatchell, - -	Qr. Master,	–	13	
Thomas Chambers, - -	D. Q. Master,	–	13	
William Brown, - -	Sw'd Master,	–	13	
Henry S. Ellis, - -	Farrier,	–	13	
John W. Rogers, - -	B. Smith,	–	13	
James Anderson, - -	Private,	–	13	
Benj'n Alexander, - -	"	–	13	
David Allmonds, - -	"	–	13	
Boston Betts, - -	"	–	13	
Richard Boran, - -	"	–	13	
Richard C. Bacon, - -	"	–	13	
John Billups, - -	"	–	13	
John Boswell, - -	"	–	13	
Thomas Batte, - -	"	–	13	
John Brown, - -	"	–	13	
James Brown, - -	"	–	13	
Anderson Bagley; - -	"	–	13	
Richard Bragg, - -	"	–	13	
Hamblin Cole, - -	"	–	13	
William Clarke, - -	"	–	13	
Field Clarke, - -	"	–	13	
Samuel Cary, - -	"	–	13	
Howell Crowder, - -	"	–	13	
Edw'd R. Chambers, -	"	–	13	
Henry P. Crenshaw, -	"	–	13	
Theophilus Denten, - -	"	–	13	
Bowler Dobbyns, - -	"	–	13	
Joseph Dupree, - -	"	–	13	
Rich'd C. Ellis, - -	"	–	13	
Benj. Edmondson, - -	"	–	13	
Hezekiah Freeman, - -	"	–	13	
William C. Fowlkes, -	"	–	13	
William J. Fowlkes, - -	"	–	13	
Thomas Fowlkes, - -	"	–	13	

NAMES.	RANK.	TIME OF SERVICE.		REMARKS.
		Months.	Days.	
Robert Garland,	Private,	–	13	
William R. Geers,	"	–	13	
Leonard Goodwin,	"	–	13	
Benj'n Gwatney,	"	–	13	
Isaiah Hawkins,	"	–	13	
Haynie Hatchell,	"	–	13	
John Hazlewood,	"	–	13	
Eaton Hudson,	"	–	13	
Valentine Hudson,	"	–	13	
Irby Hudson,	"	–	13	
Munford Hunt,	"	–	13	
Edmund Irby,	"	–	13	
Thomas Jorden,	"	–	13	
Edward Jorden,	"	–	13	
James Jorden,	"	–	13	
Branch Jorden,	"	–	13	
John Jorden,	"	–	13	
Benj'n W. Johnston,	"	–	13	
James Jennings,	"	–	13	
Thomas Knight,	"	–	13	
John Lipford,	"	–	13	
Burnett Lester,	"	–	13	
Jeremiah Morgan,	"	–	13	
Samuel B. Morgan,	"	–	13	
Reuben Morgan,	"	–	13	
Jesse Moon,	"	–	13	
Martin Peters,	"	–	13	
Jesse Pilkinton,	"	–	13	
John Ogburne,	"	–	13	
Richard L. Smithson,	"	–	13	
Jas. A. Smithson,	"	–	13	
Ralph Stegall,	"	–	13	
Wiltshire Tucker,	"	–	13	
George Tucker,	"	–	13	
Robt. Thompson,	"	–	13	
Bassfield Winn,	"	–	13	
Jonathan P. Winn,	"	–	13	
Josiah Wilson,	"	–	13	
Benjamin Wyatt,	"	–	13	
William Williams,	"	–	13	
Rich'd Williams,	"	–	13	
John J. Wells,	"	–	13	
Rowland Whitworth,	"	–	13	

PAY ROLL

Of Captain William Byrd Chamberlayne's Company of Virginia Militia, in the Service of the United States, at Camp Bottom's Bridge, attached to the First Brigade, commanded by Lieut. Col. Trueheart, from 28th August to 1st December 1814.

NAMES.	RANK.	Time of Service.		REMARKS.
		Months.	Days.	
Wm. B. Chamberlayne,	Captain,	3	3	
Edwin Burton,	Lieutenant,	3	3	
Walthall Hatcher,	"	3	3	
John Warburton,	Ensign,	3	3	
James Whitelaw,	"	3	3	
Lewis C. Tyler,	Ord. Serg't,	1	3	
Thomas Courtney,	Q. M. Serg't,	1	–	Substituted.
Martin Burton,	Ord. Serg't,	3	3	
James Quarles,	Q. M. Serg't,	3	3	
John L Turner,	Sergeant,	3	3	
David Tommerson,	"	3	3	
John L. Dandridge,	"	1	–	Substituted.
Caleb David,	"	3	3	
Thomas Jennings,	"	3	3	
Henry Philips,	Corporal,	3	3	
David Elmore,	"	3	3	
Williamson Roach,	"	3	3	
Archer Henley,	"	3	3	
Edmund H. West,	"	3	3	
Richard Clarke,	"	3	3	
Wm. W. Richardson,	"	3	3	
Elisha Garrett,	"	3	3	
John Fandrie,	Fifer,	3	3	
Joseph Eubank,	Drummer,	3	3	
Dorris Doyle,	"	1	5	
David Alley,	Private,	3	3	
William Alley,	"	3	3	
John Austin,	"	3	3	
Isham Allen,	"	1	24	Sub. for Wm. Winston.
Royall Blackburn,	"	3	3	
William P. Bowles,	"	3	3	
Thomas Bennett,	"	2	26	
John Blackburn,	"	3	3	
Claiborne Bourne,	"	3	3	
William Berry,	"	3	3	
Jno. D. G. Brown,	"	1	–	Substituted.
Edmund Bowles,	"	2	26	
Robert Cornet,	"	3	3	
Lyddall Cornet,	"	3	3	
Thomas Duke,	"	3	3	
Benjamin Duval,	"	3	3	
James Ellis,	"	3	3	
George Ellis,	"	3	3	
William Ellis,	"	2	19	
Elisha Ellis,	"	1	20	Sub. for Wm. Ellis.
Martin Ford,	"	3	3	
Zachariah Ford,	"	3	3	
Reuben Ford,	"	3	3	
Simeon Ford,	"	3	3	
Smith Fandrie,	"	2	3	Sub. for J. Dandridge.
William Ford,	"	2	3	" " S. Pointer.
Dandridge Garrett,	"	3	3	
Richard Gregory,	"	1	–	Substituted.
James Griffin,	"	3	3	

NAMES.	RANK.	Time of Service.		REMARKS.
		Months.	Days.	
James Grinstead, - -	Private,	3	3	
Joseph Green, - -	"	3	3	
Thomas Goode, - -	"	3	3	
Garland Higgason, - -	"	3	3	
Aaron Hubbard, - -	"	3	3	
William Jennings, - -	"	2	6	
David Jennings, - -	"	3	3	
Isham Jennings, - -	"	3	3	
Allen Jennings, - -	"	3	3	
George King, - -	"	1	–	Sub. for W. Jennings.
Wilson Kelley, - -	"	3	3	Substituted.
George Kelley, - -	"	3	7	
John Lawrence, - -	"	3	3	
David Melton, - -	"	3	3	
John Melton, - -	"	3	3	
John Miller, - -	"	3	3	
William Monk, - -	"	3	3	
William M. Miles, - -	"	2	26	Sub. by G. Kelly.
Joseph P. Owen, - -	"	–	7	" by T. Bennett.
David Powers, - -	"	3	3	
Spencer Padgett, - -	"	3	3	
Robert Potter, - -	"	3	3	
Sam'l Poimer, - -	"	1	–	Substituted.
John Shipman, - -	"	1	–	Transferred to U. S. service.
Wilson Staples, - -	"	3	3	
David A. Sheppard, - -	"	3	3	
Barton Smoot, - -	"	3	3	
Josiah Smoot, - -	"	3	3	
Thomas Smith, - -	"	3	3	
William Tyree, - -	"	1	24	
Allen Tyler, - -	"	3	3	
Thomas Turner, - -	"	2	19	
John Toler, - -	"	1	10	Discharged.
John Thomas, - -	"	3	3	
William Vaughan, - -	"	2	24	Sub. J. D. G. Brown.
Timothy Vaughan, - -	"	2	24	" Thos. Courtney.
John Williamson, - -	"	3	3	
Edmund West, - -	"	3	3	
Wm. W. Weymouth, - -	"	3	3	
William Winston, - -	"	2	–	Sub. by Isham Allen.
John Walton, - -	"	3	3	Or Joseph.

MUSTER ROLL

Of Captain William Cock's Troop of Cavalry of the First Regiment, Virginia Militia, in the County of Campbell, called into actual Service under the general orders of the 26th August, from 30th August to 20th September, in the year 1814.

NAMES.	RANK.	TIME OF SERVICE.		REMARKS.
		Months.	Days.	
William Cock,	Captain,	–	5	
Thomas Hunter,	Lieutenant,	–	11	
Richard Jones,	Ensign,	–	21	
John Rosser,	Sergeant,	–	21	
William W. Williams,	"	–	21	
William Hunter,	"	–	21	
Hillroy Talbot,	"	–	21	
Charles Martin,	Corporal,	–	21	
Thomas Williams,	"	–	21	
Thomas Matthews,	"	–	21	
Thomas Hamlet,	"	–	21	
Alexander Barker,	Private,	–	21	Sub. for Jas. Shannon.
John Cock,	"	–	21	
Thomas Crawford,	"	–	21	
William T. Cobbs,	"	–	21	
Thomas A. Cobbs,	"	–	21	
Simeon Cobbs,	"	–	21	
Thomas Cobbs,	"	–	21	
William W. Cobbs,	"	–	21	
Thomas S. Cheatham,	"	–	21	
Charles Depriest,	"	–	21	Sub. for Wm. Franklin.
James Daniel,	"	–	21	
Josiah Daniel,	"	–	21	
Willis D. Ellett,	"	–	21	
Isaac Foster,	"	–	21	
Larkin Foster,	"			
Michael Hubberd,	"	–	21	
Alfred Hunter,	"	–	21	Sub. for Wm. Jones.
John Hunter,	"	–	21	Sub. for Ro. Hunt.
John M. Jones,	"	–	21	
William F. Jones,	"	–	21	Sub. for Wm. Foster.
Talbot Jones,	"	–	21	Sub. for Jas. Jones.
Jesse Jones,	"	–	21	
William Jones,	"	–	21	
Abraham Irvine,	"	–	21	
Joseph Irvine,	"	–	21	
Asa Jones,	"	–	21	
James H. Irvine,	"	–	21	
Samuel Kitchen,	"	–	21	
Pleasant Kay,	"	–	21	
Michael Leason,	"	–	21	
William Lewis,	"	–	21	Sub. for Wm. Hannah.
Thomas Luster,	"	–	21	
James Maxey,	"	–	21	
Burwell Mason,	"	–	21	Sub. for John Wood.
David McKenny,	"	–	21	Sub. for Pred. Moore.
Luke Matthews,	"	–	21	Sub. for Wm. Hamlet.
Lewis D. Poindexter,	Private,	–	21	
David Robertson,	"	–	21	
Pleasant Rosser,	"	–	21	
James Reynolds,	"	–	21	
Jesse Rosser,	"	–	21	
William Rosser,	"	–	21	
John Shannon,	"	–	21	
George J. Stoball,	"	–	21	
Richmond Tatum,	"	–	21	
Merit Talbott,	"	–	21	
John Taiddie,	"	–	21	
Pleasant Talbot,	"	–	21	
Allen Talbot,	"	–	21	
William Vaughan,	"	–	21	

PAY ROLL

Of a Company of Infantry under the command of Capt. Richard Daly, of First Regiment, in the Service of the United States or State of Virginia, commanded by Lieut. Col. James Byrne, from 1st September 1814 until 30th November 1814.

NAMES.	RANK.	Time of Service.		REMARKS.
		Months.	Days.	
Dabney Collier,	Captain,	1		
Richard Daly,	"	2	4	
Hezekiah Yancey,	1st Lieutenant,	3	6	
Peter Overby,	"	3	6	
Thomas P. Pettis,	Ensign,	3	6	
Samuel S. Bugg,	"	2	24	
Edmunds Eldridge,	1st Sergeant,	3	6	
Pleasant Crew,	"	3	6	
John Cox,	"	3	6	
Freeman Weatherford,	"	3	6	
Edward Smith,	"	3	6	
Jackson M. Yancey,	Q. M. S.,	3	6	
George Jackson,	Corporal,	3	6	
James Wynne,	"	3	6	
Chastain Claybrook,	"	3	6	
Abraham Talley,	"	3	6	
James Jones,	Fifer,	3	6	
Bartlett Tillotson,	Drummer,	3	6	
Edmund Arrington,	Private,	3	6	
James M. Averett,	"	1	27	
William Averett,	"	3	6	
Richard Burnes,	"	3	6	
William Banks,	"	3	6	
Elijah Bowen,	"	3	6	
Aurelius Bowen,	"	3	6	
Mabry Bowen,	"	3	6	
Abraham Bridgwater,	"	3	6	
John P. Beasly,	"	3	6	
Henry Brame,	"	3	6	
Walter Brame,	"	3	6	
John Butler,	"	3	6	
John Blanks,	"	3	6	
Asa Certain,	"	3	6	
William Clark,	"	3	6	
William Culbreath,	"	3	6	
Thomas Culbreath,	"	3	6	
Joel Chandler,	"	3	6	
Benjamin Collier,	"	3	6	
William Childree,	"	3	6	
John Dunivant,	"	3	6	
David Dunn,	"	3	6	
William Deadman,	"	3	6	
King Elliott,	"	3	6	
Byrd Ellington,	"	3	6	
Wright Ellington,	"	3	6	
Joel Fowlkes,	"	3	6	
Anderson Green,	"	3	6	
Nathan Graves,	"	3	6	
Thomas Graves,	"	3	6	
John Griffin,	"	3	6	
Robert J. Griffin,	"	3	6	
Owen Griffin,	"	3	6	
Lewis Griffin,	"	3	6	
John Gold,	"	2		

NAMES.	RANK.	*Time of Service.*		REMARKS.
		Months.	Days.	
William O. Gillispie, - -	Private,	1	11	
Wagstaff Hurt, - -	"	3	6	
Thomas Henderick, - -	"	3	6	
Samuel Hester, - -	"	3	6	
James Hester, - -	"	3	6	
Abraham Hester, - -	"	3	6	
Chysom Hester, - -	"	3	6	
Robert Hester, - -	"	3	6	
Henry Hester, - -	"	3	6	
Willis Hyde, - -	"	3	6	
Henry H. Hyde, - -	"	3	6	
Jesse Hunt, - -	"	3	6	
John Hughes, - -	"	3	6	
Charles Hughes, - -	"	3	6	
Stephen Hudson, - -	"	3	6	
Pascal Hudson, - -	"	3	6	
Creed Hudson, - -	"	3	6	
David Holloway, - -	"	3	6	
Anderson Jeater, - -	"	3	6	
Richard Jones, - -	"	3	6	
Charles Inge, - -	"	3	6	
Thomas Leak, - -	"	2	3	
Obadiah Ligon, - -	"	2	3	
Pleasant Moore, - -	"	3	6	
William Mitchell, - -	"	3	6	
Johnson Munroe, - -	"	3	6	
Huell Matthews, - -	"	3	6	
Hampton Malone, - -	"	3	6	
Champion Marrable, - -	"	2	16	
Obadiah Neal, - -	"	3	6	
Allen Noblin, - -	"	3	24	
John Neatherry, - -	"	3	6	
Daniel Neatherry, - -	"	3	6	
David Norrington, - -	"	3	6	
Peter Overby, - -	"	3	6	
Wm. Overby, - -	"	3	6	
Herod Pierce, - -	"	3	6	
John Pritchett, - -	"	3	6	
Samuel Puryear, - -	"	3	6	
Hardiman Puryear, - -	"	3	6	
Giles Puryear, - -	"	3	6	
Gilbert Pinson, - -	"	1	6	
Burgess Pool, - -	"	3	27	
Charles Royster, - -	"	3	6	
Abel Royster, - -	"	3	6	
Robert Royster, - -	"	3	6	
Jonas Robertson, - -	"	1	20	
Christopher Singleton, -	"	3	6	
Elison Toone, - -	"	3	6	
Taviner Toone, - -	"	3	6	
James Tillotson, - -	"	3	6	
Henry Tutor, - -	"	3	6	
Willis W. Vaughan, -	"	3	6	
Spencer Vaughan, - -	"	3	6	
Thomas Wadkins, - -	"	3	6	
Richard C. Williams, - -	"	3	6	
Edward Wagstaff, - -	"	3	6	
Francis Wagstaff, - -	"	3	6	

PAY ROLL

Of Captain William Daney's Company, of the First Regiment of Virginia Militia, in the Service of the United States, from the 28th of August to the 3d of December 1814.

NAMES.	RANK.	Time of Service.		REMARKS.
		Months.	Days.	
William Daney,	Captain,	3	5	
James G. Young,	1st Lieutenant,	3	5	
Joseph W. Walton,	2d "	1	20	
Derins Robertson,	1st Ensign,	3	5	
Balaam Wills,	2d "	3	5	
William Fox,	Q. M. Serg't,	3	5	
John Massey,	1st Sergeant,	3	5	
Isham Mangram,	2d "	3	5	
Sampson A. Robertson,	3d "	3	5	
William Andleton,	4th "	2	23	
Hiram Walton,	Corporal,	3	5	
Pettypool Massey,	"	3	5	
John Shepperson,	"	3	5	
George Pike,	"	2	23	
Allen Hamblin,	Private,	2	23	
Benj. Branchcomb,	"	3	5	
William Bennet,	"	3	5	
Handy Bennet,	"	3	5	
David Burrow,	"	3	5	
William Brewer,	"	3	5	
Wiltcher Bohannon,	"	3	6	
John Cox,	"	3	5	
James Collier,	"	1		
Thomas Carrington,	"	3	5	
Frederick Collier,	"	3	5	
Benjamin Cox,	"	3	5	
Sterling Collier,	"	1		
Sterling Cato,	"	3	5	
Joseph Collier,	"	3	5	
John Clark,	"	2	23	
Nathaniel Daniel,	"	3	5	
Zachariah Doyle,	"	3	5	
Warren Dilbridge,	"	3	5	
Turner Dilbridge,	"	3	5	
Jason Futrell,	"	3	5	
George T. Fox,	"	3	5	
Jesse C. Farrar,	"	3	5	
Lockhart Fergason,	"	3	5	
Zachariah Guartney,	"	3	6	
Williamson Glover,	"	3	5	
William H. Harrison,	"	3	5	
Richard Harding,	"	3	5	
John Harrison,	"	3	5	
Hobbs Hinchea,	"	2	23	
Benjamin Johnson,	"	1		
Isham Johnson,	"	1		
Hezekiah Jordan,	"	3	5	
John M. Jordan,	"	3	5	
Henry Jenkins,	"	3	5	
James Kidd,	"	3	5	
Charles Lockhart,	"	3	5	
Thomas Lanier,	"	3	5	
Lemmon Linch,	"	3	5	
Osborne Ledbetter,	"	3	5	

NAMES.	RANK.	Time of Service.		REMARKS.
		Months.	Days.	
William Lanier,	Private,	2	23	
Benj. W. McKinny,	"	3	5	
William Massey,	"	3	5	
Richard Massey,	"	3	5	
John Murfree,	"	3	5	
Wilkinson Morriss,	"	3	5	
John Morgan,	"	3	5	
William Morgan,	"	3	5	
Benj. B. Mason,	"	2	6	
John Moseley,	"	3	5	
Chancy Mitchell,	"	2	23	
Amos Nanny,	"	3	5	
William Pair,	"	3	5	
Lewis Poarch,	"	3	5	
John Pearcy,	"	3	5	
Wilkins P. Pool,	"	3	5	
Thomas P. Pool,	"	2	23	
Harmon Rowell,	"	3	5	
William Reed,	"	3	5	
James Royster,	"	3	6	
Daniel H. Robinson,	"	2	23	
Howell Rowell,	"	2	23	
George Shehorn,	"	3	5	
Charles M. Steward,	"	3	5	
James H. Smith,	"	3	2	
Christopher Shepperson,	"	3	5	
Archer Smith,	"	3	6	
Charles Summerhill,	"	3	6	
John Spain,	"	3	1	
Elliott Spencer,	"	3	5	
Henry Tutor,	"	3	5	
Crawford Vincent,	"	3	5	
John Vincent,	"	3	5	
Alexander Vincent,	"	3	5	
Pierce Vaughan,	"	3	5	
Thomas Vaughan,	"	3	5	
John Woodroof,	"	3	5	
Harrison Wade,	"	3	5	
Allen Woodroof,	"	3	5	
Burwell B. Williamson,	"	3	5	
Williamson Westmoreland,	"	3	5	
John Warrick,	"	3	5	

Captain William Daney's Company—First Regiment.

NAMES.	RANK.	TIME OF SERVICE.		REMARKS.
		Months.	Days.	
William W. Allen,	Private,	–	10	
Michael Davis,	"	–	25	Transferred to artillery.
John J. Hinton,	"	–	25	" "
Benjamin Jones,	"	–	11	
Abel Nanny,	"	–	9	
William Richardson,	"	–	9	
Hiram Roof,	"	–	23	" "
Bartholomew Spence,	"	–	–	Deserted.
William Southern,	"	–	–	" "
Thomas Stovall,	"	–	–	" "
Johnson Thomas,	"	–	28	Enlisted in U. S. service.
Allen Thomas,	"	–	9	
Joseph Wallis,	"	–	28	Transferred to artillery.

(For rest of this company, see publication of Pay Rolls.)

PAY ROLL

Of a Company of Infantry, commanded by Capt. William Grigg, of the First Regiment of Virginia Militia, in the Service of the State of Virginia, or of the United States, from the 29th August to the 4th of December 1814, inclusive.

NAMES.	RANK.	Time of Service.		REMARKS.
		Months.	Days.	
William Grigg, - -	Captain,	3	6	
George Hardaway, - -	1st Lieutenant,	3	6	
George Powell, - -	2d "	3	6	
Edward Steagall, - -	Ensign,	3	6	
James Owen, - -	"	3	6	
James Malane, - -	1st Sergeant,	3	6	
Claiborne Malane, - -	2d "	1	7	
Robert C. Adams, - -	3d "	3	6	
Thomas Philips, - -	5th "	2	12	
John Seward, - -	2d "	3	6	
Cuthbert Smith, - -	4th "	3	6	
Gregory B. Hudson, - -	5th "	3	6	
Daniel Kelly, - -	Q. M. Serg't,	3	6	
James Preston, - -	1st Corporal,	3	6	
Wyatt M. Ezell, - -	2d "	3	6	
James Bragg, - -	3d "	3	6	
John Gresham, - -	4th "	3	6	
John Overby, - -	Drummer,	3	6	
Augustine McKinney, - -	Fifer,	3	6	
John Ashton, - -	Private,	3	6	
Reuben Allen, - -	"	3	6	
Lewis Brewer, - -	"	3	6	
John Birdsong, - -	"	3	6	
Lewis Burnett, - -	"	3	6	
John Booth, - -	"	3	6	
Allen Bennett, - -	"	3	6	
Henry Blalock, - -	"	3	6	
Yerby Brewer, - -	"	3	6	
Boling L. Bottom, - -	"	3	6	
William B. Carpenter, -	"	3	6	
Wilson Carpenter, - -	"	3	6	
John H. Chapman, - -	"	3	6	
Richard Carpenter, - -	"	3	6	
Isaac Carpenter, - -	"	3	6	
John Connell, - -	"	3	6	
John Debbridge, - -	"	3	6	
Benjamin Evans, - -	"	3	6	
Francis Evans, - -	"	3	6	
George G. Eldridge, - -	"	3	6	
Benjamin Edmondson, -	"	3	6	
Zachariah Floyd, - -	"	3	6	
Nathaniel W. Fletcher, -	"	1	5	
Edward Giles, - -	"	3	6	
Daniel Glover, - -	"	3	6	
Allen J. Green, - -	"	3	6	
William Goodrich, - -	"	3	6	
Benjamin Gee, - -	"	3	6	
Green Hull, - -	"	3	6	
John P. Harper, - -	"	3	6	
Isaac F. Hause, - -	"	3	6	
Alex'r H. Hobbs, - -	"	3	6	
Willie Hobbs, - -	"	3	6	
John Harrison, sen. - -	"	3	6	
Joseph Harrison, - -	"	3	6	

NAMES.	RANK.	Time of Service.		REMARKS.
		Months.	Days.	
Edwin Horton, - -	Private,	3	6	
Benjamin Harrison, - -	"	3	6	
John H. Joy, - -	"	3	6	
Benja. Justice, - -	"	3	6	
Henry Jackson, - -	"	3	6	
John Jackson, - -	"	3	6	
David Killy, jr. - -	"	3	6	
Wm'son Kirkland, - -	"	3	6	
Benja. W. Lashly, - -	"	3	6	
James Lane, - -	"	3	6	
William Massey, - -	"	3	6	
William Manley, - -	"	3	6	
William Moss, - -	"	3	6	
Richard Moore, - -	"	3	6	
Jno. Nicholson, - -	"	3	6	
Thomas Owen, - -	"	3	6	
William Owen, - -	"	3	6	
Drury Pearson, - -	"	3	6	
Johnson Pearson, - -	"	3	6	
William W. Pearson, - -	"	3	6	
Anthony W. Putney, - -	"	3	6	
Benjamin Pearson, - -	"	3	6	
Littleton Pearson, - -	"	3	6	
Paschal Pearson, - -	"	3	6	
James Porch, - -	"	3	6	
James Richardson, - -	"	3	6	
Thomas Richardson, - -	"	3	6	
William Saunders, - -	"	3	6	
Jno. Saunders, - -	"	3	6	
Jno. Smith, - -	"	3	6	
Elie Smith, - -	"	3	6	
Sam'l Seward, - -	"	3	6	
Joseph Ship, - -	"	3	6	
Charles Thomas, - -	"	3	6	
Edward Thrower, - -	"	3	6	
Robert Tuder, - -	"	3	6	
Labon Towns, - -	"	3	6	
John Thompson, - -	"	2	13	
Benja. Williams, - -	"	3	6	
William Williams, - -	"	3	6	
George Walker, - -	"	3	6	
Wm. L. Williams, - -	"	1	20	
Augustine Wissan, - -	"	3	6	
Alex'r Watts, - -	"	3	6	
James Webb, - -	"	3	6	
Stephen Walton, - -	"	3	6	
Wm. Walton, - -	"	3	6	
Benja. Walton, - -	"	3	6	
Thos. Walton, - -	"	3	6	
Joshua Walton, - -	"	3	6	
William Woolsey, - -	"	3	6	
Thomas Wray, - -	"	3	6	
George C. Wright, - -	"	3	6	
Robt. Williams, - -	"	3	6	
Kinchea Walton, - -	"	3	6	

Captain William Harrison's Company—First Regiment.

NAMES.	RANK.	TIME OF SERVICE.		REMARKS.
		Months.	Days.	
Lunsford Broaddus, - -	Ensign,	–	9	
Henry Philips, - -	Sergeant,	–	9	
Henry Dunn, - -	"	–	9	
Elias Taylor, - -	"	–	9	
John Cole, - -	"	–	9	
Robert Smithers, - -	Corporal,	–	9	
John Page, - -	"	–	9	
Willis Kidd, - -	"	–	9	
Reuben Sorrel, - -	"	–	9	
James Bell, - -	Private,	–	9	
Edmund Cecil, - -	"	–	9	
Larkin Duling, - -	"	–	9	
Edmond Goleman, - -	"	–	9	
Mefrom Garnet, - -	"	–	9	
William Harrison, - -	"	–	9	
John Houston, - -	"	–	9	
William Jones, - -	"	–	9	
John Key, - -	"	–	9	
Barnett Moore, - -	"	–	9	
Coleman Pitts, - -	"	–	9	
Robert Pitts, - -	"	–	9	
James Sthreshley, - -	"	–	9	
Thomas Sthreshley, - -	"	–	9	
William Sthreshley, - -	"	–	9	
Benjamin Seal, - -	"	–	9	
Hiram Sorrel, - -	"	–	9	
Geo. Trout, - -	"	2	20	

(For rest of this company, see publication of Pay Rolls.)

MUSTER ROLL

Of Captain Harry Heth's Troop of Cavalry, from the First Regiment, Virginia Militia, Chesterfield County, commanded by Lieutenant Colonel William Brown, in the Service from the 8th February to 3d March, from 27th to 29th June, and from 30th June to 1st July, 1813.

NAMES.	RANK.	TIME OF SERVICE.		REMARKS.
		Months.	Days.	
Harry Heth. - -	Captain,	1	1	
James Scott, - -	Lieutenant,	–	26	
Branch Cheatham, - -	"	1	1	
P. F. Smith, - -	"	–	5	
Harry Randolph, - -	Cornet,	–	26	
John Cobbs, - -	"	1	1	
Zachariah Brooks, - -	Qr. M. S.	1	1	
Peter McCary, - -	Sergeant,	1	1	
Edward D. Diggs, - -	"	1	1	
Robert Harris, - -	"	1	1	
William Winfree, - -	"	1	1	
Peter T. Smith, - -	Corporal,	–	26	
Matthew Burfoot, - -	"	1	1	Promoted to Corporal since 3d March 1813.
Thomas Partor, - -	"	1	1	
Samuel Woody, - -	"	–	5	
John Archer, - -	"	–	5	
Thomas Graves, - -	"	1	1	
—— Randolph, - -	Trumpeter,	–	24	
John Archer, - -	Private,	–	26	
Daniel Belcher, - -	"	–	26	
William Bradshaw, - -	"	–	5	
Thomas Ball, - -	"	–	5	
Arch'd Botts, - -	"	–	5	
John Clark, - -	"	1	1	
Is. Cunningham, - -	"	–	5	
James Flornoy, - -	"	1	1	
Thomas Farris, - -	"	1	1	
Arch'd Flornoy, - -	"	1	1	
Kennon Giles, - -	"	1	1	
Fendall Gregory, - -	"	–	26	
Matthew Graves, - -	"	–	26	
Robert Graham, - -	"	–	5	
Peter E. Graves, - -	"	–	3	
Nicho. Gordon, - -	"	–	5	
Henry Hancock, - -	"	1	1	
William Hancock, - -	"	1	1	
Egbert Harris, - -	"	1	1	
Higgason Hancock, - -	"	–	26	
Patrick Harris, - -	"	1	1	
Edward Johnson, - -	"	–	5	
John Johnson, - -	"	–	5	
Thomas Kearns, - -	"	1	1	
James Kelton, - -	"	1	1	
Francis Lockett, - -	"	–	26	
Everitt Moore, - -	"	–	26	
Jacob Michaels, - -	"	1	1	

NAMES.	RANK.	TIME OF SERVICE.		REMARKS.
		Months.	Days.	
Allen McRae, - -	Private,	1	1	
John B. Mehone, - -	"	–	26	
Collin McRae, - -	"	–	5	
John B. Morrisett, - -	"	–	5	
William Martin, - -	"	–	5	
Dan'l Pelcher, - -	"	–	5	
Joseph Price, - -	"	–	5	
William Patterson, - -	"	–	5	
H. Randolph, - -	"	–	5	
Robert Sanders, - -	"	1	1	
Theoderick Smith, - -	"	1	1	
Jordan Smith, - -	"	1	1	
Sam'l L. Sanders, - -	"	–	5	
Thomas Taylor, - -	"	–	5	
Obediah Winfree, - -	"	1	1	
Valentine Winfree, - -	"	–	26	
John Worsham, -	"	–	2	

****

PAY ROLL

Of Captain John C. Hill's Company, First Regiment, Amelia County, attached to First Regiment, First Brigade, Virginia Militia, in the Service of the United States, at Camp Bottom's Bridge, commanded by Brigadier General William Chamberlayne, from 28th August to 16th November 1814.

NAMES.	RANK.	Time of Service.		REMARKS.
		Months.	Days.	
John C. Hill,	Captain,	2	20	
Thomas Rowlett,	Lieutenant,	2	20	
William Booker,	"	2	20	
Fergusson Farmer,	Ensign,	2	20	
Robert Pescud,	"	1	6	
Thomas Powell,	Ord. Serg't,	2	20	
Chastain Raine,	Q. M. Serg't,	2	20	
Faris Marshall,	Sergeant,	2	20	
James P. Hill,	"	2	20	
Robert Dickey,	"	2	20	
Joseph Jones,	"	2	20	
Anderson Nunnally,	Corporal,	2	20	
James Allen,	"	2	20	
Peter R. Dunnivant,	"	2	20	
John Vest,	"	2	20	
Thomas W. Vaughan,	Fifer,	2	15	
Richard Allen,	Private,	2	20	
William Bragg,	"	2	20	
Baugh Bartlett,	"	2	20	
James Booker,	"	2	20	
Reynard Bevel,	"	2	20	
Sutton E. Belcher,	"	2	20	
William Butler,	"	2	20	
Newby Belcher,	"	1	20	
Samuel Bridgewater,	"	2	20	
William Clyborne,	"	2	20	
Spencer Chandler,	"	2	20	
John L. Cowardin,	"	2	20	
Rowlett Dearen,	"	2	20	
Francis Dunnavant,	"	2	20	
John Dunnavant,	"	2	20	
John Dunkin,	"	2	20	
Royal Fergusson,	"	2	20	
John Frith,	"	2	20	
John Farley,	"	2	20	
Micajah French,	"	2	20	
Jesse Franklin,	"	2	20	
Lewis Goodwyn,	"	2	20	
William B. Giles,	"	2	20	
Henry Garrett,	"	2	20	
Waller Garrett,	"	2	20	
Thomas Hudson,	"	2	20	
Walter B. Hughes,	"	2	20	
William Howell,	"	2	20	
Osborne Jones,	"	2	20	
John Lynch,	"	2	20	
Jacob A. Lockett,	"	2	20	
James W. Muse,	"	2	20	
William McGlasson,	"	2	20	
John Marsfiall,	"	2	20	
Daniel Snelayes,	"	2	20	
John M Friiren,	"	2	20	
Littlebes FriNeale,	"	2	20	
AndersFridleride,	"	2	20	

NAMES.	RANK.	Time of Service.		REMARKS.
		Months.	Days.	
Francis Pride, - -	Private,	2	20	
Francis Powell, - -	"	2	20	
Laban Pritchard, - -	"	2	20	
Isaac Pollard, - -	"	2	20	
John Rayborne, - -	"	2	20	
Williamson D. Seay, - -	"	2	20	
James C. Stranger, - -	"	2	20	
Peter D. Sublett, - -	"	2	20	
John Smith, - -	"	2	20	
William Timberlake, - -	"	2	20	
William H. Vaughan, - -	"	2	20	
William Weeks, - -	"	2	20	
William Waldrop, - -	"	2	20	

Captain John C. Hill's Company—First Regiment.

NAMES.	RANK.	TIME OF SERVICE.		REMARKS.
		Months.	Days.	
John C. Hill, - -	Captain,	–	14	
Thomas Rowlett. - -	Lieutenant,	–	14	
William Booker, - -	"	–	14	
Ferguson Farmer, - -	Ensign,	–	14	
Robert Pescud, - -	"	–	14	
Thomas Powell, . - -	Or. Sergeant,	–	14	
Raine Chastain, - -	Q. M. Serg't,	–	14	
Marshall Fariss, - -	Sergeant,	–	14	
James P. Hill, - -	"	–	14	
Robert Dickers, - -	"	–	14	
Joseph Jones, - -	"	–	14	
Anderson Nunally, - -	Corporal,	–	14	
James Allen, - -	"	–	14	
Peter R. Dunnavant, -	"	–	14	
John Vest, - -	"	–	14	
Thomas W. Vaughan, -	Fifer,	–	14	
Richard Allen, - -	Private,	–	14	
William Bragg, - -	"	–	14	
Bartlett Baugh, - -	"	–	14	
James Booker, - -	"	–	14	
Bernard Brivill, - -	"	–	14	
Littleton E. Belcher, -	"	–	14	
William Butler, - -	"	–	14	
Samuel Bridgewater, -	"	–	14	
William Clayborne, - -	"	–	14	
Spencer Chandler, - -	"	–	14	
John L. Cowardin, - -	"	–	14	
Rowlett Dearen, - -	"	–	14	
Francis Dunevant, - -	"	–	14	
John Dunevant, - -	"	–	14	
John Dunkin, - -	"	–	14	
Royall Fergason, - -	"	–	14	
John Farley, - -	"	–	14	
John Frith, - -	"	–	14	
Micajah French, - -	"	–	14	
Jessee Franklin, - -	"	–	14	
Lewis Goodwin, - -	"	–	14	
William B. Giles, - -	"	–	14	
Henry Garrett, - -	"	–	14	
Walter L. Garrett, - -	"	–	14	
Thomas Hudson, - -	"	–	14	
Walter B. Hughes, - -	"	–	14	
William Howlet, - -	"	–	14	
Osborne Jones, - -	"	–	14	
John Lynch, - -	"	–	14	
Jacob A. Lockett, - -	"	–	14	
Wm. Meglafon, - -	"	–	14	
John Marshall, - -	"	–	14	
Daniel J. Mayes, - -	"	–	14	
John McLaren, - -	"	–	14	
Littleberry Neal, - -	"	–	14	
Francis Pride, - -	"	–	14	
Anderson Pride, - -	"	–	14	
Francis Powell, - -	"	–	14	

NAMES.	RANK.	TIME OF SERVICE.		REMARKS.
		Months.	Days.	
Laban Pitchford, - -	Private,	–	14	
Isaac Pollard, - -	"	–	14	
John Rayborne, - -	"	–	14	
Wm'son D. Sears, - -	"	–	14	
James C. Stranger, - -	"	–	14	
Peter D. Sublett, - -	"	–	14	
John Smith, - -	"	–	14	
William Timberlake, -	"	–	14	
William H. Vaughan, -	"	–	14	
William Werks, - -	"	–	14	
William Waldrop, - -	"	–	14	

(For rest of this company, see publication of Pay Rolls.)

PAY ROLL

Of a Troop of Cavalry, commanded by Captain Tilmon E. Jeter, from the First Regiment of Virginia Militia, of the County of Amelia, under the command of Major John T. Woodford, from 28th August to 14th November 1814.

NAMES.	RANK.	Time of Service. Months.	Days.	REMARKS.
Tilmon E. Jeter,	Captain,	2	17	
Anthony Webster,	Lieutenant,	2	17	
James P. Cocke,	"	2	17	
Herbert Eanes,	Cornet,	2	17	
Thomas W. Webster,	Sergeant,	2	17	
Fabius Lawson,	"	2	17	
Robert Woodson,	"	2	17	
Edward Berry,	"	2	6	
Willis Johnson,	Corporal,	2	17	
Henry Ligon,	"	–	10	Promoted to serg't in Maj. Holcombe's staff.
Joseph B. Anderson,	"	2	17	
Anderson Nunnally,	"	–	7	Sub. by W. Eggleston.
Thomas Carter,	"	2	17	Sub. for Jos. Haskew.
Joseph Foster,	"	2	17	
William Wright,	"	2	17	Sub. for N. Crenshaw.
Edmund B. Walker,	"	2	17	Sub. for Geo. Walker.
William Murray,	"	1	24	Sub. by John Ogilby.
Samuel Williams,	Musician,	2	17	
Robert Johnson,	Farrier,	2	17	
Daniel Booker,	Private,	2	17	
William Baird,	"	2	12	Sub. for Pleasant Baird.
Edward Claybrook,	"	2	17	
Patrick H. Chapman,	"	2	17	
John Cousins,	"	2	17	
Allen J. Crenshaw,	"	2	17	
William Cooper,	"	2	17	
Peter L. Chieves,	"	2	17	
Simeon Cobbs,	"	2	17	Sub. for John Webster.
William J. Dunn,	"	2	17	Sub. for A. S. Wright.
William Eggleston,	"	2	10	Sub. for Anderson Nunnally.
George N. Foster,	"	2	17	
Francis Flippin,	"	2	17	Sub. for Wm. Jackson.
Paschal Green,	"	2	17	Sub. for Ed. Green.
Pleasant Gills,	"	2	17	
John S. Hardaway,	"	–	13	Promoted to surgeon's mate in Col. Greenhill's staff.
James Hill,	"	2	17	Sub. for Grief Truly.
David Johnson,	"	2	17	Sub. for Arm. Green.
Edmund Jeter,	"	2	17	
Richard Johnson,	"	2	17	
Thomas Morriss,	"	2	17	Sub. for Wm. Mottley.
Ire McGlasson,	"	2	7	
William O. Magee,	"	2	17	
John Ogilby,	"	–	21	Sub. for Wm. Murray.
Peter F. Ogilby,	"	2	17	Sub. for Jos. Hundley.
Robert Pollard,	"	2	17	
John Pollard,	"	2	17	
William A. Powell,	"	2	17	
Christopher H. Price,	"	2	17	
Edward Perkins,	"	2	17	Sub. for Rich. Webster.
William Peay,	"	2	19	Sub. for Jno. Williams.
John A. Robertson,	"	2	17	

NAMES.	RANK.	*Time of Service.*		REMARKS.
		Months.	Days.	
John Roberts, - -	Private,	2	17	
George B. Seay, - -	"	2	17	Sub. for Ed. Atkinson.
William Sadler, - -	"	2	17	
Allen Tharpe, - -	"	2	17	Sub. for Wm. Nance.
Armistead T. Townes, -	"	–	7	Promoted in Col. Holcombe's staff.
Elijah Vasser, - -	"	2	17	Sub. for Wm. C. Anderson.
Henry H. Vaughan, - -	"	2	17	Sub. for W. Gregory.
Arthur Wadmore, - -	"	2	17	Sub. for Rich. Dabbs.
Joel Williams, - -	"	2	17	Sub. for Josiah Foster.
George Wright, - -	"	2	19	
Daniel Wilson, - -	"	2	17	Sub. for H. Anderson.

Captain Tilmon E. Jeter's Troop of Cavalry—First Regiment.

NAMES.	RANK.	TIME OF SERVICE.		REMARKS.
		Months.	Days.	
Anderson Jeter, - -	Private,	–	27	
Thomas Wilson, - -	"	–	27	

(For rest of this company, see publication of Pay Rolls.)

PAY ROLL

Of a Company of Virginia Militia, under the command of Captain William Jones, of the First Regiment, First Brigade, in the Service of the State of Virginia, commanded by Col. James Byrne, from 28th of August to 30th November 1814.

NAMES.	RANK.	Time of Service.		REMARKS.
		Months.	Days.	
William Jones, - -	Captain,	3	5	
John M. Jeffris, - -	1st Lieutenant,	3	5	
Timothy Thorp, - -	2d "	3	5	
Erancis E. Williamson, - -	1st Ensign,	3	5	
Lewis Thorp, - -	2d "	3	5	
Teschanner Degraffenreid, -	Q. Master,	3	5	
Hartwell Ivy, - -	1st Sergeant,	3	4	
Daniel Fisher, - -	2d "	3	4	
Jaquelin Goodwin, - -	3d "	3	4	
Thomas Keaton, - -	4th "	3	5	
Elisha Eastus, - -	5th "	3	5	
John Smith, - -	1st Corporal,	3	4	
Boling Grigg, - -	2d "	3	4	
Thomas Jones, - -	3d "	3	5	
James A. Watson, - -	4th "	3	4	
John Barnes, - -	Drummer,	3	4	
Bennett Barnes, - -	Fifer,	3	4	
Jeremiah Brown, - -	Private,	3	4	
Henry Batt, - -	"	3	4	
Littleton Bailey, - -	"	3	4	
Gardner Batt, - -	"	3	4	
Jonathan Bailey, - -	"	3	5	
John H. Boothe, - -	"	3	5	
Charles Driver, - -	"	3	4	
Goodwin G. Daniel, - -	"	3	4	
Drury Dunn, - -	"	3	4	
Ramsey J. Dunivant, - -	"	3	5	
Stephen Dowdy, - -	"	3	5	
Sloman Davis, - -	"	3	5	
Charles Edwards, - -	"	3	4	
William Edmonds, - -	"	3	4	
Jerman Eanes, - -	"	3	5	
John Evans, - -	"	3	5	
John Edmonson, - -	"	3	5	
Daniel Easley, - -	"	3	4	
Edward Fisher, - -	"	3	4	
Josiah Farlow, - -	"	3	4	
Francis Gent, - -	"	1	27	
James Gee, - -	"	3	5	
John S. Gordan, - -	"	3	5	
Williamson Graves, - -	"	3	4	
Drury Gill, - -	"	3	5	
James S. Gordan, - -	"	3	4	
Elias Goodrich, - -	"	3	2	
John Haris, - -	"	3	4	
Gilbert Hays, - -	"	3	4	
Harison Hobbs, - -	"	3	4	
David Hunt, - -	"	3	4	
David Harmon, - -	"	3	5	
Daniel Harmon, - -	"	3	5	
John Harding, - -	"	3	5	
Thomas Holt, - -	"	3	5	
Collin Harison, - -	"	3	4	
Patrick Johnson, - -	"	3	4	

NAMES.	RANK.	Time of Service. Months.	Days.	REMARKS.
Daniel M. Jolley, - -	Private,	3	5	
Julius Johnson, - -	"	3	5	
Benjamin Johnson, - -	"	3	5	
Stephen Justice, - -	"	3	5	
Jacob Lester, - -	"	3	5	
John H. Lucas, - -	"	3	2	
Nathaniel W. Lucas, - -	"	3	4	
Abner Lakier, - -	"	3	4	
Joseph Lunsford, - -	"	3	5	
Jabez Lambert, - -	"	3	5	
Gravet Lefoe, - -	"	3	5	
Frederick Lester, - -	"	3	5	
Barnet Lester, - -	"	3	5	
James Mason, - -	"	3	4	
Benj. Mirack, - -	"	3	4	
David Moore, - -	"	3	5	
Thomas McDaniel, - -	"	3	5	
Robert Matthews, - -	"	3	5	
Riggin Newsome, - -	"	3	4	
Thomas Newsome, - -	"	1	3	
Booker Nevils, - -	"	3	5	
John W. Poole, - -	"	3	5	
Benj. Palmer, - -	"	3	5	
Matthew Peace, - -	"	3	5	
Richard Pepper, - -	"	3	4	
Redmond Reece, - -	"	3	4	
Henry Rollings, - -	"	3	4	
Benj. Rudder, - -	"	3	5	
Edward Redford, - -	"	3	5	
Peter Rutledge, - -	"	2	2	
Robertson Ryland, - -	"	3	5	
George Reece, - -	"	3	5	
Charles H. Steward, - -	"	3	4	
John J. Sturdivant, - -	"	3	4	
Evans Spencer, - -	"	3	4	
John Snead, - -	"	3	5	
Jesse Steagall, - -	"	3	5	
Zebulon Singleton, - -	"	3	5	
Bartlet Stokes, - -	"	3	5	
Edward Slaughter, - -	"	3	1	
Thomas Stone, - -	"	3	1	
William Saunders, - -	"	3	4	
Woodson Sulivant, - -	"	3	5	
Mack. Ship, - -	"	3	5	
William Thomas, - -	"	3	4	
Benjamin Thomas, - -	"	3	4	
John Tunstall, - -	"	3	4	
William Tatum, - -	"	3	5	
Drury Townsend, - -	"	3	5	
Robert Ward, - -	"	3	5	
Gideon Walker, - -	"	3	5	
Samuel Williams, - -	"	3	5	
Benj. Wilkins, - -	"	3	4	
Nathaniel Warmack, - -	"	3	5	
Daniel Walker, - -	"	3	4	

PAY ROLL

Of a Company of Virginia Militia, commanded by Capt. John J. Moore, of the First Regiment, in the Service of the United States, from the 31st August to the 30th November 1814, both days inclusive, under the command of James Byrne, Colonel Commandant.

NAMES.	RANK.	Time of Service.		REMARKS.
		Months.	Days.	
John J. Moore, - -	Captain,	3	5	
Warner Moore, - -	1st Lieutenant,	3	5	
David Moss, - -	2d "	1	29	
John Johnson, - -	1st Ensign,	3	5	
John H. Knight, - -	2d "	3	5	
Newman Dortch, - -	Q. M. Sergt,	3	5	
Churchwell Curtis, - -	1st Sergeant	3	5	
Isham Nance, - -	2d "	3	5	
Williamson Rainey, - -	3d "	3	5	
Jesse Parish, - -	4th "	3	5	
Robert F. Bridgforth, - -	5th "	3	5	
Joseph Lett, - -	1st Corporal,	3	5	
Zachariah Curtis, - -	2d "	3	5	
Varney Andrews, - -	3d "	3	5	
Edwin P. Smith, - -	4th "	3	5	
James Carrell, - -	Drummer,	3	5	
Charles Taylor, - -	Fifer,	3	5	
Isaac Arnold, - -	Private,	3	5	
Edward Algood, - -	"	3	5	
Jarriott Avery, - -	"	3	5	
Joseph Bohannon, - -	"	3	5	
William H. Bugg, - -	"	3	5	
John J. Bugg, - -	"	3	5	
Jordan Bowin, - -	"	3	5	
Pleasant Burnett, - -	"	3	5	
Alexander Butler, - -	"	3	5	
William Burnett, - -	"	3	5	
Richard Butler, - -	"	3	5	
Gray Blackbourn, - -	"	3	5	
Edward Cole, - -	"	3	5	
Benjamin Carrel, - -	"	3	5	
James Coleman, - -	"	3	5	
Thomas Crutchfield, - -	"	3	5	
Samuel Crutchfield, - -	"	3	5	
Charles D. Cleaton, - -	"	3	5	
Richard Crowder, - -	"	3	5	
James Day, - -	"	3	5	
William Davis, - -	"	3	5	
Francis Edmonson, - -	"	3	5	
Covington Edmonson, -	"	3	5	
Benjamin T. Edmonson, -	"	3	5	
Thomas Farrar, - -	"	3	5	
Peter T. Fagerson, - -	"	3	5	
John Farrar, - -	"	3	5	
Joseph Hargrove, - -	"	3	5	
Obadiah Hatchel, - -	"	3	5	
David Horn, - -	"	3	5	
Benjamin Hatchel, - -	"	3	5	
Richard Hazelwood, - -	"	3	5	
Benjamin Heavlin, - -	"	3	5	
George Holmes, - -	"	3	5	
Thomas Johnson, - -	"	3	5	
Charles Jones, - -	"	3	5	
Woodson N. Johnson, -	"	3	5	

NAMES.	RANK.	Time of Service.		REMARKS.
		Months.	Days.	
Sandy Johnson, - -	Private,	3	5	
Ludwell E. Jones, - -	Artificer,	3	5	
Joseph Jones, - -	Private,	3	5	
Sack H. Jones, - -	"	3	5	
Joseph Keeton, - -	"	3	5	
John Lipford, - -	"	3	5	
Howel Mallet, - -	"	3	5	
Robert McLaughlin, - -	"	3	5	
John Morgan, - -	"	3	5	
William McDaniel, - -	"	3	5	
Isaac Nance, - -	"	3	5	
Edmond Noel, - -	"	3	5	
William Nash, - -	"	3	5	
William Oliver, - -	"	3	5	
Hartwell S. Overby, - -	"	3	5	
William Osling, - -	"	3	5	
Josiah Ogbourn, - -	"	3	5	
William Powel, - -	"	3	5	
Charles Palmer, - -	"	3	5	
James Pully, - -	"	3	5	
John Phillips, - -	"	3	5	
Pettus Phillips, - -	"	2	27	
William Roberts, - -	"	1	23	
Samuel D. Roffe, - -	"	3	5	
Buswell Rice, - -	"	3	5	
Samuel Robert, - -	"	2	25	
Anselm Roberts, - -	"	3	5	
John Rudd, - -	"	3	5	
George Steegall, - -	"	3	5	
Edward Simmons, - -	"	3	5	
Samuel Simmons, - -	"	2		
Thomas Sanders, - -	"	3	5	
Frederick Short, - -	"	3	5	
Thomas W. Smith, - -	"	3	5	
Edmond Simmons, - -	"	3	5	
Vines Short, - -	"	3	5	
Thomas Sketchley, - -	"	3	5	
William Short, - -	"	3	5	
William N. Smith, - -	"	3	5	
Freeman Short, - -	"	3	5	
William Turner, - -	"	3	5	
Lewis G. Thomas, - -	"	3	5	
Paschal Thomas, - -	"	3	5	
John Toon, - -	"	3	5	
Edward Thompson, - -	"	3	5	
Daniel Tucker, - -	"	3	5	
Richard Tally, - -	"	3	5	
Benjamin Tanner, - -	"	3	5	
George Thompson, - -	"	1	23	
George Thomerson, - -	"	3	5	
Worsham Tucker, - -	"	1	12	
Lemuel Vaughan, - -	"	1	25	
Bushrod Webb, - -	"	3	5	
Edwin Willis, - -	"	3	5	
Banister Winn, - -	"	3	5	
Sherod Wilson, - -	"	3	5	
Woodson Winn, - -	"	3	5	
John Waller, - -	"	3	5	

MUSTER ROLL

Of Captain William Moseley's Company of Cavalry, attached to the First Regiment, Virginia Militia, in the Service of the United States, from the 29th August to 13th of Sept, 1814.

NAMES.	RANK.	TIME OF SERVICE.		REMARKS.
		Months.	Days.	
William Moseley, - -	Captain,	–	16	
Charles Moseley, - -	Lieutenant,	–	16	
Thomas Jurticum, - -	"	–	16	
Bernard Booker, - -	Cornet,	–	16	
Thomas Cobbs, -	1 Sergeant,	–	12	
Samuel Gordon, - -	2 "	–	16	
Robert Bonderant, - -	3 "	–	16	
Nathan Spencer, - -	4 "	–	16	
Pleasant Abbott, - -	Private,	–	16	
Felix Brown, - -	"	–	16	
John Chadsin, - -	"	–	–	On wagon guard.
James Coleman, - -	"	–	16	
Richard W. Chick, - -	"	–	16	
Matthew W. Cason, - -	"	–	16	
William J. Dunn, - -	"	–	16	
George W. Eldridge, - -	"	–	16	
Thomas Eldridge, - -	"	–	16	
Stephen Fossee, - -	"	–	16	
William B. Gray, - -	"	–	16	
William Gordon, - -	"	–	16	
John Gibson, - -	"	–	16	
Obediah Gordon, - -	"	–	16	
William Harris, - -	"	–	–	On wagon guard.
Peter Hales, - -	"	–	16	
James Holbeman, - -	"	–	16	
Henry Hall, - -	"	–	16	
William H. Jones, - -	"	–	16	
William B. Jones, - -	"	–	16	
William D. Jones, - -	"	–	–	On vidette.
Thomas Jeffries, - -	"	–	16	Sub. for Thos. Rush.
Josas Jones, - -	"		–	Sub. for Wm. Moore.
Robert B. Jones, - -	"	–	16	
James W. Jones, - -	"	–	16	
David Johnson, - -	"	–	16	
John Linticum, - -	"	–	16	
Thomas Lewis, - -	"	–	16	
David Murriner, - -	"	–	16	
Merit Milton, - -	"	–	16	
Charles May, - -	"	–	16	
Matthew Moseley, - -	"	–	16	
John Moore, - -	"	–	16	
Thomas Nowlin, - -	"	–	16	Sub. for R. Patterson.
Miller Copton, - -	"	–	16	
Edward Perkins, - -	"	–	16	
Turner H. Patterson, - -	"	–	–	On vidette.
Stephen Pankey, - -	"	–	16	
Thomas Saunders, - -	"	–	16	
Francis Saunders, - -	Private,	–	16	
Samuel Saunders, - -	"	–	16	
Absalom Stephens, - -	"	–	16	
Thomas Stephens, - -	"	–	16	
Arthur Woodmore, - -	"	–	16	
Geo. W. Word, - -	"	–	16	
Geo. Wooldridge, - -	"	–	16	
Robert Walker, - -	"	–	16	
Geo. Webb, - -	"	–	16	
Joseph Walker, - -	"	–	16	
Robert Walton, - -	"	–	16	
Thomas Walton, - -	"	–	16	
Walter C. Wilkerson, -	"	–	16	

PAY ROLL

Of a Company commanded by Captain Baker Pegram, of the First Regiment of Virginia Militia, in the Service of the United States, under the command of Colonel James Byrne, from the 28th August to 30th November 1814.

NAMES.	RANK.	Time of Service.		REMARKS.
		Months.	Days.	
Baker Pegram, - -	Captain,	3	4	
Jacob L. Clapdore, - -	Lieutenant,	3	4	
Giles Wells, jun. - -	"	3	4	
Robert Strange, - -	"	3	4	
Thomas Terrell, - -	"	3	4	
William L. Griffin, - -	Q. M. Serg't,	3	4	
Ebenezer Watts, - -	Ord. Sergeant,	3	4	
John B. Tunstill, - -	"	2	13	
Joseph Tenn, - -	Sergeant,	3	4	
Thomas Tenn, - -	"	3	4	
Patrick H. Wells, - -	"	3	4	
Roberts B. Daniel, - -	"	3	4	
Benjamin Archer, - -	"	2	13	
Hiram Goodwyn, - -	"	2	13	
John Green, - -	Corporal,	3	4	
Peter D. Gibbs, - -	"	3	4	
Patrick R. Smith, - -	"	3	4	
Thos. Pitt, - -	"	3	4	
John W. Baird, - -	"	3	4	
William G. Jones, - -	"	3	4	
John S. Eler, - -	"	3	4	
Geo. W. Tenn, - -	"	3	4	
John Brooks, - -	"	2	13	
Terry Gill, - -	"	2	13	
Robert Newsum, - -	"	2	13	
John Clements, - -	"	2	13	
Frederick H. Brooks, - -	Drummer,	3	4	
Wm. Barber, - -	Fifer,	1	1	
Cad. W. Archer, - -	Private,	3	4	
John Andrews, - -	"	3	4	
Parham Adams, - -	"	3	4	
Amaza Barker, - -	"	3	4	
Stephen Barrenzino, - -	"	2	13	
John Brown, - -	"	3	4	
Clotworthy Barbour, - -	"	2	13	
Edward Crostick, -	"	3	4	
Sampson Clements, - -	"	3	4	
James Carry, - -	"	3	4	
David Cougar, - -	"	3	5	
Thos. Christopher, - -	"	3	5	
John W. Christopher, - -	"	3	5	
James Crowder, - -	"	3	4	
James Collier, - -	"	3	6	
Sterling Collier, - -	"	3	4	
John Daniel, - -	"	3	4	
Ephraim Daniel, - -	"	3	4	
Michael Davis, - -	"	2	11	
George Dilworth, - -	"	2	13	
Benjamin Davis, - -	"	2	13	
Thos. H. Elam, - -	"	3	4	
Robert Fuller, - -	"	3	3	
Thos. Gill, - -	"	3	4	
Thos. Garland, - -	"	3	4	
Uriah Grantham, - -	"	2	13	

NAMES.	RANK.	Time of Service.		REMARKS.
		Months.	Days.	
Richard F. Griffin, - -	Private,	3	4	
Chesley Hardy, - -	"	3	4	
A. Henderson, - -	"	3	4	
John I. Hinton, - -	"	2	11	
George Harlan, - -	"	2	13	
Michael C. Heath, - -	"	2	13	
James Hardiman, - -	"	2	13	
Cary Hobbs, - -	"	2	13	
James Ives, - -	"	3	5	
Wiley Jones, - -	"	3	4	
Benj. Johnson, - -	"	2	6	
Isham Johnson, - -	"	2	6	
Eaton Lamb, - -	"	3	4	
Stephen Leath, - -	"	3	4	
Jesse Lantrup, - -	"	3	4	
William S. Lucas, - -	"	3	4	
Daniel Lamb, - -	"	2	13	
John Lockridge, - -	"	2	13	
Loyde Marsh, - -	"	3	4	
Thomas Marsh, - -	"	3	4	
John Mahaffey, - -	"	3	4	
Spencer McKinney, - -	"	3	4	
John Michaels, - -	"	3	4	
Charles Mingg, - -	"	3	5	
Curtis McCleaster, - -	"	2	13	
Peter Nixon, - -	"	3	4	
Jonathan Percy, - -	"	3	4	
Storkey Perkins, - -	"	3	5	
Jeremiah Prichett, - -	"	3	4	
Allen Pearmore, - -	"	2	13	
Saml. Roberts, - -	"	3	4	
Geo. W. Roberts, - -	"	3	4	
Beverly Randolph, - -	"	3	4	
Harrison Randolph, - -	"	3	4	
Hiram Roffe, - -	"	2	9	
Samuel G. Smith, - -	"	3	4	
Robert Stephens, - -	"	3	4	
William Sterdivant, - -	"	3	5	
John E. Shermon, - -	"	3	4	
Henry Tucker, jun. - -	"	3	5	
Henry Tucker, sen. - -	"	3	4	
Wm. B. Tunstill, - -	"	3	4	
Peter Vaughan, - -	"	3	4	
Herbert L. Vaughan, - -	"	3	4	
Andrew Waugh, - -	"	3	4	
Collin Wallace, - -	"	3	4	
Joseph Wallace, - -	"	2	6	
William West, - -	"	3	4	
Thomas Wilkerson, - -	"	3	2	
Thomas Wood, - -	"	3	4	
Baker Woodward, - -	"	3	4	
Thos. Worsham, - -	"	3	4	
Henry Wright, - -	"	3	4	
Thos. G. Wynn, - -	"	3	5	
John H. Wells, - -	"	2	13	
Walker Watkins, - -	"	2	13	

Captain Baker Pegram's Company—First Regiment.

NAMES.	RANK.	TIME OF SERVICE.		REMARKS.
		Months.	Days.	
Billy, - - -	Driver,	2	16	
Chavers, - - -	"	3	4	

(For rest of this company, see publication of Pay Rolls.)

PAY ROLL

Of a Troop of Cavalry, Virginia Militia, in the United States Service, of the State of Virginia, commanded by Captain Philip Pryor, from 28th August to 22d November 1814. (First Regiment.)

NAMES.	RANK.	Time of Service. Months.	Days.	REMARKS.
Philip Pryor,	Captain,	3	6	
Green Hill,	1st Lieutenant,	3	6	
Henry Stith,	2d "	3	6	
Green Jackson,	Cornet,	3	6	
Dand'ge Spotswood,	"	3	5	
David Hobbs,	Sword Master,	3	4	
Erasmus Kennon,	Riding Master,	3	6	
George Steed,	1st Sergeant,	3	5	
Benjamin Pegrum,	2d "	3	4	
Thomas Blackburn,	3d "	3	6	
James A. M. Stewart,	4th "	3	6	
Benjamin Moody,	5th "	3	4	
Thomas J. Oliver,	1st Corporal,	3	4	
David Westmoreland,	2d "	3	4	
Benjamin H. Bass,	3d "	3	4	
William Boswell,	4th "	3	4	
Lyne S. Kemp,	5th "	3	2	
William B. Pryor,	6th "	3	4	
William Wilkinson,	7th "	3	4	
Isaac Mason,	8th "	3	4	
Henry Mitchell,	Saddler,	3	4	
William J. Gibbon,	Farrier,	3	4	
Luke Pryor,	Q. M. Serg't,	3	4	
John Abernethy,	B. Smith,	3	4	
John Andrews,	Private,	3	3	
John J. Brawn,	"	3	4	
John Brawn,	"	3	3	
James J. Blanks,	"	3	3	
Edmund T. Brodnax,	"	3	1	
William J. Barney,	"	3	4	
William E. Booth,	"	3	2	
Joel Baugh,	"	3	4	
William Bowden,	"	3	2	
Green Burge,	"	3	3	
William J. Barner,	"	3	4	
Richard M. Cunningham,	"	1	18	
Robert Chappell,	"	3	3	
Robert Chesly,	"	3	4	
Richard Collier,	"	3	4	
Alexander Closwell,	"	3		
John Clarke,	"	3	3	
Thomas Clarke,	"	3	3	
George W. Clarke,	"	3	3	
George B. Collier,	"	3	4	
Hamlen Cole,	"	3	3	
Thomas Comer,	"	3	3	
John W. Deadman,	"	2	28	Enlisted in U. States service 26th Nov. '14.
Allan Drummond,	"	3	4	
William Edmunds,	"	3	4	
William D. Floyd,	"	3	4	
John Goodwyn,	"	3	3	
John Grubbs,	"	3	4	
Peterson Hatten,	"	3	3	
Braxton Harrison,	"	3	3	
Turner Hamlett,	"	3	4	

NAMES.	RANK.	Time of Service.		REMARKS.
		Months.	Days.	
William Holloway, - -	Private,	3	4	
Hartwell Hitchcock, - -	"	3	2	
Burwell Hitchcock, - -	"	3	2	
Litt'y Hatton, - -	"	3	4	
James J. Harrison, - -	"	3	4	
Matthew M. Harrison, - -	"	1	18	
Hartwell Heath, - -	"	3	3	
Eldred Johnson, - -	"	3	4	
William Jett, - -	"	3	4	
James Jones, - -	"	3	4	
Hartwell Johnson, - -	"	3	3	
Reuben F. Johnson, - -	"	3	4	
John Kirkland, - -	"	3	3	
Robert B. Lacy, - -	"	3	4	
John Lanthrop, - -	"	3	3	
Lewis Matthews, - -	"	3	4	
Richard Morriss, - -	"	3	4	
William Nelson, - -	"	3	6	
John Nelson, - -	"	1	17	
Buckner Overby, - -	"	3	4	
John J. Parish, - -	"	3	4	
Claudius Piatt, - -	"	3	4	
William Pentecost, - -	"	3	4	
Wyatt Parish, - -	"	3	4	
Benjamin B. Perkins, - -	"	3	4	
Edward H. Pegram, - -	"	2	24	
Benjamin Rawlings, - -	"	3	4	
Burwell Robinson, - -	"	3	4	
Daniel Reese, - -	"	3	3	
Samuel Short, - -	"	3	3	
Edmund Short, - -	"	3	3	
Thomas Smith, - -	"	1	16	
Philip Shelby, - -	"	3	3	
Williamson Smith, - -	"	3	4	
William Shepperson, - -	"	3	4	
Anthony W. Smith, - -	"	3	2	
Robert Spires, - -	"	3	3	
Hugh T. Simmons, - -	"	3	3	
Benjamin Simmons, - -	"	3	3	
Turner Saxon, - -	"	3	4	
William Tewry, - -	"	1	17	
Thomas H. Walpoole, - -	"	3	4	
John Walpoole, - -	"	3	4	
Thomas J. Wyche, - -	"	3	4	
Henry Williams, - -	"	3	4	
Cary Wilkinson, - -	"	3	4	
Colson T. Wilks, - -	"	3	4	
Robert W. Woodruff, - -	"	3	4	
Edmund Wells, - -	"	3	3	
Alexander Wells, - -	"	3	3	
Farleigh Wade, - -	"	3	6	
Edmund Wilkins, - -	"	3	3	
William Wallace, - -	"	3	3	
Matthew Wren, - -	"	3	4	
Benjamin Wyatt, - -	"	3	3	
Joshua T. Whitcomb, - -	"	3	3	
William Young, - -	"	3	3	

PAY ROLL

Of a Company of Light Infantry, commanded by Captain John B. Rice, of the First Regiment of Virginia Militia, in the Service of the State of Virginia, or of the United States, from 29th August to 3d December 1814.

NAMES.	RANK.	Time of Service.		REMARKS.
		Months.	Days.	
John B. Rice, - -	Captain,	3	5	
Benjamin Harrison, - -	1st Lieutenant,	3	5	
John Hanserd, - -	2d "	3	5	
Andrew Lucy, - -	Ensign,	3	5	
Lewis A. Collier, - -	"	3	5	
Edward C. Smith, - -	Q. M. Serg't,	3	5	
Rany Jesse, - -	1st Sergeant,	3	5	
Dudley Publis, - -	2d "	3	5	
Benja. Harris, - -	3d "	3	5	
Benja. Gladish, - -	4th "	3	5	
William Reid, - -	5th "	3	5	
Rawley Abernathy, - -	1st Corporal,	3	5	
George I. Stainback, - -	2d "	3	5	
Ephraim Bass, - -	3d "	3	5	
James Ried, - -	4th "	3	5	
Rich'd F. Bennet, - -	Fifer,	3	5	
Nathaniel Rany, - -	Drummer,	3	5	
Elisha Abernathy, - -	Private,	3	5	
James W. Atkerson, - -	"	3	5	
Wyatt Adams, - -	"	3	5	
James Allen, - -	"	3	5	
Joel Atkerson, - -	"	3	5	
William Adams, - -	"	3	5	
William S. Bass, - -	"	3	5	
Nathaniel Bass, - -	"	3	5	
John N. Bishop, - -	"	3	5	
Coleman Brewer, - -	"	3	5	
Joseph Browder, - -	"	3	5	
Robert Bass, - -	"	3	5	
Jabez N. Brown, - -	"	3	5	
Caleb Browder, - -	"	3	5	
William P. Booker, - -	"	3	4	
Edward Branch, - -	"	2		
John Camp, - -	"	3	5	
Howel Cain, - -	"	3	5	
Thomas Coosey, - -	"	3	5	
Robert Connelly, - -	"	3	5	
Giles Crook, - -	"	3	5	
Thomas Chisman, - -	"	3	5	
Joseph Crook, - -	"	3	5	
Thomas A. Chambliss, -	"	3	5	
Henry Dugger, - -	"	3	5	
Joseph Dugger, - -	"	2	23	
Jesse Edwards, - -	"	3	5	
David Edwards, - -	"	3	5	
Peter Edwards, - -	"	3	5	
John Elmore, - -	"	3	5	
Allen Floyd, - -	"	3	5	
Daniel Griffis, - -	"	1	16	
Clement Hall, - -	"	3	5	
Richmond W. House, - -	"	3	5	
Edward Hall, - -	"	3	5	
John House, - -	"	3	5	
William Heartwell, - -	"	3	5	

NAMES	RANK.	Time of Service.		REMARKS.
		Months.	Days.	
Wm. R. P. Hunnicutt, - -	Private,	3	5	
Micajah Hawthorn, - -	"	3	5	
Asa W. Hood, - -	"	3	5	
Bolling Hawthorn, - -	"	3	5	
James Hawks, - -	"	3	4	
John Hawks, - -	"	3	4	
Marcus Hardiway, - -	"	3	4	
Thomas Hanks, - -	"	3	5	
Hardimant S. Ivey, - -	"	3	5	
Marcum Kirklan, - -	"	3	5	
William Kennedy, - -	"	3	5	
Samuel D. Kelley, - -	"	3	5	
Edmunds T. Lucus, - -	"	3	5	
James Lanier, - -	"	3	5	
David Lanier, - -	"	3	5	
Richard Lock, - -	"	3	5	
William Lewis, - -	"	3	5	
Michael Maidlen, - -	"	3	5	
Benjamin Miller, - -	"	3	5	
James Maton, - -	"	3	5	
Thomas Nunnally, - -	"	3	5	
James B. Parrish, - -	"	3	5	
John Parrish, - -	"	3	5	
Frederick Peebles, - -	"	3	5	
David S. Parrish, - -	"	3	5	
Sterling Parsons, - -	"	3	5	
Jesse Peebles, - -	"	1	9	
William Ridout, - -	"	3	5	
Thomas Ridout, - -	"	3	5	
Benjamin Ridout, - -	"	3	5	
Thomas Sanders, - -	"	3	5	
John Shelley, - -	"	3	5	
Griffin Stegal, - -	"	3	5	
David Smith, - -	"	3	4	
Hardiway Stainback, - -	"	3	5	
Daniel Stone, - -	"	3	5	
John Smith, - -	"	3	5	
George Stainback, - -	"	3	5	
Harvey Smith, - -	"	3	5	
Major Short, - -	"	3	5	
John Scoggin, - -	"	3	5	
Wilson Turbyfill, - -	"	3	5	
David Taylor, - -	"	3	5	
James Trotter, - -	"	3	5	
John Underhill, - -	"	3	5	
Jesse C. Vaughan, - -	"	3	5	
Robert Vaughan, - -	"	3	5	
Jasper R. Walker, - -	"	3	5	
Joel Wynne, - -	"	3	5	
Leroy Williams, - -	"	3	5	
Isham Wills, - -	"	3	5	
Freman Wynne, - -	"	3	5	
William C. White, - -	"	3	4	
James White, - -	"	1	7	

MUSTER ROLL

Of Captain John B. Royall's Troop of Cavalry, from the First Regiment, Virginia Militia, Halifax County, in the Service of the United States, from the 30th of August to 21st September, 1814, commanded by Lieutenant Colonel P. Halcomb.

NAMES.	RANK.	TIME OF SERVICE.		REMARKS.
		Months.	Days.	
John B. Royall, - -	Captain,	–	22	
R. D. Palmer, - -	Lieutenant	–	22	
William Collins, - -	Cornet,	–	22	
John Abbott, - -	Sergeant,	–	22	
J. D. Spragins, - -	"	–	22	
D. P. Snead, - -	"	–	22	
Elisha Collins, - -	"	–	22	
William P. Carr, - -	Corporal,	–	22	
Lorenzo Thomas, - -	"	–	22	
John Wilbourne, - -	"	–	22	
James M. Cooper, - -	Musician,	–	22	
Fleming Mayard, - -	"	–	22	
Charles Bardette, - -	Private,	–	22	
James Bomar, - -	"	–	22	
Joseph Bass, - -	"	–	22	
James Bower, - -	"	–	22	
Samuel Barley, - -	"	–	22	
John Beadle, - -	"	–	22	
John Barley, - -	"	–	22	
William Bunting, - -	"	–	22	
Edward Baptist, - -	"	–	22	
Thomas Clarke, - -	"	–	22	
Allen Claybrooke, - -	"	–	22	
Robert Claybrooke, -	"	–	22	
John Carr, - -	"	–	22	
Thomas T. Carr, - -	"	–	22	
Thomas Carr, sr. - -	"	–	22	
Philip Clay, - -	"	–	22	
Joseph M. Crews, - -	"	–	22	
George M. Crews, - -	"	–	22	
John B. Callahan, - -	"	–	22	
Drury Dunaway, - -	"	–	22	
James Elam, - -	"	–	22	
Mark L. Elam, - -	"	–	22	
Henry Fisher, - -	"	–	22	
James Y. Franklin, - -	"	–	22	
John Faris, - -	"	–	22	
William Fletcher, - -	"	–	22	
John Glascock, - -	"	–	22	
Elisha Hodges, - -	"	–	22	
Nathan Hensley, - -	"	–	22	
James Hankley, - -	"	–	22	
John Hubbard, - -	"	–	22	
Frederick Hodges, - -	"	–	22	
Joel Hubbard, - -	"	–	22	
Isaac Kirk, - -	"	–	22	

NAMES.	RANK.	TIME OF SERVICE.		REMARKS.
		Months.	Days.	
Curtis D. Kates, - -	Private,	–	22	
William Lee, - -	"	–	22	
William Moore, - -	"	–	22	
Edmund Martin, - -	"	–	22	
Zachariah Martin, - -	"	–	22	
William Martin, - -	"	–	22	
Philip McKenny, - -	"	–	22	
Thomas Meret, - -	"	–	22	
James Pettey, - -	"	–	22	
Banister Pridie, - -	"	–	22	
William Prindle, - -	"	–	22	
John Prindle, - -	"	–	22	
Banister J. Pindle, - -	"	–	22	
Hardaway Pindle, - -	"	–	22	
Lewis D. Poindexter, -	"	–	22	
Samuel Price, - -	"	–	22	
William Royall, - -	"	–	22	
James Rudder, - -	"	–	22	
William Ridgeway, - -	"	–	22	
Geo. Reaves, - -	"	–	22	
Francis Smith, - -	"	–	22	
Parhan Seamore, - -	"	–	22	
Paul Street, - -	"	–	22	
John Shuffield, - -	"	–	22	
William Tins, - -	"	–	22	
Elijah Vasser, - -	"	–	22	
Joseph Wilker, - -	"	–	22	
John Walker, - -	"	–	22	
Henry Wade, - -	"	–	22	
John Walne, - -	"	–	22	
Ambrose Walker, - -	"	–	22	
Robert L. Wilbourn, - -	"	–	22	
John Yates, - -	"		22	
Joel Younger, - -	"	–	22	
Thomas Younger, - -	"	–	22	
Wm'son Younger, - -	"			

PAY ROLL

Of Capt. Alexander Taylor's Company, of the First Regiment of Virginia Militia, in the Service of the United States, from 13th February to 3d March 1813, and from 1st September to 31st October 1814.

NAMES.	RANK.	Time of Service.		REMARKS.
		Months.	Days.	
Alexander Taylor,	Captain,	2	25	
John Williams,	Lieutenant,	2	25	
Thomas N. Cameron,	Lieutenant,	2	2	
Archibald Todd,	Ensign,	2	25	
Joseph Traylor,	Q. M. Serg't,	2	25	
William Shannon,	Sergeant,	2	16	
John Wilson,	"	2	25	
Peter Franklin,	"	2	25	
Lewis L. Marks,	"	2	25	
Mackie D. Janson,	"	2	25	
Elijah T. Smith,	Corporal,	2	25	
John H. Osborne,	"	2	25	
John M. Banister,	"	2	2	
Nathan Harned,	"	2	25	
Henry Weideimeyer,	Pl. Musician,	1		
Abner P. Bates,	Musician,	2	25	
Herbert Baird,	"	2	2	
Andrew Barnard,	"	2	2	
Thomas Clarke,	"	2	2	
Benjamin Cooke,	"	2	2	
Ira A. Easter,	"	2	2	
Anthony Mullen,	"	2	2	
Stephen Parr,	"	2	2	
David Rosser,	"	2	25	
Ethewald Sanford,	"	2	2	
James Cholson,	Drummer,	2	2	
William Yancey,	Fifer,	2	2	
Archibald Anderson,	Private,	2	2	
William Allison,	"	2	2	
Hezekiah R. Anderson,	"	2	2	
Ellis G. Blake,	"	2	2	
Robert Batte,	"	2	2	
Ralph C. Blake,	"	2	2	
William Bradley,	"	2	2	
John H. Brewer,	"	2	2	
William Burton,	"	2	2	
James Bagley,	"	2	2	
Augustine Burge,	"	2	25	
James Cate,	"	2	2	
James Cabaniss,	"	2	2	
John Camm,	"	2	2	
William Cain,	"	2	2	
James B. Cogbill,	"	2	2	
William Clarke,	"	2	2	
Samuel Cooper,	"	2	2	
Samuel Cross,	"	2	2	
William Davis,	"	2	2	
Daniel Dugger,	"	2	2	
Nathaniel Denby,	"	2	2	
Samuel Delworth,	"	2	2	
William Edwards,	"	2	2	
James Ennes,	"	2	2	
John A. Ezell,	"	2	2	
James R. Farrar,	"	2	2	

NAMES.	RANK.	Time of Service.		REMARKS.
		Months.	Days.	
William H. Fernandoes,	Private,	2	2	
John Gill,	"	2	2	
Alexander M. Green,	"	2	25	
William D. Godfrey,	"	2	2	
George Grundy,	"	2	2	
Dinwiddie Goodwyn,	"	2	2	
Michael Haffey,	"	2	9	
Roderick Haffey,	"	2	2	
Joseph M. Heath,	"	2	2	
John Hubbard,	"	2	2	
Charles Hunt,	"	2	2	
Arthur Johnson,	"	2	2	
Roderick Joiner,	"	2	2	
Joseph H. Lee,	"	2	2	
Arthur Leith,	"	2	2	
Robert Leith,	"	2	2	
Samuel M. Lewis,	"	2	2	
Abraham S. Lockhead,	"	2	2	
Randolph Mattox,	"	2	2	
William Matthews,	"	2	2	
Richard McRae,	"	2	2	
Benj. W. Moss,	"	2	25	
Robert Manly,	"	2	2	
Benjamin Middleton,	"	2	2	
John McLean,	"	2	2	
Joseph C. Noble,	"	2	2	
William Old,	"	1	19	
Nathaniel M. Osborne,	"	2	2	
John Owens,	"	2	2	
Chichester Owens,	"	2	2	
Samuel Peele,	"	2	2	
Moses B. Pillsborough,	"	2	2	
Robert Prentis,	"	2	2	
William Richards,	"	2	25	
Samuel Raines,	"	2	2	
William Robertson,	"	2	2	
John Roane,	"	2	2	
Thomas Rosser,	"	2	2	
William H. Russell,	"	2	2	
Elgan Russell,	"	2	2	
T. P. Roberts,	"	2	2	
Alden B. Spooner,	"	2	2	
Daniel Stringer,	"	2	2	
William Stewart,	"	2	2	
Ezra Stith,	"	2	2	
William Stephenson,	"	2	2	
Edwin B Stoat,	"	2	2	
John B. Taliaferro, jr.	"	2	2	
Theodore Tresvant,	"	2	2	
Martin Thayer,	"	2	2	
William Tufts,	"	2	2	
John B. Underhill,	"	2	25	
Claiborne Vaughan,	"	2	2	
William Wells,	"	2	25	
William Welch,	"	2	25	
William H. Wells,	"	2	14	
Nathaniel H. Whitlow,	"	2	2	
E. R. Whiting,	"	2	2	
Nathaniel Wells,	"	2	2	
John Warrick,	"	2	2	
William Wilkinson,	"	2	2	
Francis G. Yancey,	"	2	2	
Jonathan Zimmerman,	"	2	2	

Captain Alexander Taylor's Company.

NAMES.	RANK.	TIME OF SERVICE.		REMARKS.
		Months.	Days.	
Reuben Moss, - -	Ensign,	–	23	
Daniel Pegram, - -	Corporal,	–	23	
John Anderson, - -	Private,	–	23	
Wylie Burge, - -	"	–	23	
William Cameron, - -	"	–	23	
Patrick Durkin, - -	"	–	23	
Samuel Davis, - -	"	–	23	
David Fowler, - -	"	–	23	
Joseph Gray, - -	"	–	23	
Theodore Hart, - -	"	–	23	
Benjamin Johnson, - -	"	–	23	
John Joiner, - -	"	–	23	
Thomas Lockhead, - -	"	–	23	
Francis Pace, - -	"	–	23	
John B. Ponsonby, - -	"	–	23	
Ro. G. Simmons, - -	"	–	23	
Thomas Taylor, - -	"	–	23	
William Worsham, - -	"	–	23	
Davis Wills, - -	"	–	23	
William B. Wills, - -	"	–	6	

(For rest of this company, see publication of Pay Rolls.)

PAY ROLL

Of Captain Charles Thompson's Company, of the First Regiment, First Brigade of Virginia Militia, in the Service of the United States, commanded by Col. Wm. Trueheart, at Camp Bottom's Bridge, and under the command of Brigadier-General William Chamberlayne, from 23d August to 16th November 1814.

NAMES.	RANK.	Time of Service.		REMARKS.
		Months.	Days.	
Charles Thompson, - -	Captain,	2	24	
William Langhorne, - -	Lieutenant,	2	19	
Rich'd H. Frayser, - -	"	2	22	
Henry H. Jones, - -	Ensign,	2	24	
Anthony Matthews, - -	"	2	22	
George S. Netherland, -	Ord. Serg't,	2	24	
Thomas Swift, - -	Q. M. Serg't,	2	24	
Charles Barker, - -	1st Sergeant,	2	24	
Reuben George, - -	2d "	2	24	
George V. Angel, - -	3d "	2	22	
John Wilson, - -	4th "	2	22	
Elijah Phillips, - -	1st Corporal,	2	19	
Wm. A. Thompson, - -	2d "	2	24	
Thomas Childrey, - -	3d "	2	22	
Thomas Goode, - -	4th "	2	22	
Matt. Vaughan, - -	5th "	2	22	
Wm. Q. Pleasants, - -	6th "	2	24	
Joseph Jenkins, - -	7th "	2	22	
Robert Askew, - -	Private,	2	24	
James Austin, - -	"	2	22	
William Austin, - -	"	2	22	
William Baughan, - -	"	2	24	
Robert Belvin, - -	"	2	19	
Thomas Barbour, - -	"	2	22	
Levy Beacham, - -	"	2	19	
Turner Bottoms, - -	"	2	22	
William Barker, - -	"	1	19	
William Callis, - -	"	2	24	
Richard Callis, - -	"	2	24	
William Corker, - -	"	2	24	
Jno. S. Crutchfield, - -	"	2	24	
Theodorick Carter, - -	"	2	24	
John Carter, - -	"	2	22	
William Cogbill, - -	"	2	22	
Joel Cox, - -	"	2	19	
Robert Dunn, - -	"	2	19	
John Drewry, - -	"	2	19	
Thomas Emmerry, - -	"	2	19	
Nat. Enroughty, - -	"	2	22	
William Enroughty, - -	"	2	22	
Edmund Eppes, - -	"	2	22	
Thomas Epperson, - -	"	2	22	
Martin Fussel, - -	"	2	22	
William Fussel, - -	"	2	22	
George Fussel, - -	"	2	22	
John Gentry, - -	"	2	3	
Anderson Garthright, - -	"	2	22	
Henry Howard, - -	"	1	2	
William Howard, - -	"	1	9	
James E. Hardiman, - -	"	2	22	
Gideon Hanes, - -	"	2	24	
John Higgason, - -	"	2	24	
Richard Higgason, - -	"	2	24	
James Hogg, - -	"	1	9	

NAMES.	RANK.	Time of Service.		REMARKS.
		Months.	Days.	
Thomas Holmes, - -	Private,	2	22	
Thomas Hamlet, - -	"	2	22	
Samuel R. Jones, - -	"	2	24	
Rich'd F. Jones, - -	"	2	24	
John Insley, - -	"	2	19	
John Jordan, - -	"	2	22	
Claiborne Jennings, - -	"	2	22	
John R. Lee, - -	"	2	19	
Heartwell McManners, -	"	2	22	
Arthur Nicholson, - -	"	2	19	
James Parker, - -	"	2	19	
Edmund Powers, - -	"	2	19	Deserted.
Charles Paul, - -	"	2	19	
Robert Radford, - -	"	2	22	
David Simms, - -	"	2	24	
William Stanley, - -	"	2	24	
Jno. H. Skinner, - -	"	2	19	
Thomas Skinner, - -	"	2	19	
Robert Sharp, - -	"	2	22	
Price Sharp, - -	"	2	22	
William Shum, - -	"	2	22	
Wilson Storrs, - -	"	2	19	
William Stakes, - -	"	1	9	
Thomas Sammon, - -	"	2	22	
Richmond Terrell, - -	"	2	24	
Isaac Truman, - -	"	2	22	
Jacob Truman, - -	"	2	22	
Andrew Tencer, - -	"	2	22	
Lapole Tencer, - -	"	2	22	Or Leopold.
John Valentine, - -	"	2	22	
Thomas Watkins, - -	"	2	19	
John Wroughton, - -	"	2	19	
William Wright, - -	"	2	19	
John Warriner, - -	"	2	22	
Samuel Warriner, - -	"	2	22	
Elisha Williams, - -	"	2	22	

MUSTER ROLL

Of Captain John L. Townes' Company of Mounted Infantry, of the First Corps d'Elite, commanded by Colonel Thomas M. Randolph, in the Service of the State of Virginia, from the 30th August to 14th September, in the year 1814.

NAMES.	RANK.	TIME OF SERVICE.		REMARKS.
		Months.	Days.	
John L. Townes, - -	Captain,	–	15	
Benjamin L. Meade, -	Lieutenant,	–	15	
John Robertson, - -	Ensign,	–	15	
Peter Rison, - -	Sergeant,	–	15	
Thomas Bolt, - -	"	–	15	
John T. Leigh, - -	"	–	15	
Joseph R. Robertson, -	"	–	15	
Francis Anderson, - -	Private,	–	15	
Wm. Anderson - -	"	–	15	
Benjamin Bridgforth, -	"	–	15	
Richerson Booker, - -	"	–	15	
Richard Booker, - -	"	–	15	
Richard Bibb, - -	"	–	15	
John P. Bolling, - -	"	–	15	
Robert F. Branch, - -	"	–	15	
John Chaffin, - -	"	–	15	
George Craddock, - -	"	–	15	
Armstead Coleman, - -	"	–	15	
Wm. H Eggleston, - -	"	–	15	
Alford O. Eggleston, -	"	–	15	
Ca's H. Featherston, -	"	–	15	
Edward Ford, -	"	–	15	
Marston Foster, - -	"	–	15	
Nathan Hawkins, - -	"	–	15	
Nathaniel Harrison, - -	"	–	15	
Benjamin M. Harrison, -	"	–	15	
Phil. Wm. H. Holcombe, -	"	–	15	
John W. Jones, - -	"	–	15	
Seth W. Jones, - -	"	–	10	
Benjamin Lawson, - -	"	–	15	
Wm. G. Overton, - -	"	–	15	
Leonard Puckett, - -	"	–	15	
John S. Quarles, - -	"	–	15	
John R. Robertson, - -	"	–	15	
Edward Randolph, - -	"	–	15	
Thomas Wiley, - -	"	–	15	
John Webster, - -	"	–	15	
John F. Wiley, - -	"	–	15	

MUSTER ROLL

Of Captain James Underwood's Troop of Cavalry, of the Fourth Regiment, in the County of Hanover, in the Service of the United States, from 31st August to 13th September, 1814.

NAMES.	RANK.	TIME OF SERVICE.		REMARKS.
		Months.	Days.	
James Underwood, - -	Captain,	–	14	
Arch'd B. Dandridge, - -	Lieutenant,	–	14	
Ro. A. Dandridge, - -	"	–	14	
John C. Underwood, - -	Cornet,	–	14	
John King, - -	Sergeant,	–	14	
John G. Childers, - -	"	–	14	
Nath. W. Dandridge, - -	"	–	14	
Joseph Woodsong, - -	"	–	14	
Fred. Shoemaker, - -	Corporal,	–	14	
Thomas Elmore, - -	"	–	14	
Nath. Anthony, jr. - -	"	–	14	
Charles Childress, - -	"	–	14	
John H. Priddy, - -	Trumpeter,		14	
Thos. S. Aail, - -	Private,	–	14	
Thos. Atkinson, - -	"	–	14	
Robt. S. Austin, - -	"	–	14	
Samuel J. Bulliam, - -	"		14	
Ambrose Brooks, - -	"	–	14	
Thomas Bowles, - -	"	–	14	
Nath'l Crenshaw, - -	"	–	14	
Spotswood Childers, - -	"	–	14	
Peter Copeland, - -	"	–	14	
Pendleton R. Childress, -	"	–	14	
Ed. Camron, - -	"	–	14	
James Denton, - -	"	–	14	
Nath'l Dogan, - -	"	–	14	
Allen Denton, - -	"	–	14	
John England, - -	"	–	14	
William Ford, - -	"	–	14	
Solomon Harris, - -	"	–	14	
Pleasant Hattan, - -	"	–	14	
Ed. W. Kimbrough, - -	"	–	14	
Alexander Loving, - -	"	–	14	
John Mallory, jr. - -	"	–	14	
John Mann, - -	"	–	14	
Overton W. Mallory, - -	"	–	14	
Benj. Mann, - -	"	–	14	
Nath. Mills, - -	"	–	14	
Stephen Mallory, - -	"	–	14	
John Nuckols, - -	"	–	14	
Nath. Nuckols, - -	"	–	14	
David Nuckols, - -	"	–	14	
John Nash, - -	"	–	14	
Ben. Perkins, - -	"	–	14	
William Sayre, - -	"	–	14	
Jesse Sayre, - -	"	–	14	
Christian Stone, - -	"	–	14	

NAMES.	RANK.	TIME OF SERVICE.		REMARKS.
		Months.	Days.	
John H. Taylor, - -	Private,	–	14	
Garland Thompson, - -	"	–	14	
Francis Underwood, - -	"	–	14	
Rich'd A. Woodson, - -	"	–	14	
Reuben Wood, - -	"	–	14	

PAY ROLL

Of Capt. James Leftwich's Company, of Virginia Militia, attached to the command of Major J. T. Woodford, in the Service of the United States, Bedford County, from the 3d September to the 28th November 1814.

NAMES.	RANK.	Time of Service.		REMARKS.
		Months.	Days.	
James Leftwich, - -	Captain,	2	27	
Henry Jones, - -	Lieutenant,	2	27	
Jesse Clarke, - -	"	2	27	
William W. Austin, - -	Cornet,	2	27	
Nicholas Wilkinson, - -	Sergeant,	2	27	
John Robinson, - -	"	2	27	
Peter Austin, - -	"	2	27	
Cornelius Owen, - -	"	2	27	
Richard Harvey, - -	Corporal,	2	27	
James Noel, - -	"	2	27	
Robert M. Clayton, - -	"	2	27	
Paschal B. Wade, - -	"	2	27	
Stith Mead, - -	Trumpeter,	2	27	
Patrick Austin, - -	Private,	2	27	
Jno. W. Bagwell, - -	"	2	27	
Nicholas Bagwell, - -	"	2	27	Sub. for Rich'd Jones.
Waller Bunch, - -	"	2	27	
Wilshire Burton, - -	"	2	27	
Arch'd Bradfute, - -	"	2	27	
Benjamin Botts, - -	"	2	27	
Jesse A. Bramlet, - -	"	2	27	Sub. for A. Franklin.
Anthony Christian, - -	"	2	27	
James Cobbs, - -	"	2	27	Sub. for Archer Waide.
James Cundiffe, - -	"	2	27	
David Douglas, - -	"	2	27	
Joseph Dearen, - -	"	2	27	Or Joel.
Nimrod Daniel, - -	"	2	27	Or Darniel.
Barney A. Eidson, - -	"	2	27	Sub. for Thos. D. Sherman.
Elias M. Enbank, - -	"	2	27	
Geo. W. Eubank, - -	"	2	27	
Caleb Fuqua, - -	"	2	27	
Anderson C. Faris, - -	"	2	27	
Gilbert Gibbs, - -	"	2	27	
Thomas Greenwood, - -	"	2	27	Sub. for Isaac Wade.
William Gibson, - -	"	2	27	Sub. for Alex. B. Price.
Daniel Gregory, - -	"	2	27	
John Goode, - -	"	2	27	
Warner Hewett, - -	"	2	27	
Sylvanus Howard, - -	"	2	27	
Powell Hawkins, - -	"	2	27	Sub. for Francis L. Lee.
Stephen Hewett, - -	"	2	27	
John Jones, - -	"	2	27	Sub. for Wm. B. Harris.
William Minor, - -	"	2	27	Sub. for Wm. Minor.
Stephen E. Mitchell, - -	"	2	27	
William Marsh, - -	"	2	27	
James Marsh, - -	"	2	27	
Jno. R.				
Jno. R. North, - -	"	2	27	
Jno. Nowel, - -	"	2	27	
Caleb Noell, - -	"	2	27	
Simon M. Noell, - -	"	2	27	
William L. Otey, - -	"	2	27	
Lewis Parker, - -	"	2	27	
Jno. A. Price, - -	"	2	27	Sub. for N. H. Price.

NAMES.	RANK.	Time of Service.		REMARKS.
		Months.	Days.	
Harden Perkins, - -	Private,	2	27	
Daniel L. Price, - -	"	2	27	Sub. for Elijah Weeks.
Abram B. Pullen, - -	"	2	27	Sub. for Jacob Dawson.
William W. Quarles, - -	"	2	27	Received in exchange
Richard Roberts, - -	"	2	27	for Jas. Culland.
John Rucker, - -	"	2	27	
William Rucker, - -	"	2	27	
William Ransone, - -	"	1	18	
Nath'l S. Strange, - -	"	2	27	
Philip Turpin, - -	"	2	27	
John A. White, - -	"	2	27	
Alexander Wade, - -	"	2	27	
Owen Wilkinson, - -	"	2	27	
Jno. H. Wright, - -	"	2	27	
William Woodford, - -	"	2	8	
James Wilkinson, - -	"	2	8	

PAY ROLL

Of Captain Walter Otey's Company, from the Tenth Regiment of Virginia Militia, Bedford County, in the Service of the United States, at Camp Mitchell's Spring, under Major Woodford, and at Hampton, under the command of General John H. Cocke, from the 31st August 1814 to the 28th February 1815.

NAMES.	RANK.	Time of Service.		REMARKS.
		Months	Days.	
Walter Otey, - -	Captain,	6		
Samuel Quarles, - -	Lieutenant,	6		
Arch'd Stratton, - -	"	6		
Armistead Otey, - -	Cornet,	6		
James Campbell, - -	Sword Master,	6		
Alexander Smith, - -	Sergeant,	2	27	
Jubal Cundiff, - -	"	6		
Garland Rucker, - -	"	6		
William Leftwich, - -	"	2	16	
John Smith, - -	"	6		
Dabney Tucker, - -	"	6		
Jubal Jourdan, - -	Corporal,	6		
Thomas Pegram, - -	"	6		
Eben Nelms, - -	"	6		
John Preston, - -	"	6		
James Leftwich, - -	Trumpeter,	6		
James Ailiff, - -	Private,	6		
Geo. W. Baldwin, - -	"	6		
Jacob Burton, - -	"	6		
Philip Bowsman, - -	"	6		
John Brown, - -	"	6		
Richard Boothe, - -	"	6		
John W. Baylor, - -	"	2	21	
James Coleman, - -	"	6		
James Calland, - -	"	2	13	Sub. for Edw. Perkins.
William Drake, - -	"	6		
John Dent, - -	"	6		
John Drewry, - -	"	6		
Thomas Davis, - -	"	3	8	
Robert Elliott, - -	"	6		
Peregrine Echols, - -	"	6		
James H. Echols, - -	"	6		
Joel Elliott, - -	"	6		
Peter Feller, - -	"	6		
Bird Flournoy, - -	"	6		
William Gooldy, - -	"	6		
Hampton Haynes, - -	"	6		
Jesse Hackworth, - -	"	6		
Simon Hancock, - -	"	6		
John Hancock, - -	"	6		
Jeremiah Jourdan, - -	"	6		
Jonas Irvine, - -	"	6		
Merriman Lunsford, - -	"	6		
Aug. Leftwich, - -	"	–	24	Sub. for Ro. Mitchell.
Morgan Morgan, - -	"	6		
Dotson Minor, - -	"	6	–	Or Dobson.
Leroy Minor, - -	"	6		
Joseph Mills, - -	"	6		
Andrew Miller, - -	"	6		
John Madrey, - -	"	5	16	
Henry Moss, - -	"	6		
John McGeorge, - -	"	6		
James Maze, - -	"	6		
James Murphy, - -	"	5	4	Sub. for Isaac Shilman.

NAMES.	RANK.	Time of Service.		REMARKS.
		Months.	Days.	
Pleasant Murphy, t -	Private,	6		
Robert Mitchell, - -	"	1	6	Substituted Aug. Leftwich.
Charles Nelms, - -	"	6		
Amos Nelms, - -	"	6		
William Nelms, - -	"	6		
Isaac Nichols, - -	"	5	6	
John Nichols, - -	"	6		
Michael Overfelt, - -	"	6		
Chistopher Preston, - -	"	6		
Charles Perrin, - -	"	6		
John Pearce, - -	"	6		
Thomas Rucker, - -	"	6		
Anthony Rucker, - -	"	6		
Lewis Suttle. - -	"	6	–	Or Settle.
Fielding Suttle, - -	"	6		
Francis Suttle, - -	"	6		
Henry Smith, - -	"	6		
John H. Smith, - -	"	2		
William Thomas, - -	"	6		
William S. Wright, - -	"	6		
James Wright, - -	"	5	6	
John Wright, - -	"	6		
Charles Whitely, - -	"	2		
Henry Williamson, - -	"	4	16	

Captain Walter Otey's Company—Tenth Regiment.

NAMES.	RANK.	TIME OF SERVICE.		REMARKS.
		Months.	Days.	
William Woodford, - -	Serg't Major,	1	14	
Thomas Moorman, - -	Private,	6		
Benj. H. Mansfield, - -	"	6		
William McGeorge, - -	"	6		
Edward Perkins, - -	"	3	17	Substitute for James Calland.
William Smith, - -	"	–	–	Substitute for Thomas Pegram.

(For rest of this company, see publication of Pay Rolls.)

MUSTER ROLL

Of the Field and Staff Officers of the Twentieth Regiment of Virginia Militia, commanded by Lieutenant Colonel James Robinson, from 6th to 18th February, from 8th to 15th March, and from 5th to 28th September, in the year 1813.

NAMES.	RANK.	TIME OF SERVICE.		REMARKS.
		Months.	Days.	
James Robinson, - -	Lt. Colonel,	1	15	
William Nimmo, - -	Major,	–	21	
James D. Moseley, - -	Surg. Mate,	1	15	
Jonathan Hopkins, - -	Qr. Master,	2	2	
Jacob Valentine, - -	Q. M. Sergt.	–	21	
Willam Davis, - -	"	–	18	

MUSTER ROLL

Of Captain Moses Fentress's Company of the Twentieth Regiment, Virginia Militia, commanded by Lieutenant Colonel James Robinson, in the Service of the United States, from the 5th to 13th February, from 10th to 15th March, and from 24th to 29th September, 1813.

NAMES.	RANK.	TIME OF SERVICE.		REMARKS.
		Months.	Days.	
Moses Fentress, - -	Captain,	–	15	
Henry Lewis, - -	Lieutenant,	–	15	
Benjamin Cason, - -	Ensign,	–	15	
Thomas Harrison, - -	Sergeant,	–	15	
Thomas Henley, - -	"	–	15	
John Harrison, - -	"	–	15	
John James, - -	"	–	10	
William B. Day, - -	Corporal,	–	15	
Peter Whitehurst, - -	"	–	9	
Thomas Woodhouse, -	"	–	10	
Hilley Brown, - -	"	–	15	
Simon M. Etheredge, -	"	–	5	
William Axstead, - -	Private,	–	5	
James Brown, - -	"	–	15	
William Brown, - -	"	–	10	
Thomas Brown, - -	"	–	15	
Peter Brown, - -	"	–	15	
Hilley Cason, - -	"	–	10	
Joshua Cannon, - -	"	–	10	
John Fentress, sr. - -	"	–	13	
William Fentress, - -	"	–	13	
John Fentress, jr. - -	"	–	10	
Peter Fentress, - -	"	–	15	
Willoughby Flanagan, -	"	–	15	
Robert Holmes, - -	"	–	15	
Emperor James, - -	"	–	15	
Edward Kays, - -	"	–	15	
Willis Langley, - -	"	–	15	
Reubin Land, - -	"	–	10	
Henry Land, - -	"	–	5	
Henry Liggatt, - -	"	–	10	
William McClanen, - -	"	–	10	
Joshua McClanen, - -	"	–	15	
Demcey McClanen, - -	"	–	15	
Thomas McClanen, - -	"	–	10	
John Malbone, - -	"	–	10	
Abner Malbone, - -	"	–	12	
Batson Malbone, - -	"	–	15	
Jessee Malbone, - -	"	–	10	
William Moore, - -	"	–	15	
Tulley Moore, - -	"	–	10	
James Moore, - -	"	–	5	
William Newman, - -	"	–	15	
Etheridge M. Simon, -	"	–	10	
James Simpson, - -	"	–	5	

PAY ROLL

Of Captain John Jones's Company, of the Twelfth Regiment Virginia Militia, Fluvanna County, stationed at Camp Holly, under the command of Major William Armistead, and afterwards of Col. John H. Cocke, from 23d March to 17th August 1813.

NAMES.	RANK.	Time of Service.		REMARKS.
		Months.	Days.	
John Jones, - - -	Captain,	3	26	
Valentine Mayo, - -	Lieutenant,	3	26	
James G. Mayo, - -	Ensign,	3	26	
Callom Jones, - -	"	3	26	
Richard Holland, - -	Sergeant,	3	26	
David Wildy, - -	"	2	26	
Robert Kent, - -	"	3	26	
Alfred Wren, - -	"	3	26	
Allen R. Bernard, - -	"	3	26	
John Baily, - -	Corporal,	2		
Reuben Martin, - -	"	3	26	
Nelson Parrish, - -	"	3	26	
David Ross, - -	"	3	26	
James Ross, - -	"	3	26	
Thomas Mayo, - -	"	3	26	Or Mays.
Henry Taylor, - -	Drummer,	3	26	
Bart. K. Johnson, - -	Fifer,	3	26	
James Alston, - -	Private,	3	26	
William R. Allen, - -	"	3	26	
Mark Blincoe, - -	"	3	26	
James Bartlett, - -	"	3		
John Bernard, - -	"	2		
David Brown, - -	"	3	26	
Obadiah Branson, - -	"	3	26	Or Brannon.
Stephen Fitzgerald, - -	"	3	26	
Dudley Gilman, - -	"	2	26	
Henry Ham, - -	"	1		
Joseph Holland, - -	"	3	26	
Samuel Hardesty, - -	"	3	26	
William B. Howard, - -	"	3	26	
Joshua Harlow, - -	"	3	26	
James Jones, - -	"	3	26	
John Loving, - -	"	3	26	
Armager Lilly, - -	"	3	26	
Elijah Lowry, - -	"	1	26	
Thomas Snead, - -	"	3	26	
William Saunders, - -	"	3	26	
Thomas Sadler, - -	"	3	26	
William D. Statham, - -	"	3	26	
William Tencer, - -	"	2		
John Thomas, - -	"	3	26	
William Thomas, - -	"	3	26	
Henry Taylor, - -	"	1	26	
John Venable, - -	"	3	26	
Garland White, - -	"	3	26	
Dabney White, - -	"	3	26	

Captain John Jones' Company—Twelfth Regiment.

NAMES.	RANK.	TIME OF SERVICE.		REMARKS.
		Months.	Days.	
John Jones,	Captain,			
Valentine Mayo,	Lieutenant,			
James G. Mayo,	Ensign,			
Richard Holland,	Sergeant,			
David Wildy,	"			
Robert Kent,	"			
Callom Jones,	"			
Alfred Wren,	"			
John Bailey,	Corporal,			
Reubin Martin,	"			
Wilson Parrish,	"			
Allen R. Bomard,	"			
David Ross,	"			
John Lovins,	Drummer,			
Bartholomew K. Johnston,	Fifer,			
James Aston,	Private,			
William R. Allen,	"			
Mark Blumcoe,	"			
James Bartlett,	"			
David Brown,	"			
Obadiah Bransam,	"			
Stephen Fitzgerald,	"			
Dudley Gilman,	"			
Joseph Holland,	"			
Samuel Hardesty,	"			
William B. Howard,	"			
Joshua Harlow,	"			
James Jones,	"			
Armager Lilly,	"			
Elijah Lowry,	"	–	–	Sub for David Wildy.
Thomas Mayo,	"			
James Ross,	"			
Thomas Snead,	"			
William Saunders,	"			
William D. Statham,	"			
Thomas Sadler,	"			
Benj. Smith,	"	–	12	
William Tencer,	"			
John Thomas,	"			
William Thomas,	"			
Henry Taylor,	"			
John Venable,	"			
Garland White,	"			
Dabney White,	"			

(For rest of this company, see publication of Pay Rolls.)

Captain Richard H. L. Lawson's Company—Twentieth Regiment.

NAMES.	RANK.	TIME OF SERVICE.		REMARKS.
		Months.	Days.	
Richard H. L. Lawson,	Captain,	–	28	
Simon Hancock,	Lieutenant,	1	2	
William T. Nimmo,	Ensign,	1	3	
James Scarfe,	Sergeant,	1	12	
Charles Moseley,	"	1	12	
Henry A. Dalbey,	"	1	12	
William Corbell,	"	1	12	
Henry K. Manning,	"	–	26	
Thomas Barkwell,	"	–	28	
James Johnston,	"	–	13	
James Hunter,	"	–	21	
James Throwgood,	Corporal,	1	12	
Hillary M. Hunter,	"	–	15	
Geo. T. Hall,	"	1	22	
Hillary Snale,	"	–	13	
James Walmsley,	"	–	25	
Thomas Fountain,	"	–	11	
Stephen Bonney,	Private,	1	16	
James Bryant,	"	1	2	
Amos Benson,	"	–	28	
Thaddeus Bowman,	"	–	29	
John Bevin,	"	1	2	
Geo. Bashaw,	"	1	2	
Joseph Benthall,	"	–	18	
John Care,	"	1	3	
Joel Cuterell,	"	1	2	
James Collins,	"	1	2	
Lemuel Collins,	"	2		
Jessee Cartwright,	"	1	12	
William Core,	"	–	26	
Jeremiah Cain,	"	–	13	
Benjamin Dixon,	"	1	16	
Samuel Drayton,	"	1	2	
Geo. Dudley,	"	–	25	
Ralph Dixon,	"	–	27	
William Ellegood,	"	1	2	
Thomas Ewell,	"	1	2	
John Edmonds,	"	1	2	
James Ewell,	"	1	2	
Thomas Fountain,	"	1	12	
Geo Fentress,	"	–	13	
John Gains,	"	1	2	
James Haynes,	"	1	19	
William Harrison,	"	1	2	
John Holmes,	"	1	12	
John Haynes,	"	–	13	
John Henderson,	"	–	13	
James Jarrell,	"	1	2	
James Johnston,	"	–	28	
Edmond Johnston,	"	–	28	
James Kellum,	"	–	28	
Major Kellum,	"	1	2	
John Kellum,	"	–	11	
William Lockwood,	"	1	12	

NAMES.	RANK.	TIME OF SERVICE.		REMARKS.
		Months.	Days.	
Henry Lemount, - -	Private,	1	12	
John Lester, - -	"	1	12	
John McDonald, - -	"	1	2	
John Mills, - - -	"	1	19	
Nathaniel Mears, - -	"	1	14	
John Moore, - - -	"	1	8	
Bagwell Moore, - -	"	–	24	
Leven Pettet, - -	"	1	16	
Richard Pebworth, - -	"	1	12	
Henry Pebworth, - -	"	1	16	
Erasmus Smith, - -	"	1	12	
Wesley Smith, - -	"	1	12	
Enoch Smith, - -	"	1	12	
Hillary Snale, - -	"	–	20	
David Scott, - -	"	–	27	
Geo. Throp, - -	"	1	12	
John B. Vaughan, - -	"	–	25	
Moses Williams, jr. - -	"	–	28	
James Walmsley, - -	"	–	3	
Jacob Hunter, - -	"	–	13	

(For rest of this company, see publication of Pay Rolls.)

PAY ROLL

Of Captain Benjamin Allen's Company, of the Seventeenth Regiment, attached to the First Regiment, First Brigade of Virginia Militia, in the Service of the United States, at Camp Bottom's Bridge, commanded by Col. William Trueheart, from 28th August to 3d December 1814.

NAMES.	RANK.	Time of Service.		REMARKS.
		Months.	Days.	
Benjamin Allen, - -	Captain,	3	26	
Nathan Glenn, - -	Lieutenant,	3	23	
Robert Stratton, - -	"	3	26	
John England, - -	Ensign,	3	26	
John Seayres, - -	"	3	26	
John Anderson, - -	Sergeant,	3	26	
James Allen, - -	"	3	26	
John Seayres, - -	"	3	26	
Anderson Booker, - -	"	3	26	
William Farmer, - -	"	3	26	
Ben. T. Davis, - -	"	3	26	
Ro. S. Coleman, - -	Corporal,	3	26	
John T. Johns, - -	"	3	26	
Nathan Glenn, - -	"	3	26	
Matthew Hendrick, - -	"	3	26	
Andrew Anglen, - -	"	3	26	
Thomas Dowdy, - -	"	3	26	
John S. Phillips, - -	"	2	17	
James Dowdy, - -	"	3	26	
Simeon Allen, - -	Private,	3	26	
Henry Amos, - -	"	3	23	
John Amos, - -	"	3	23	
Meadow Bootwright, - -	"	3	26	
Edward Bootwright, - -	"	3	26	
Park Baily, - -	"	1	6	
John Bosher, - -	"	3	26	
Rich'd Bellamy, - -	"	3	26	
Stephen Benson, - -	"	1	22	
William Childress, - -	"	3	26	
William Coleman, - -	"	3	26	
John Cooper, - -	"	3	26	
Alexander Davis, - -	"	3	26	
John Dowdy, - -	"	3	26	
Robert Deane, - -	"	3	26	
Thos. Dowdy, Sr. or Jr., -	"	3	23	
Philip Durnford, - -	"	3	26	
Robert England, - -	"	3	26	
Major D. Epperson, - -	"	3	26	
James Farmer, - -	"	3	26	
Charles Faris, - -	"	3	26	
Bernard Guthrey, - -	"	3	26	
Daniel Goodsey, - -	"	3	26	
William Giles, - -	"	3	26	
Thomas Gill, - -	"	3	26	
John Hammontree, - -	"	3	26	
William Y. Hendrick, - -	"	3	26	
Zepheniah Hall, - -	"	3	26	
John Hambleton, - -	"	3	26	
David Hendrick, - -	"	3	26	
Samuel Hill, - -	"	3	26	
Hiram Hudson, - -	"	3	26	
John Isbell, - -	"	3	26	
Francis B. Junior, - -	"	3	26	
Allen Jenkins, - -	"	3	26	

NAMES.	RANK.	Time of Service.		REMARKS.
		Months.	Days.	
Dabney Kerr, - -	Private,	3	26	
Daniel W. Kerr, - -	"	3	26	
Samuel Mountcastle, - -	"	3	26	
Elisha Maxey, - -	"	3	26	
Henry Martin, - -	"	3	26	
Jesse Martin, - -	"	3	26	
Elijah North, - -	"	3	26	
Stephen Noel, - -	"	3	26	
Matthew Orange, - -	"	3	26	
Richard Osborne, - -	"	3	26	
John A. Oslin, - -	"	3	26	
John R. Palmore, - -	"	3	26	
Martin Richardson, - -	"	3	26	
Tully Scruggs, - -	"	3	26	
John Smith, - -	"	3	26	
William Smith, - -	"	3	26	
Anderson H. Tribue, - -	"	3	26	
Thomas Wisdom, - -	"	3	26	
John Whitt, - -	"	3	26	
William Walton, - -	"	3	26	
Lyddall Wilkinson, - -	"	3	26	

Captain John Miller's Company—Seventeenth Regiment.

NAMES.	RANK.	TIME OF SERVICE.		REMARKS.
		Months.	Days.	
Edmund Lee, - -	Private,	1	4	
James Wilkinson, - -	"	1	6	Sub. for Carter Wilkinson,
John Woodson, - -	"	1	4	

(For rest of this company, see publication of Pay Rolls.)

Captain Samuel Steele's Company—At Camp Holly.

NAMES.	RANK.	TIME OF SERVICE.		REMARKS.
		Months.	Days.	
James Blair, - -	Private,	–	–	No time given.
William Howman, - -	"			
Amos Pharp, - -	"			

(For the rest of this company, see publication of Pay Rolls.)

PAY ROLL

Of Captain Allen Wilson's Company, Seventeenth Regiment, Cumberland, attached to the First Regiment, First Brigade Virginia Militia, in the Service of the United States, commanded by Colonel William Trueheart, at Camp Bottom's Bridge, under the command of Brigadier General William Chamberlayne, from 28th August to 30th November 1814.

NAMES.	RANK.	Time of Service.		REMARKS.
		Months.	Days.	
Allen Wilson, - -	Captain,	3	27	
Joseph Carson, - -	Lieutenant,	3	27	
Jacob Bransford, - -	"	3	27	
Anthony Hughes, - -	Ensign,	3	27	
Charles A. Ballow, - -	"	3	27	
Thomas Tuggle, - -	Sergeant,	3	27	
A. M. Davenport, - -	"	3	27	
John Bagby, - -	"	3	27	
Rowland L. Hobson, - -	"	3	27	
Alexander Johns, - -	"	3	27	
Richard Webber, - -	"	3	27	
William T. Ballow, - -	Corporal,	3	27	
Henry Hobson, - -	"	3	27	
Richard B. Eggleston, - -	"	3	27	
John R. Stratton, - -	"	3	27	
John Hughes, - -	"	3	27	
John Wilkerson, - -	"	3	27	
Merrit Booker, - -	"	3	27	
Joseph Ransone, - -	"	3	27	
James Armistead, - -	Private,	3	27	
Joel Adcock, - -	"	3	27	
Wright Adams, - -	"	3	27	
Richard Alderson, - -	"	3	27	
Richard Anderson, - -	"	1	14	Deserted.
Harrison Armistead, - -	"	3	27	
William A. Burton, - -	"	3	27	
Daniel Bootwright, - -	"	3	27	
Langhorn Bootwright, - -	"	3	27	
Leonard Bootwright, - -	"	3	27	
William Burton, - -	"	3	27	
Meredith Blanton, - -	"	3	27	
Turner Brown, - -	"	3	27	
Thomas H. Brackett, - -	"	2	26	
Reuben Clopton, - -	"	3	27	
Thomas Coleman, - -	"	3	27	
James Corley, - -	"	3	27	Or Cosby.
Joseph E. Carter, - -	"	3	27	Or G.
Abram Charlton, - -	"	3	27	
William Crisp, - -	"	3	27	
Joseph Davidson, - -	"	3	27	
David Dunkin. - -	"	3	27	
Nathaniel Darney, - -	"	3	27	
John E. Edwards, - -	"	3	27	
William Earnest, - -	"	3	27	
Robert Fuqua, - -	"	3	27	
John Garrett, - -	"	3	27	
Samuel Goodman, - -	"	3	27	
Daniel Horner, - -	"	3	27	
Thomas Hudson, - -		3	27	
Samuel Hobson, - -	"	3	27	
Thomas Harris, - -	"	3	27	
Henry Hughes, - -	"	3	27	
John Huddleston, - -	"	3	27	

NAMES.	RANK.	Time of Service.		REMARKS.
		Months.	Days.	
Daniel Jamieson, - -	Private,	3	27	
Mosby Jenkins, - -	"	3	27	
Jacob Johnson, - -	"	3	27	
Anderson Johnson, - -	"	3	27	
John Jesse, - -	"	3	27	
Samuel Lightfoot, - -	"	1	24	
Henry Lightfoot, - -	"	3	27	
William Liggon, - -	"	3	27	
Wm. H. Moody, - -	"	1	7	
Henry Mason, - -	"	1	7	
Reuben Murray, - -	"	1	7	
Jesse Melton, - -	"	3	27	
Osborne Morris, - -	"	3	27	
Henry B. Montague, - -	"	3	27	
Daniel Martin, - -	"	3	27	
Drury Nixon, - -	"	3	27	
Randolph Newton, - -	"	3	27	
Samuel Newton, - -	"	3	27	
John Newton, - -	"	3	27	
Claiborne Nash, - -	"	3	27	
Anthony North, - -	"	3	27	
William Owen, - -	"	3	27	
John Price, - -	"	3	27	
Henry M. Penick, - -	"	3	27	
John Powers, - -	"	3	27	
Ben. H. Powell, - -	"	3	27	
John J. Reynolds, - -	"	1	22	
Thomas Robertson, - -	"	2	23	
James M. Smith, - -	"	3	27	
Hales Steger, - -	"	3	27	
Edward Scully, - -	"	1	10	
John Swann, - -	"	3	27	
Thomas Taylor, (S.) - -	"	3	27	
Thomas Taylor, (S. T.) -	"	3	27	
James M. Taylor, - -	"	3	27	
Daniel Taylor, - -	"	3	1	
William Wade, - -	"	3	27	
Josiah Ward, - -	"	3	27	
Wilson Wray, - -	"	3	27	
William Wray, - -	"	3	27	
Creed Wray, - -	"	2	23	
William Winfree, - -	"	3	27	
Peter Winfree, - -	"	3	27	
Ben. Woodson, - -	"	3	27	
William Walton, Sr., - -	"	2	20	

Captain Allen Wilson's Company—Seventeenth Regiment.

NAMES.	RANK.	TIME OF SERVICE.		REMARKS.
		Months.	Days.	
John T. Anderson, - -	Private,	–	9	
Francis Armistead, - -	"			
Reuben Austin, - -	"	–	29	
William Armistead, - -	"	–	15	
George Bigby, - -	"	–	15	
William Bigby, - -	"	–	15	
Samuel Browning, - -	"	–	15	
William Clarke, - -	"	–	15	
George Godwin, - -	"			
Christo. Hudson, - -	"	–	15	
Samuel Hudson, - -	"	2	20	
Francis F. James, - -	"	–	15	
Carter Johnson, - -	"	–	15	
Chesley Key, - -	"	–	15	
William L. Montague, -	"	–	15	
Robert Moore, - -	"			
Fleming Palmer, - -	"	–	15	
Hugh Watson, - -	"	–	15	
Maurice L. Wood, - -	"	–	15	
William H. Watkins, - -	"	–	15	

(For rest of this company, see publication of Pay Rolls.)

MUSTER ROLL

Of the Quarter Master General and Hospital Departments, in the City of Richmond, in the Service of the United States from the 29th day of November 1814, when last mustered, to the 28th of February 1815.

NAMES.	RANK.	TIME OF SERVICE.		REMARKS.
		Months.	Days.	
James Maurice, - -	Adj't Gen'l,	2	25	
Nathaniel Cargill, - -	Q. M. Gen'l,	3		
George Blow, - -	A. D. Q. M. Gen'l,	–	15	
Robert Rochelle, - -	"	3		
Carter B. Page, - -	P. F. Master,	3		
M. B. Poitiaux, - -	Ass't F. Master	3		
Ptolemy L. Watkins, -	Ass't T. Master	5	18	
John L. Duffel, - -	Ass't T. Master	2	22	
Jesse Burton, - -	P. W. Master,	1	8	
James Jones, - -	Surg. General,	–	17	
Philip Thornton, - -	Hosp'l Surg.	–	17	
M. Clark, - -	H. Surg. Mate,	–	18	
M. Fox, - - -	H. L. Mate,	3		
H. Jones, - - -	H. Steward,	–	10	
John T. Anderson, - -	Ward Master,	2	22	

MUSTER ROLL

Of Captain Samuel G. Adams' Company of Militia of the Nineteenth Regiment, commanded by Lt. Colonel John Ambler, in the Service of the United States from the 18*th to the* 27*th March, and from the* 27*th day of June to the* 3*d day of July* 1813.

NAMES.	RANK.	TIME OF SERVICE.		REMARKS.
		Months.	Days.	
Samuel G. Adams,	Captain,	–	16	
John S. Stubbs,	Lieutenant,	–	16	
Jacob Weisiger,	Ensign,	–	16	
Thomas Anslow,	Sergeant,	–	16	
Charles Kelley,	"	–	10	
John Yore,	"	–	10	
Francis J. Lewis,	"	–	16	
Geo. Watt,	"	–	6	
John Oram,	"	–	6	
William B. Lupton,	Corporal,	–	16	
Richard Finch,	"	–	10	
Charles Word,	"	–	10	
Thomas Turner,	"	–	6	
Crosher Graves,	"	–	6	
Samuel Quay,	"	–	6	
James S. Smithers,	"	–	6	
Nathan Abbott,	Private,	–	16	
Francis Austin,	"	–	16	
James Adams,	"	–	16	
Ignatius H. Allen,	"	–	16	
James Aspey,	"	–	10	
Bently Anderson,	"	–	10	
Thos. H. Alley,	"	–	10	
Edward Brown,	"	–	16	
William Brown,	"	–	16	
William W. Brown,	"	–	4	
Thos. Briggs,	"	–	16	
Alex. Barker,	"	–	6	
Joshua Brotherhood,	"	–	16	
Jason J. Brightwell,	"	–	16	
Joseph Bertrand,	"	–	4	
Geo. Brock,	"	–	4	
John Baptist,	"	–	4	
Amos Bemis,	"	–	10	
Ely Bennet,	"	–	10	
Samuel Bowers,	"	–	10	
John Clarke,	"	–	16	
William Coggin,	"	–	16	
John Cramey,	"	–	6	
Andrew Dunn,	"	–	16	
Joshua Doing,	"	–	16	
Benj. Darby,	"	–	16	
Berkett Doudall,	"	–	16	
John Drinkard,	"	–	6	
Charles Daniel,	"	–	4	
James Enders,	"	–	6	
James Earle,	"	–	16	

NAMES.	RANK.	TIME OF SERVICE.		REMARKS.
		Months.	Days.	
Thomas M. Everson,	Private,	–	16	
Charles Elliott,	"	–	6	
Pleasant Franklin,	"	–	16	
Ralph Fenn,	"	–	16	
William Fleming,	"	–	16	
Sam'l Gathwright,	"	–	16	
John Gathwright,	"	–	4	
Chas. F. Gretter,	"	–	16	
Major T. Garnett,	"	–	16	
Thomas Green,	"	–	6	
William Garraw,	"	–	4	
Sam'l D. Hart,	"	–	16	
Geo. B. Haines,	"	–	4	
Sam'l Houston,	"	–	6	
Noah Jones,	"	–	16	
John Johnston,	"	–	13	
William S. Johnston,	"	–	6	
Thomas Jones,	"	–	4	
Thomas Kesey,	"	–	6	
Joseph Key,	"	–	16	
Daniel Lucas,	"	–	16	
John Lancaster,	"	–	6	
Nath'l Long,	"	–	16	
William Miller,	"	–	16	
John McElligott,	"	–	4	
Geo. Myers,	"	–	4	
Thomas Oliver,	"	–	16	
Reuben Pleasants,	"	–	16	
Robert Pleasants,	"	–	16	
Geo. W. Payne,	"	–	16	
Philip Peach,	"	–	16	
Laurance Ryan,	"	–	16	
Jonathan Rogers,	"	–	6	
William Sheran,	"	–	16	
Charles Smith,	"	–	16	
Geo. Smith,	"	–	16	
Stephen Smith,	"	–	16	
John Sexsmith,	"	–	16	
Reuben M. Sizer,	"	–	16	
Jonas P. Slade,	"	–	16	
John Starr,	"	–	5	
Francis Sharp,	"	–	4	
Baylor Stubbs,	"	–	4	
Abner W. Turner,	"	–	16	
Richard Turner,	"	–	16	
Roddy Towers,	"	–	16	
Ambrose Turner,	"	–	16	
Joseph Thompson,	"	–	5	
John West,	"	–	16	
Cornelius West,	"	–	4	
Robert White,	"	–	4	
Beverly T. Wells,	"	–	16	
John Worrock,	"	–	16	
Thomas Whitlow,	"	–	16	
John Willock,	"	–	6	
John Wright,	"	–	16	
Edm'd Wright,	"	–	16	
Alex'r Parker,	"	–	10	
Henry Wright,	"	–	10	
Charles Hughes,	"	–	10	
James Snell,	"	–	10	
Joseph Palmer,	"	–	10	
Wyatt Hines,	"	–	10	
Hugh Warder,	"	–	10	

NAMES.	RANK.	TIME OF SERVICE.		REMARKS.
		Months.	Days.	
Francis Childress, - -	Private,	–	10	
Levy Pickrell, - -	"	–	10	
Purley Hughes, - -	"	–	10	
Ephraim Leonard, - -	"	–	10	
William J. Williams, -	"	–	10	
Nath'l Miller, - -	"	–	10	
Joseph New, - -	"	–	10	
Geo. N. Haynes, - -	"	–	10	
William Massie, - -	"	–	10	
John Nettles, - -	"	–	10	
John Grantland, - -	"	–	10	
Philip Holtz, - -	"	–	10	
John Oram, - -	"	–	10	
Joseph Murdock, - -	"	–	10	
William Kesee, - -	"	–	10	
Jabez Parker, - -	"	–	10	
William Tate, - -	"	–	10	
James Gibbs, - -	"	–	10	
Geo. Watt, - -	"	–	10	
Nicholas Scherer, - -	"	–	10	
Samuel Sherer, - -	"	–	10	
Geo. Reed, - -	"	–	10	
James Whitefield, - -	"	–	10	
William Mitchell, - -	"	–	10	
Christ. Drummond, - -	"	–	10	
Crosher Graves, - -	"	–	10	
Benj. Hubbard, - -	"	–	10	
Martin Turner, - -	"	–	10	
Geo. Merry, - -	"	–	10	

PAY ROLL

Of a Company commanded by Capt. George Booker, of the 19th Regiment Virginia Militia, in the Service of the United States, from 26th August to 30th September 1814.

NAMES.	RANK.	Time of Service.		REMARKS.
		Months.	Days.	
George Booker, - -	Captain,	1	6	
John Drewry, - -	Lieutenant,	1	6	
John Goddin, - -	Sergeant,	1	6	
Lewis Taylor, - -	Corporal,	1	6	
Hickerson Hancock, - -	"	1	6	
Eugene V. Lavert, - -	"	1	6	
William Cook, - -	Drummer,	1	6	
Rob't B. Armstead, - -	Private,	1	6	
Gilliam Anderson, - -	"	1	6	
Anderson Barrett, - -	"	1	6	
Samuel Baker, - -	"	1	6	
Simon Z. Block, - -	"	1	6	
Thomas Cook, - -	"	–	19	Transferred to Capt. Turner's company.
Ezekiel Daws, - -	"	1	6	
Henry Drewry, - -	"	1	6	
Samuel Doyle, - -	"	1	6	
Adolph Dill, - -	"	1	6	
Daniel Ellis, - -	"	1	6	
Samuel Greenhow, - -	"	1	6	
John Guthrie, - -	"	1	6	
John Hipkins, - -	"	1	6	
Josiah Hill, - -	"	1	6	
Thomas Keran, - -	"	1	6	
Miles F. King, - -	"	1	6	
Roger N. Lipscomb, - -	"	1	6	
Frank Mills, - -	"	1	6	
George Myers, - -	"	1	6	
William Powell, - -	"	1	6	
Jonathan Richards, - -	"	1	6	
Thomas Richardson, - -	"	1	6	
A. L. Robertson, - -	"	1	6	
George W. Spooner, -	"	1	6	
Jonah Slade, - -	"	1	6	
John Tharp, - -	"	1	6	
Thomas Tinsley, - -	"	1	6	
Caleb Tyree, - -	"	1	6	
John Tinsley, - -	"	1	6	
William Wingo, - -	"	1	6	
Josiah Williams, - -	"	1	6	

Captain George Bookers' Company—Nineteenth Regiment.

NAMES.	RANK.	TIME OF SERVICE.		REMARKS.
		Months.	Days.	
George Booker, - -	Captain,	–	10	
John Drewry, - -	Lieutenant,	–	10	
William Taylor, - -	Ensign,	–	10	
Joseph S. James, - -	"	–	24	
John Kenedy, - -	"	–	22	Promoted.
M. B. Portiaux, - -	Lieutenant,	–		
Francis Wood, - -	"	–	24	
Thomas Clarke, - -	Sergeant,	–	10	
William Boler, - -	"	–	10	
John Goddin, - -	"	–	10	
Lewis Atkinson, - -	"	–	22	
Christopher Irvine, - -	"	–	12	
Thomas Jude, - -	"	–	12	Transferred to comp'y as assistant.
Joshua Lomax, - -	"	–	24	
John Wood, - -	"	–	16	
Ebenezer Jones, - -	"	–	24	
John Parkhill, - -	"	–	24	
Robert B. Fife, - -	"	–	24	
Adolph Dill, - -	Corporal,	–	10	
Anderson Barrett, - -	"	–	10	
Abner Robinson, - -	"	–	10	
Francis Mills, - -	"	–	10	
John Powell, - -	"	–	12	
George W. Holmes, - -	"	–	12	Transferred to comp'y as assistant.
William Dickerson, - -	"	–	12	
Henry Pollard, - -	"	1	6	
John Southall, - -	"	–	24	
Henry Cower, - -	"	–	24	
John Rynax, - -	"	–	24	
Moses H. Judah, - -	"	–	24	
Samuel Andrews, - -	Private,	–	24	
James C. Anthony, - -	"	–	24	
Leary Andrews, - -	"	–	1	
David Allen, - -	"	–	10	
Gilliam Anderson, - -	"	–	10	
Lewis Atkinson, - -	"	–	10	
John G. Beck, - -	"	–	24	
Robert Bullington, - -	"	–	12	
Edward Bradley, - -	"	–	12	
William Baker, - -	"	–	10	
William Bosher, - -	"	–	2	Joined Capt. Stevenson's company.
Samuel Bingham, - -	"	–	10	
Thomas Baker, - -	"	–	10	
John Bosher, - -	"	–	10	
C. Baker, - -	"	–	10	
Benjamin Baker, - -	"	–	10	
Joshua Beale, - -	"	–	10	
J. Blair, - -	"	–	10	
James Bexhall, - -	"	–	10	
John Benson, - -	"	–	10	
William Badger, - -	"	–	2	Left the company.

NAMES.	RANK.	TIME OF SERVICE.		REMARKS.
		Months.	Days.	
William Bush,	Private,	–	2	
Charles Christian,	"	–	24	
Thomas Conclain,	"	–	25	Deserted.
Charles A. Cox,	"	–	–	Joined Capt. Wirt's F. artillery.
Milton Clarke,	"	–	24	
Elisha Copland,	"	–	24	
J. B. Cotton,	"	–	14	
William Crane,	"	–	24	
Henry Clarke,	"	–	24	
Frederick Clarke,	"	–	24	
Thomas Clark,	"	–	11	
Richardson Curle,	"	–	2	Joined some other company.
Reuben Crealy,	"	–	10	
James Cannon,	"	–	10	
Andrew Carleton,	"	–	4	
William W. Dickerson,	"	–	24	
William Dabney,	"	1	4	
Samuel Dunn,	"	–	10	
Charles Dunbar,	"	–	10	
Samuel Dayle,	"	–	10	
William Ellis,	"	–	10	
James Epperson,	"	–	10	
Ambrose Edwards,	"	–	4	Joined some other company.
James Edwards,	"	–	4	Joined some other company.
Daniel Ellis,	"	–	22	
William Elliott,	"	–	2	Joined another company.
Macon Ford,	"	–	24	
William Finch,	"	–	24	
Philip Fister,	"	–	24	
Elijah Folks,	"	–	24	
Nelson Farrar,	"	–	12	
William Foster,	"	–	14	Joined Capt. Wrist's (or Wirt's) artillery.
William Ford,	"	–	10	
Robert Fuller,	"	–	10	
R. B. Gwathney,	"	–	17	
James Gray,	"	–	24	
R. H. Goldthwait,	"	–	24	
John Garth,	"	–	24	
Mathew Gentry,	"	–	6	
Samuel Greenho[illegible],	"	–	10	
William Guy,	"	–	10	
John A. Glass,	"	–	4	
John S. Hughes,	"	–	24	
Wyatt Hynes,	"	–	24	
John F. Hendley,	"	–	12	
John Hanley,	"	–	22	
William L. Hedenburgh,	"	–	–	Deserted.
George Hamilton,	"	–	10	
James Holcroft,	"	–	10	
Leopold Jones,	"	–	24	
Edwin James,	"	–	24	
Dexter Jones,	"	–	10	
Christ. Irvine,	"	–	10	
Henry King,	"	–	24	
Daniel Lipscomb,	"	–	24	
Oliver Lipscomb,	"	–	21	Deserted.
William Lawrence,	"	–	24	
James Lowns, jr.	"	–	24	
Roger Lipscomb,	"	–	10	

NAMES.	RANK.	TIME OF SERVICE.		REMARKS.
		Months.	Days.	
John Miller,	"	–	16	
Thomas Massie,	"	–	24	
Sublett McGruder,	"	–	24	
W. G. Meriwether,	"	–	18	
William McEnry,	"	–	24	
Thomas Michall,	"	–	10	
Joseph Mays,	"	–	10	Appointed Serg. Maj.
Otis Mason,	"	–	10	
Peter Mayse,	"	–	1	
John Noel,	"	–	24	
Hector Organ,	"	–	24	
James Oldham,	"	–	10	
Asa Otis,	"	–	11	
Henry Owen,	"	–	22	
Thomas Ponsenbuy,	"	–	5	
Lawson Puckett,	"	–	24	
Charles Paine,	"	–	18	
George Parker,	"	–	4	Deserted.
John Puryear,	"	–	12	Transferred to company as assistant.
David Perry,	"	–	12	
Thomas Prosser,	"	–	10	
William Powell,	"	–	10	
Lindley Quesy,	"	–	10	
Richard Roddy,	"	–	9	Deserted.
Lodovicus Reed,	"	–	11	
William Richards,	"	–	24	
Elias Reed,	"	–	21	
Tho. Richardson,	"	–	3	Joined some other company.
Paschal Robertson,	"	–	10	
Samuel Stillman,	"	–	24	
John Slade,	"	–	24	
William Sheppard,	"	–	24	
Nathaniel Sheppard,	"	1	4	
William Saunderson,	"	–	21	
Samuel Swan,	"	–	24	
John Scott,	"	–	12	
Philip Sturdivant,	"	–	4	Joined Capt. Wrist's (or Wirt's) artillery.
Nath'l Shapard,	"	–	12	
George Spooner,	"	–	10	
John Sims,	"	–	10	
Yancy Thompson,	"	–	12	
William Tyree,	"	–	10	Deserted.
Caleb Tyree,	"	–	10	
W. P. Thatcher,	"	–	18	
Thos. Tinsley,	"	–	10	
Edward Valentine,	"	–	10	
R. C. Wortham,	"	–	24	
Harvie Williams,	"	–	24	
Edward Walford,	"	–	24	
Orin Williams,	"	–	24	
Isaac White,	"	–	24	
John Wright,	"	–	24	
Charles William,	"	–	24	
William Wild,	"	–	19	
Christopher Whiting,	"	–	12	
David Wood,	"	–	–	Deserted.
Josiah Williams,	"	–	10	
Henry Williams,	"	–	1	Joined some other company.
Thomas Winston,	"	–	10	
Thomas Ware,	"	–	10	

(For rest of this company, see publication of Pay Rolls.)

PAY ROLL

Of a Company commanded by Capt. Wilson Bryan, of the Nineteenth Regiment of Virginia Militia, in the Service of the United States, from the 28th June to 3d July 1813, *and from the 26th August to 30th September* 1814.

NAMES.	RANK.	Time of Service.		REMARKS.
		Months.	Days.	
Wilson Bryan, - -	Captain,	1	11	
John Lipscomb, - -	Lieutenant,	1	11	
Thomas B. Conway, - -	Ensign,	1	5	
Thomas Mieure, - -	Sergeant,	1	5	
Joseph Carter, - -	"	1	12	
Peter Ralston, - -	"	1	5	
William Tace, - -	Corporal,	1	5	
Richard Edwards, - -	"	1	11	
James Apperson, - -	Private,	1	5	
Samuel Ball, - -	"	1	7	
Robert Bradfute, - -	"	1	5	
Hickman Batcheldor, - -	"	1	5	
Robert Bouldin, - -	"	1	5	
John Carter, - -	"	1	11	
Obadiah Duvall, - -	"	1	11	
Hillary Driver, - -	"	1	11	
Samuel Dycher, - -	"	1	5	
Thomas Hooper, - -	"	1	5	
John Hollins, - -	"	1	7	
Anthony K. Johnson, - -	"	1	5	
John Jones, - -	"	1	11	
Frederick Jude, - -	"	1	7	
Richard Kimbrough, - -	"	1	5	
David Lemon, - -	"	1	11	
B. B. Lipscomb, - -	"	1	11	
George Mackey, - -	"	1	5	
McCuein, - -	"	1	5	
Hugh Moore, - -	"	1	9	
Abraham Mallack, - -	"	1	5	
James Oliver, - -	"	1		
Thomas Peede, - -	"	1	5	
William Pollard, - -	"	1	5	
Thomas Ritchie, - -	"	1	5	
John Robinson, - -	"	1		
James Seal, - -	"	1	11	
Joseph Spencer, - -	"	1	5	
Hairfield Timberlake, - -	"	1	5	
Amos Vibert, - -	"	1	7	
Jacob Valentine, - -	"	1	2	
Lewis Wingfield, - -	"	1	7	
George West, - -	"	1	5	
Rodney Walters, - -	"	1	5	

MUSTER ROLL

Of Ensign G. M. Carrington's Company, in the Nineteenth Regiment of Virginia Militia, commanded by Lieutenant Col. John Ambler, called into the Service of the United States, from the 27th day of August to the 7th day of September, in the year 1814.

NAMES.	RANK.	TIME OF SERVICE.		REMARKS.
		Months.	Days.	
G. M. Carrington,	Ens'n Comd't,	–	13	Transferred to Captain Turner.
Joseph Mayo,	Lieut. by brev.,	–	13	
N. K. Thomas,	Ens'n by "	–	13	
F. G. Crenshaw,	Sergeant,	–	13	" " "
Chas. T. Toomer,	"	–	13	" " "
Reuben Ragland,	"	–	13	" " "
Dan'l P. Organ,	"	–	13	" " "
Richard Anderson,	Private,	–	5	" " "
John Armistead,	"	–	13	" " "
William Barksdall,	"	–	2	
Simon Block,	"	–	13	" " "
Alexander Brown,	"	–	13	" " "
John Cline,	"	–	13	" " "
William M. Chick,	"	–	13	" " "
William H. Carroll,	"	–	11	
Nathaniel Dunlop,	"	–	10	
William Dunn,	"	–	13	" " "
Russel Dutton,	"	–	13	" " "
Geo. W. Hill,	"	–	13	" " "
Daniel Higginbotham,	"	–	6	" " "
John Henderson,	"	–	3	" " "
Edward Hallam,	"	–	13	" " "
John James,	"	–	13	" " "
Nathaniel M. Johnson,	"	–	13	" " "
Bennett Kirby,	"	–	13	" " "
William F. Micou,	"	–	8	Deserted.
John McMarra,	"	–	13	Transferred to Captain Turner.
Lewis Minor,	"	–	13	" " "
Elisha May,	"	–	9	" " "
John Marques,	"	–	13	" " "
Chas. M. Mitchell,	"	–	13	" " "
Daniel Mitchell,	"	–	13	" " "
Philip McGathy,	"	–	13	" " "
John Perkins,	"	–	13	" " "
John B. Ogg,	"	–	7	" " "
John Rowland,	"	–	13	" " "
Edward W. Roots,	"	–	13	" " "
Geo. Read,	"	–	13	" " "
Alexander Reid,	"	–	7	" " "
David Roper,	"	–	13	" " "
Mathew H. Rice,	"	–	8	" " "
Seamore Scott,	"	–	6	" " "
Larkin Smith,	"	–	13	" " "

NAMES.	RANK.	TIME OF SERVICE.		REMARKS.
		Months.	Days.	
Samuel Sublett, - -	Private,	–	10	
Samuel Shepheard, - -	"	–	13	Transferred to Captain
Alexander Sharp, - -	"	–	13	Turner,
Edward W. Trent, - -	"	–	13	" " "
Hez'h Veach, - -	"	–	13	" " "
Jos. W. Vaughan, - -	"	–	7	" " "
Conquest Wyott, - -	"	–	13	" " "
Sylvester Walkley, - -	"	–	13	" " "
James Watson, - -	"	–	8	" " "

Captain Wilson Bryan's Company—Nineteenth Regiment.

NAMES.	RANK.	TIME OF SERVICE.		REMARKS.
		Months.	Days.	
Wilson Bryan, - -	Captain,	–	10	
John Lipscomb, - -	Lieutenant,	–	10	
John Perry, - -	"	1	5	
Daniel Hutchinson, - -	Ensign,	–	14	
Jacob Weisiger, - -	"	–	23	
Thomas Ritchie, - -	Sergeant,	–	6	
Chauncey Carter, - -	"	–	14	
Charles Christian, - -	"	–	5	
Warner Thomas, - -	"	–	6	
John H. Jude, - -	"	–	9	
Robert Snuden, - -	"	–	24	
Thomas Hatcher, - -	"	–	23	
William Butler, - -	"	–	23	
John Quarles, - -	"	–	23	
Wilman Gilman, - -	"	–	10	
John L. Turner, - -	"	–	10	
Richard Scott, - -	"	–	10	
Samuel Evans, - -	Corporal,	–	16	
Peter Letellier, - -	"	–	6	
Alex'r Grant, - -	"	–	6	
Thomas Atkinson, - -	"	–	10	
William Tyree, - -	"	–	3	
Richard Edwards, - -	"	–	10	
George Boasher, - -	"	–	23	
William Granberry, - -	"	–	24	
Ellis Carlton, - -	"	–	5	
Nelson G. Phillips, - -	"	–	23	
Madison McLauren, - -	"	–	23	
Reuben Nash, - -	"	–	12	
James H. Royster, - -	"	–	12	
Samuel Queay, - -	"	–	8	
J. New, - -	Drummer,	–	17	
Robert Andrews, - -	Private,	–	23	
Thomas M. Ambler, - -	"	–	23	
Charles Anderson, - -	"	–	5	
Thomas Atkerson, - -	"	–	2	
George Atkerson, - -	"	–	3	
Charles J. Bingham, - -	"	–	5	
George Boswell, - -	"	–	12	
Royall Brown, - -	"	1		
James Bailess, - -	"	–	7	
William Barnes, - -	"	–	23	
John Benson, - -	"	–	2	
John Bransford, - -	"	–	6	
Samuel J. Bagby, - -	"	–	12	
Thomas Butler, - -	"	–	5	
G. H. Bacchus, - -	"	–	23	
Thomas Baish, - -	"	–	23	
Daniel Baugh, - -	"	–	23	
Wilson Bracket, - -	"	–	23	
James Brock, - -	"	–	23	
Samuel Brame, - -	"	–	23	
William Burke, - -	"	–	23	
Charles Bennet, - -	"	–	22	
Joshua Brotherhood, - -	"	–	23	
William Bressie, - -	"	–	23	
Samuel Bull, - -	"	–	1	

NAMES.	RANK.	TIME OF SERVICE.		REMARKS.
		Months.	Days.	
John Bath,	Private,	–	3	
James Booker,	"	–	1	
John Barnes,	"	–	1	
Joseph Butler,	"	–	1	
James Burchell,	"	–	4	
Jonathan Collingworth,	"	–	16	
Robert Cracker,	"	–	6	
Ralph Crutchfield,	"	–	14	
Henry Calloway,	"	–	7	
James Connelly,	"	–	2	
John Craw,	"	–	3	
Geo. R. Cocks,	"	–	23	
Samuel Churchill,	"	–	23	
Samuel N. Cardozo,	"	–	23	
B. W. Coleman,	"	–	23	
George Carter,	"	–	23	
Charles Carter,	"	–	13	
Edward Cunningham,	"	–	7	
Walter Cameron,	"	–	24	
John Carter,	"	–	10	
Joseph Carter,	"	–	10	
Charles Christian,	"	–	10	
Anthony Croussell,	"	–	3	
Thomas Cook,	"	–	3	
William Cousins,	"	–	1	
John J. Dickenson,	"	–	10	
John Dean,	"	–	9	
Abraham Delape,	"	–	12	
Alex'r S. Dean,	"	–	6	
John Durham,	"	–	6	
Richard Davis,	"	–	23	
John Drinkard,	"	1	3	
Andrew Dunn,	"	–	23	
Benjamin Daiby,	"	–	12	Or Dailey.
William Darning,	"	–	4	
Obediah Duvall,	"	–	10	
Hilary Driver,	"	–	13	
John Enders,	"	–	23	
Charles Ellis,	"	–	14	
Theodorick Fergason,	"	–	23	
Alexander Fulcher,	"	–	23	
James Grassett,	"	–	9	
Michael H. Gilliam,	"	–	12	
John Goode,	"	–	23	
William Garrow,	"	–	23	
John Grantland,	"	–	23	
Francis Gilmer,	"	–	4	
John G. Gamble,	"	–	2	
Alexander Grant,	"	–	10	
Mich'l W. Hancock,	"	–	16	
Garland Haynes,	"	–	16	
William Harding,	"	–	14	
Major Horner,	"	–	16	
William Haynes,	"	–	2	
Samuel Hawkins,	"	–	5	
Thomas Hedrick,	"	–	18	
James Herron,	"	–	23	
John Hove,	"	–	3	
John Hollins,	"	–	10	
William Holloway,	"	–	12	
Martin Holloway,	"	–	3	
Henry Huxford,	"	–	23	
Isaac Harnard,	"	–	23	
Daniel Jones,	"	1	3	

NAMES.	RANK.	TIME OF SERVICE.		REMARKS.
		Months.	Days.	
John Jamerson,	Private,	–	2	
John Jude,	"	–	2	
Richard Jeffries,	"	–	4	
Charles A. Jacob,	"	–	23	
John Jones,	"	–	3	
John Johnson,	"	–	23	
Harrison Jones,	"	–	12	
Benjamin Johnston,	"	–	1	
Fred. Jude,	"	–	10	
John M. Key,	"	–	23	
Bashforth Irvin,	"	–	1	
Yancy Lipcomb,	"	–	4	
William Loyall,	"	1	19	
Thomas Letellier,	"	–	6	
Charles Lamgmead,	"	–	12	
Nathaniel Long,	"	–	23	
Thomas Lee,	"	–	23	
Isaac Leonard,	"	–	23	
Francis Lewis,	"	–	2	
David Lemmon,	"	–	10	
Austin Lipscomb,	"	–	10	
Beverly B. Lipscomb,	"	–	10	
Peter Letellier,	"	–	10	
John Murphy, jr.	"	–	16	
Alex'r McKim,	"	1	16	
John Marcus,	"	–	14	
Patrick McDonough,	"	–	16	
John Moore,	"	–	16	
Archelaus Mays,	"	–	16	
Samuel Meridith,	"	–	6	
James M. Morris,	"	–	2	
John McBride,	"	–	4	
Charles J. McMurdo,	"	–	23	
James McAllister,	"	–	23	
Alexander Morris,	"	–	23	
William Massenburg,	"	–	23	
Archelaus Mays,	"	–	18	
William Morrissett,	"	–	10	
Reuben Merideth,	"	–	10	
Samuel Mallory,	"	–	10	
John McCurne,	"	–	1	
Hugh Moore,	"	–	10	
Edmond S. Norvell,	"	–	23	
Reubin Nash,	"	–	11	
Robert McCracken,	"	–	10	
Joseph Neale,	"	–	11	
George Olphin,	"	–	10	
Richard Olphin,	"	–	10	
James Oliver,	"	–	2	
John Ormond,	"	–	6	
Daniel G. Pleasants,	"	–	12	
Joseph Perryman,	"	–	4	
Anthony Perryman,	"	–	6	
Edward Peticole,	"	–	23	
Jabez Parker,	"	–	23	
Thomas Peckrill,	"	–	23	
Daniel G. Pleasant,	"	–	12	
Noblin Puryear,	"	–	10	
Thomas Puryear,	"	–	2	
Samuel Quay,	"	–	15	
Nathan H. Rice,	"	–	16	
John Rutherfoord,	"	–	6	
Samuel Roberts,	"	–	2	
Richard Redford,	"	–	23	

NAMES.	RANK.	TIME OF SERVICE.		REMARKS.
		Months.	Days.	
John Roberts, - -	Private,	-	23	
James H. Royster, - -	"	-	11	
Thomas Ritchie, - -	"	-	10	
John Robertson, - -	"	-	10	
James Rudd, - -	"	-	10	
Thomas E. Sanford, - -	"	-	16	
William Shapard, - -	"	-	2	
James Seal, - -	"	-	10	
Briton Sharpe, - -	"	-	1	
Thomas Skidmore, - -	"	-	5	
William C. Shield, - -	"	-	23	
Samuel Smith, - -	"	-	23	
George Smith, - -	"	-	23	
William Sharan, - -	"	-	23	
James Snell, - -	"	-	23	
Solomon Simon, - -	"	-	23	
Charles Smith, - -	"	-	23	
Jacob Smith, - -	"	-	23	
Reuben M. Sizer, - -	"	-	13	
Joseph Trent, - -	"	1	3	
John L. Turner, - -	"	-	2	
Zachariah Tyler, - -	"	-	1	
Caleb Tyre, - -	"	-	2	
Thomas Warner, - -	"	-	2	
Chiles Terrell, - -	"	-	23	
Thomas Wilson, - -	"	-	23	
William Talley, - -	"	-	9	
James Taylor, - -	"	-	23	
Thomas Benaja, - -	"	-	23	
Michael Tucker, - -	"	-	23	
Watson Tyler, - -	"	-	23	
Amos Vibert, - -	"	-	3	
Jacob Valentine, - -	"	-	10	
William Wright, - -	"		6	
Jesse Willis, - -	"	-	16	
David Wallace, - -	"	-	13	
John Watkins, - -	"	-	16	
William Wirt, - -	"	-	10	
Erasmus Welsh, - -	"	-	10	
Lewis Wingfield, - -	"	-	10	
Samuel Winston, - -	"	-	23	
John Warrick, - -	"	-	23	
Benjamin Waller, - -	"	-	23	
Hugh Warden, - -	"	-	23	
Edmond Warner, - -	"	-	23	
Ambrose Watkins, - -	"	-	21	
Charles Word, - -	"	-	2	

Captain William Byrd Chamberlayne's Company—First Brigade.

NAMES.	RANK.	TIME OF SERVICE.		REMARKS.
		Months.	Days.	
William W. Christian, -	Private,	3	24	
John Turner, - -	"	1	5	
Jesse Willis, - -	"	-	8	Transferred to Army.

(For rest of this company, see publication of Pay Rolls.)

PAY ROLL

Of Captain William Coleman's Company, of the Ninetieth Regiment of Virginia Militia, Amherst County, belonging to the Detachments commanded by Major William Armistead and Colonel John H. Cocke, at Camp Holly, from the 25th of March to the 21st of August 1813.

NAMES.	RANK.	Time of Service. Months.	Days.	REMARKS.
William Coleman, - -	Captain,	3	27	
Dudley Sandidge, - -	Lieutenant,	3	27	
James S. Pendleton, - -	Ensign,	3	27	
Wiatt Duncan, - -	Sergeant,	3	27	
Dabney Ware, - -	"	3	27	
Robert Carter, - -	"	3	27	
Joshua Sandidge, - -	"	3	27	
Gideon Powell, - -	"	3	27	
George T. Williams, - -	"	3	27	
Charles W. Christian, - -	Corporal,	2		
Wm. H. McCulloch, - -	"	1		
William Turner, - -	"	3	27	
Ezekiel B. Gilbert, - -	"	3	27	
James M. Smith, - -	"	3	27	
John P. Brown, - -	"	3	27	
Wm. B. Walker, - -	Drummer,	3	27	
Wesley E. Christian, - -	"	2		
Willis Mays, - -	Fifer,	3	27	
Robert Allen, - -	Private,	1		
John Birch, - -	"	3	27	
William Bryant, - -	"	3	27	
George Binks, - -	"	1		
John C. Banks, - -	"	3	27	Or Blanks.
Uriah Bobbett, - -	"	2		
Lacey Bobbett, - -	"	1	27	
Mahlon Clements, - -	"	3	27	
Jack Carter, - -	"	2		
Jesse Cash, - -	"	3	27	
Littleberry Coleman, - -	"	3	27	
John Creasy, - -	"	3	27	
James B. Coflin, - -	"	3	27	Or Coffin.
Robert Douglas, - -	"	2		
Joseph Davenport, - -	"	2	27	
Barnett Edwards, - -	"	3	27	
Nicholas Gilliam, - -	"	1		
James Gilliam, - -	"	3	27	Or Gilman.
John Goolsby, - -	"	3	27	
Edward Guthrie, - -	"	3	27	
Archer Gilliam, - -	"	2	–	Or Archillaus.
Charles Haynes, - -	"	3	27	
William Henderson, - -	"	3	27	
James Halton, - -	"	1	27	
John Langhorne, - -	"	2		
George Langhorne, - -	"	3	27	
William Lyon, - -	"	1	27	
Joshua Mays, - -	"	2		
Tarpley Mitchell, - -	"	2		
David Maxwell, - -	"	2		
Wiatt Moon, - -	"	2		
William Massie, - -	"	3	27	
Thomas Massie, - -	"	3		
Robert McCullock, - -	"	3	27	
Lewis Martin, - -	"	3	27	
Jesse Massie, - -	"	3	27	

NAMES.	RANK.	Time of Service.		REMARKS.
		Months.	Days.	
James Mitchell, - -	Private,	1		
John Mitchell, - -	"	1	27	
Thomas Nowell, - -	"	3	27	Or Norvell.
David Price, - -	"	3	27	
Charles Palmer, - -	"	2		
John Rowsey, - -	"	3	27	
James Roundtree, - -	"	1		
Peter Robinson, - -	"	1	27	
David W. Robinson, - -	"	1	27	Or David M.
Morris Roberts, - -	"	1	27	
Waller Sandidge, - -	"	3	27	
Ro. T. Sandidge, - -	"	3	27	
Obadiah Scruggs, - -	"	3	27	
William Sherman, - -	"	2		
Nicholas Shoemaker, - -	"	3	27	
Nat. Stewart, - -	"	3	27	
Daniel Snoddy, - -	"	3	27	
William Snead, - -	"	3	27	
Hugh Taggott, - -	"	3	27	Or Tyget.
Moses Taylor, - -	"	2		
Geo. W. Taylor, - -	Blacksmith,	3	27	
Landon Tooley, - -	"	3	27	
William Tucker, - -	"	3	27	
John Tooley, - -	"	3	27	
Wm. Tankersley, - -	"	3	27	
Shadrack Tennison, - -	"	3	27	
Robert Wingfield, - -	"	3	27	
John Wright, - -	"	3	27	
Ben. Wright, - -	"	3	27	
Curtis Watts, - -	"	3	27	
William Watts, - -	"	3	27	
James Whittenton.				
Edmund Williamson, - -	"	3	27	

Captain William Coleman's Company—Ninetieth Regiment.

NAMES.	RANK.	TIME OF SERVICE.		REMARKS.
		Months.	Days.	
Dennis Enzy, - -	Corporal,	1		
James Daily, - -	Drum Major,	1		
James Edwards, - -	Fife Major,	1		
Lunsford Carter, - -	Private,	1	27	
Dennis Ensy, - -	"	1		
Jacob Gilliam, - -	"	1		
Thomas Gilbert, - -	"	1	27	
Wright Robinson, - -	"	1		
Walter Williams, - -	"	2	27	

(For rest of this company, see publication of Pay Rolls.)

MUSTER ROLL

Of Captain Robert Gamble's Troop of Cavalry, from the 19th Regiment, Virginia Militia, commanded by Lieutenant Colonel John Ambler, in the Service of the United States, at different periods in the years 1813, and 1814.

NAMES.	RANK.	TIME OF SERVICE.		REMARKS.
		Months.	Days.	
Robert Gamble, - -	Captain,	2	15	
Alexander Fulton, - -	1st Lieutenant,	1	20	
Benjamin Shepard, - -	2d "	–	27	
James Sheppard, - -	2d "	1	18	
Jacq'ne B. Harvie, - -	Cornet,	–	27	
Richard Randolph, - -	"	1	18	
John B. Hillard, - -	S. Master,	–	27	
Thomas Burton, - -	Q. M. Serg't,	–	27	
William Bootright, - -	Sergeant,	–	27	
Reuben Johnston, - -	"	1	13	
Thomas Guy, - -	"	–	27	
Thomas Diddep, - -	"	–	27	
James H. Lynch, - -	"	1	18	
Gabriel Ralston, - -	"	1	18	
James Currie, - -	"	1	13	
William Randolph, - -	Corporal,	1	18	
Macon Green, - -	"	1	18	
Henry Heath, - -	"	–	16	
James Seldon, - -	"	1	8	
Thomas H. Harris, - -	"	–	27	
Peter Chevallie, - -	"	–	27	
Hall Melson, - -	"	–	27	
John Woodfin, - -	"	–	27	
Theodorick, - -	Trumpeter,	1	13	
Frank Washington, - -	"	1	2	
Jedediah Allen, - -	Private,	2	15	
Spencer Alvis, - -	"	–	27	
P. Aylett, - -	"	1	2	
Thomas Bohannon, - -	"	2	15	
John Burton, - -	"	2	15	
Richard Brooks, - -	"	1	20	
William Burksdale, - -	"	–	27	
Thomas Burton, - -	"	1	18	
William Bootwright, - -	"	1	16	
Reubin Burton, - -	"	1	18	
J. D. Brown, - -	"	1	16	
J. Buckner, - -	"	2	1	
James Currie, - -	"	–	27	
Charles Childree, - -	"	2	15	
B. F. Cocke, - -	"	2	13	
John Craddock, - -	"	–	27	
William Colquahoon, - -	"	–	2	
Joel Colice, - -	"	–	27	
Richard Crouch, - -	"	–	27	
Peter Chevallie, - -	"	1	5	
John Collins, - -	"	1	18	
Richard Darrington, - -	"	–	2	

NAMES.	RANK.	TIME OF SERVICE.		REMARKS.
		Months.	Days.	
J. F. Dennis, - -	Private,	2	15	
James Dick, - -	"	1	20	
Martin Drury, - -	"	2	15	
William Dupriest, - -	"	1	3	
John Dove, - -	"	–	27	
David Dorrington, - -	"	2	8	
William Derrough, - -	"	1	18	
Edward C. Davis, - -	"	1	18	
William Dornin, - -	"	–	6	
John S. Ellis, - -	"	2	15	
Francis Ellis, - -	"	1	18	
Samuel Frazer, - -	"	2	15	
Thomas Foster, - -	"	1	13	
William Frost, - -	"	–	6	
W. H. Fitzhugh, - -	"	1	2	
Macon Green, - -	"	–	27	
William Good, - -	"	1	13	
James Gwathmey, - -	"	1	13	
John Gatewood, - -	"	1	12	
Thomas Guy, - -	"	1	18	
John Gunn, - -	"	1	12	
George Hendree, - -	"	–	27	
Geo. M. Hopkins, - -	"	–	27	
Charles Hay, - -	"	2	15	
Thomas H. Harris, - -	"	1	12	
John B. Hillard, - -	"	–	16	
J. Harwood, - -	"	–	10	
J. B. Harvey, - -	"	–	16	
J. Haynes, - -	"	1	2	
R. Harwood, - -	"	1	2	
Lightfoot Janney, - -	"	1	16	
Ambrose Jenkins, - -	"	–	16	
P. W. Jackson, - -	"	–	12	
Robert K. Jones, - -	"	–	25	
Nichl's Kimbrough, - -	"	1	12	
Caleb Lownes, - -	"	1	3	
Jacob Lyon, - -	"	2	13	
James Lynch, - -	"	2	13	
William Lambert, - -	"	–	6	
William Mann, - -	"	2	15	
Jo. H. Mays, - -	"	2	15	Or Mayo.
Elijah Marquis, - -	"	2	15	
Wade Mosby, jr. - -	"	–	27	
William Miller, - -	"	1	12	
James Morris, - -	"	1	18	
John McAllister, - -	"	1	18	
Nath'l Nelson, - -	"	1	18	Or James.
Hall Neilson, - -	"	–	10	
Geo. Pickett, - -	"	1	20	
Mann Page, - -	"	–	27	
William B. Page, - -	"	1	17	
Francis Pratte, - -	"	1	18	
Whitley Preston, - -	"	1	18	
Thos. H. Puryear, - -	"	–	10	
G. Payne, - -	"	1	2	
William Randolph, - -	"	–	27	
Gabriel Ralston, - -	"	–	27	
Jas. B. Roddy, - -	"	1	13	
Isaac Raphael, - -	"	–	27	
Wm. B. Randolph, - -	"	–	27	
William Richardson, jr. -	"	2	15	
John M. Redford, - -	"	1	18	
Timothy Redmond, - -	"	1	18	
P. Roane, - -	"	1	2	

NAMES.	RANK.	TIME OF SERVICE.		REMARKS.
		Months.	Days.	
James Selden,	Private,	–	27	
John Strother,	"	1	7	
John Stagg,	"	2	5	
Walter Shelton,	"	1	3	
John Schermerhorn,	"	1	3	
Lenews Smith,	"	1	13	
N. Smith,	"	1	5	
John S. Shelton,	"	2	15	
John Shippard,	"	1	5	
Robert Smith,	"	1	18	
P. Shevallia,	"	1	2	Or Chevallie.
M. Smith,	"	1	2	
Saml. H. Smith,	"	–	6	
Claiborne Thomas,	"	1	14	
Henry Tompkins,	"	2	15	
John Taylor,	"	–	18	
James Talley,	"	1	13	
Ezra Talmadge,	"	1	13	
William Temple,	"	1	18	
Thomas Watson,	"	2	15	
Nathaniel White,	"	2	15	
John Watson,	"	2	9	
Daniel Warwick,	"	1	13	
John Woodfin,	"	1	12	
James Whitlock,	"	1	18	
Thomas Williams,	"	–	6	
Isaac Webster,	"	1	8	
Thomas Underwood,	"	1	8	

MUSTER ROLL

Of Captain John R. Jones' Company, of the Nineteenth Regiment, Virginia Militia, in the County of Henrico, commanded by Lieutenant Colonel John Ambler, in the Service of the United States, from 18th to the 27th March, 1813, and from 26th August to 8th September, 1814.

NAMES.	RANK.	TIME OF SERVICE.		REMARKS.
		Months.	Days.	
John R. Jones,	Captain,	–	24	
Patrick Coutts,	Lieutenant,	–	23	
David Haynes,	Ensign,	–	17	
Francis Wood,	"	–	23	
Joshua Lomax,	Sergeant,	–	13	
John Parkhill,	"	–	13	
Ebenezer Jones,	"	–	13	
John Wood,	"	–	13	
Sublett Magruder,	"	–	10	
James Williams,	"	–	10	
Charles Keesee,	"	–	10	
Francis Wood,	"	–	10	
Henry Robinson,	Corporal,	–	23	
John Parkhill,	"	–	10	
John Wood.	"	–	10	
Samuel T. Chandler,	"	–	10	
William Crane,	"	–	13	
Charles J. Payne,	"	–	13	
John Southall,	"	–	13	
Samuel Andrews,	Private,	–	13	
S. Alaquin,	"	–	10	
Edward Adams,	"	–	10	
Samuel Adams,	"	–	10	
Andrew Bryson,	"	–	10	
Richard Bohannan,	"	–	10	
Campbell Blades,	"	–	10	
Arch'd Blair,	"	–	10	
John G. Beck,	"	–	13	
Benj. W. Coleman,	"	–	10	
Marcus Cochran,	"	–	10	
William Crane,	"	–	10	
Frs. W. Coleman,	"	–	10	
Joseph B. Colton,	"	–	10	
Henry Clarke,	"	–	10	
Geo. W. Clarke,	"	–	10	
Frederick Clarke,	"	–	13	
Josephus B. Colton,	"	–	13	
Elisha Copland,	"	–	13	
Milton Clarke,	"	–	13	
William Dixon,	"	–	10	
Thos. S. Dicken,	"	–	10	
William Dabney,	"	–	23	
Edw'd Eubank,	"	–	23	
Saml. C. Faulkner,	"	–	10	

NAMES.	RANK.	TIME OF SERVICE.		REMARKS.
		Months.	Days.	
Richard Fitzgerald, - -	Private,	–	10	
William Finch, - -	"	–	15	
Macon Ford, - -	"	–	23	
John B. Finley, - -	"	–	10	
Thomas Foster, - -	"	–	10	
Simon Frayser, - -	"	–	10	
James Gray, - -	"	–	13	
A. T. Gordon, - -	"	–	10	
James Gentry, - -	"	–	10	
Robert H. Goldthwaite, -	"	–	13	
Th. P. Hutchinson, - -	"	–	10	
And. Hetherton, - -	"	–	10	
John C. Hobson, - -	"	–	10	
C. Hubbard, - -	"	–	10	
John S. Hughes, - -	"	–	13	
Wyatt Hynes, - -	"	–	11	
George Irwin, - -	"	–	10	
John Johnson, - -	"	–	10	
L. Jones, - -	"	–	10	
Moses Jackson, - -	"	–	10	
John Jenks, - -	"	–	10	
Ellis Juan, - -	"	–	10	
Philip Jackson, - -	"	–	10	
Moses H. Judah, - -	"	–	13	
Jacob King, - -	"	–	15	Transferred to flying artillery.
John Kelso, - -	"	–	10	
Henry King, - -	"	–	13	
Caleb Lownes, - -	"	–	10	Transferred to cavalry.
Geo. B. Lafong, - -	"	–	10	
Joshua Lomax, - -	"	–	10	
Joseph Lovell, - -	"	–	10	
John Ludden, - -	"	–	5	Transferred to flying artillery.
William Lenieve, - -	"	–	13	
James Lownes, jr. - -	"	–	13	
Caleb Lownes, - -	"	–	5	
John Miller, - -	"	–	23	
Thomas Massie, - -	"	–	10	
Hector M. Organ, - -	"	–	23	
Asa Otis, - -	"	–	10	
Geo. B. Poe, - -	"	–	10	
Benjamin Poe, -	"	–	10	
Thomas A. Ponsonby, -	"	–	13	
Bernard Phillips, - -	"	–	8	
Reuben Ragland, - -	"	–	10	
L. Read, - -	"	–	10	
Nath. Ragland, - -	"	–	10	
Theod'k Robinson, - -	"	–	10	
Nicholas Rind, - -	"	–	13	
William Richard, - -	"	–	13	
Henry Rogers, - -	"	–	5	
John Rynax, - -	"	–	13	
Elias Reed, - -	"	–	13	
Richard Reddy, - -	"	–	6	
F. Sydnor, - -	"	–	10	
Wm. Sanderson, - -	"	–	10	
Burnett Scott, - -	"	–	10	
Robert Shapard, - -	"	–	10	
William Shapard, - -	"	–	10	
Edward Staples, - -	"	–	10	
William Shepherd, - -	"	–	10	
C. Vail, - -	"	–	10	
Otway Wilkinson, - -	"	–	10	

NAMES.	RANK.	TIME OF SERVICE.		REMARKS.
		Months.	Days.	
Isaac White, - -	Private,	–	10	
Edward Walford, - -	"	–	10	
Edward Williams, - -	"	–	10	
David Wilson, - -	"	–	10	
William Wild, - -	"	–	10	
Austin Williams, - -	"	–	10	

(For rest of this company, see publication of Pay Rolls.)

MUSTER ROLL

Of Captain Samuel Jones' Company, of the Nineteenth Regiment, Virginia Militia, commanded by Lieutenant Colonel John Ambler, in the Service of the United States, from the 18th to the 27th March, and from the 28th June to the 3rd day of July, 1813.

NAMES.	RANK.	TIME OF SERVICE.		REMARKS.
		Months.	Days.	
Samuel Jones, - -	Captain,	–	16	
John B. Ogg, - -	Lieutenant,	–	10	
John H. Royster, - -	Ensign,	–	16	
John W. Wood, - -	Sergeant,	–	13	
N. K. Thomas, - -	"	–	13	
Thomas Oliver, - -	"	–	16	
Trebourne Crenshaw, -	"	–	10	
F. J. Crenhard, - -	"	–	6	Or Crenshaw.
G. H. Bacchus, - -	"	–	6	
James Armstrong, - -	"	–	3	
A. Wiley, - -	Corporal,	–	3	
George Davis, - -	"			
James Laughline, - -	"	–	6	
D. Ball, - -	"	–	4	
Charles Anthony, - -	Private,	–	10	
Richard Anderson, - -	"	–	16	
Myer Alden, - -	"	–	10	
James Armstrong, - -	"	–	3	
Samuel J. Blair, - -	"	–	14	
Simon Block, - -	"	–	16	
Gurdon H. Bacchus, - -	"	–	13	
James Burley, - -	"	–	10	
George W. Bristow, - -	"	–	10	
James Bennett, - -	"	–	10	
Albert Booker, - -	"	–	10	
Hillary Baker, - -	"	–	13	
Wm. Bradley, - -	"	–	16	
Robert Bullington, - -	"	–	10	
William Barksdale, - -	"	–	6	
Samuel Brooks, - -	"	–	4	
James Bailey, - -	"	–	4	
Leo. Bowers, - -	"	–	3	
Lewis Brawner, - -	"	–	3	
William Crawford, - -	"	–	16	
William Caulfield, - -	"	–	16	
Joseph R. Crouch, - -	"	–	10	
Andrew Crew, - -	"	–	16	
William Colquhoun, - -	"	–	16	
William H. Carroll, - -	"	–	16	
Seaman Charlton, - -	"	–	10	
Jonathan Carlile, - -	"	–	13	
William H. Carlile, - -	"	–	16	
James A. Campbell, - -	"	–	16	
Peter Cotton, - -	"	–	6	
Robert Craig, - -	"	–	6	
Nathan. Dunlop, - -	"	–	16	
William Dunn, - -	"	–	16	

NAMES.	RANK.	TIME OF SERVICE.		REMARKS.
		Months.	Days.	
Charles Doyle,	Private,	–	16	
George Dabney,	"	–	10	
William Davenport,	"	–	16	
George Davis,	"	–	10	
Jos. W. Dickenson,	"	–	16	
Saml. C. Dickenson,	"	–	16	
Thos. T. Dickenson,	"	–	16	
Russell Dutton,	"	–	6	
William Dandridge,	"	–	6	
Geo. W. Fuzzell,	"	–	16	
William Foushee, jr.	"	–	16	
James Fellows,	"	–	16	
Francis Graves,	"	–	16	
James Gray,	"	–	16	
William Gentry,	"	–	16	
John B. Green,	"	–	16	
John Gray,	"	–	6	
Edward Gay,	"	–	6	
Edward Hallam,	"	–	16	
Ellis Hudnall,	"	–	16	
John Henry,	"	–	16	
George W. Hill,	"	–	16	
Gideon Hatcher,	"	–	16	
John Holderfield,	"	–	16	
James Howard,	"	–	16	
Charles Hubbard,	"	–	16	
Axiom Hubbard,	"	–	16	
Richard Hines,	"	–	10	
James Henderson,	"	–	16	
Robert Hughes,	"	–	10	
Robert Henderson,	"	–	16	
Richard Henderson,	"	–	16	
D. Higginbotham,	"	–	3	
John Ireson,	"	–	12	
Solomon Jacobs,	"	–	13	
Richard Jordan,	"	–	11	
John James,	"	–	16	
Harrison James,	"	–	13	
John Jones,	"	–	10	
Abraham Kimball,	"	–	16	
Bennett Kirby,	"	–	16	
Frederick Kuhn,	"	–	16	
John King,	"	–	16	
Henry King,	"	–	10	
John Leslie,	"	–	16	
James Lughlam,	"	–	10	
Isaac Leabetts,	"	–	10	
Conrad Lotz,	"	–	4	
Isaac Leadbetter,	"	–	6	
Gamaliel Monroe,	"	–	16	
John McMarra,	"	–	16	
James McKildoe,	"	–	16	
James McNally,	"	–	16	
Andrew Moore,	"	–	16	
William S. Murphy,	"	–	13	
Thomas Montague,	"	–	13	
Adam Maury,	"	–	10	
Charles M. Mitchell,	"	–	13	
Garland Mitchell,	"	–	10	
Afid. Murray,	"	–	3	
Elijah May,	"	–	3	
B. Morrison,	"	–	6	
J. G. Mosby,	"	–	6	
Littleberry Mosby,	"	–	6	

NAMES.	RANK.	TIME OF SERVICE.		REMARKS.
		Months.	Days.	
Matthew Mosby, - -	Private,	–	6	
Andrew Moorland, - -	"	–	6	
Opie Norris, - -	"	–	16	
William Neckervis, - -	"	–	16	
D. P. Organ, - -	"	–	6	
Samuel Pointed, - -	"	–	10	
Allen Pollock, - -	"	–	16	
Jonathan Palmer, - -	"	–	16	
Sherloch Palmer, - -	"	–	16	
Munford Perks, - -	"	–	13	
Fleming Park, - -	"	–	13	
James Pakes, - -	"	–	10	
John Parker, - -	"	–	13	
F. D. Peters, - -	"	–	1	
John Perkins, - -	"	–	3	
John Rowland, - -	"	–	13	
Leonard Rowlett, - -	"	–	10	
Edward W. Rootes, - -	"	–	16	
Alexander Reed, - -	"	–	13	
Samuel Read, - -	"	–	13	
Pascal Robinson, - -	"	–	10	
G. H. Stanback, - -	"	–	16	
Nathaniel Smith, - -	"	–	10	
George W. Smith, - -	"	–	10	
John M. Smith, - -	"	–	16	
Jacob Stally, - -	"	–	10	
Wm. M. Samuel, - -	"	–	10	
Jos. Smith, - -	"	–	6	
William Scott, - -	"	–	6	
Alexander Sharp, - -	"	–	6	
John Southall, - -	"	–	6	
Edward W. Trent, - -	"	–	13	
James Talley, - -	"	–	10	
Robert Tucker, - -	"	–	13	
Exra Talmadge, - -	"	–	10	
John L. Thomas, - -	"	–	10	
John Vaughan, - -	"	–	16.	
Hez. Veach, - - -	"	–	16	
Geo. W. Valentine, -	"	–	16.	
Joseph A. Weed, - -	"	–	13	
Edward Wanton, - -	"	–	16	
William W. Walker, -	"	–	16	
David Woodward, - -	"	–	16	
Ro. Wilson, - -	"	–	6	
Sylvester Walkley, - -	"	–	6	
Alex. Wiley, - -	"	–	3	

MUSTER ROLL

Of Captain William McCabe's Company, from the Nineteenth Regiment, Virginia Militia, commanded by Lieutenant Colonel John Ambler, in the Service of the United States, from the 18th to the 27th March, 1813.

NAMES.	RANK.	TIME OF SERVICE.		REMARKS.
		Months.	Days.	
William McCabe, - -	Captain,	–	10	
Archelaus Hughes, - -	Lieutenant,	–	10	
John McPherson, - -	Ensign,	–	10	
Richard Crouch, - -	Sergeant,	–	10	
David Hanna, - -	"	–	10	
Robert Triplett, - -	"	–	10	
Joshua Crump, - -	"	–	10	
Christian Bohn, - -	Private,	–	10	
James Wallace, - -	"	–	10	
Charles J. Shelton, - -	"	–	10	
John Southall, - -	"	–	10	
James Lucadoe, - -	"	–	10	
David Mason, - -	"	–	10	
James Roberts, - -	"	–	10	
Matthew Moody, - -	"	–	10	
William Franklin, - -	"	–	10	
Leroy Hipkins, - -	"	–	10	
James McBride, - -	"	–	10	
Beverly Gale, - -	"	–	10	
Jos. W. Vaughan, - -	"	–	10	
Richard Archer, - -	"	–	10	
Charles Ellis, - -	"	–	10	
Joseph Todd, - -	"	–	10	
Walker Y. Meriwether, -	"	–	10	
Robert Poore, - -	"	–	10	
David Poore, - -	"	–	10	
John Cooley, - -	"	–	10	
Edmund Leneve, - -	"	–	10	
James Atkinson, - -	"	–	10	
Thomas W. Walker, -	"	–	10	
David Merry, - -	"	–	10	
Robert Walker, - -	"	–	10	
Westwood James, - -	"	–	10	
John Anderson, - -	"	–	10	
Benjamin Read, - -	"	–	10	
Thomas Hatcher, - -	"	–	10	
William Matthew, - -	"	–	10	
James Barnes, - -	"	–	10	
Graves Matthews, - -	"	–	10	
William T. Archer, - -	"	–	10	
Geo. W. Spooner, - -	"	–	10	
William Price, - -	"	–	10	
Edward Cunningham, -	"	–	10	
Geo. Atkinson, - -	"	–	10	
Benj. James Harris, - -	"	–	10	
James Bridges, - -	"	–	10	
Michael Gretter, - -	"	–	10	

NAMES.	RANK.	TIME OF SERVICE.		REMARKS.
		Months.	Days.	
Leonard Wheeler, - -	"		10	
Samuel Hawkins, - -	"		10	
Alexander Brander, - -	"		10	
Gustavus Lucke, - -	"		10	
William H. Hubbard, - -	"		10	
Horatio H. Chittenden, -	"		10	
David Timberlake, - -	"		10	
Jessee Higginbottom, - -	"		10	
George Winston, - -	"		10	
Caleb Terrell, -	"		10	
Samuel Winston, - -	"		10	
Cyrus Christian, - -	"		10	
Walter Childers, - -	"		10	
John Winston, - -	"		10	
Valerius Campbell, - -	"		10	
Lewis Webb, - -	"		10	
George Stillman, - -	"		10	
Hugh McNamare, - -	"		10	
James S. Smithers, - -	"		10	
John Hill, - -	"		10	
John D. Miller, - -	"		10	
Samuel D. Daniel, - -	"		10	
Thomas E. Brown, - -	"		10	
Osmond Bowler, - -	"		10	
John H. Sublett, - -	Private,		10	
James Scott, - -	"		10	
James Rent, - -	"		10	
Thomas Hubbard, - -	"		10	
William Rhodes, - -	"		10	
Jacob Cheadle, - -	"		10	
John L. Buckner, - -	"		10	
John Hockiday, - -	"		10	
Joseph S. James, - -	"		10	

MUSTER ROLL

Of Captain John McPherson's Company, from the Nineteenth Regiment, Virginia Militia, commanded by Lieutenant Colonel John Ambler, in the Service of the United States, from 26th August to the 7th day of September, 1814.

NAMES.	RANK.	TIME OF SERVICE.		REMARKS.
		Months.	Days.	
John McPherson, - -	Captain,	–	14	
John Bootwright, - -	Lieutenant,	–	14	
John Perry, - -	Ensign,	–	14	
Jos. S. James, - -	Sergeant,	–	14	
James Reat, - -	"	–	14	
Joshua Crump, - -	"	–	14	
Thos. Cushing, - -	"	–	14	
Westwood W. James, -	Corporal,	–	14	
Josiah Poore, - -	"	–	6	Joined Aug. 28, 1814.
David Reat, - -	"	–	4	" 31, "
William Poe, - -	"	–	4	" 31, "
Richard Archer, - -	Private,	–	9	Joined the blues Sep. 3.
Richard Allfin, - -	"	–	8	
Christian Bohn, - -	"	–	9	Flying artillery Sept. 3.
William Boulware, - -	"	–	19	" " "
Water Childress, - -	"	–	19	" " "
Wilson B. Clark, - -	"	–	8	" " "
Edwin Clark, - -	"	–	19	" " "
Michael Gretter, - -	"	–	19	" " "
Parke Glenn, - -	"	–	14	
Thos. Gillian, - -	"	–	9	" " "
Jessee Higginbotham, -	"	–	9	Appointed secretary Sept. 3.
David Hanna, - -	"	–	9	Appointed serg't major Sept. 3.
James Hubbard, - -	"	–	9	Flying artillery.
Isaac Harper, - -	"	–	9	" "
Thomas Hill, - -	"	–	3	" "
John Hill, - -	"	–	4	" "
William Jones, - -	"	–	14	
Nath'l Ireson, - -	"	–	4	Transferred.
David Kenney, - -	"	–	14	
Read Kire, - -	"	–	14	
Gustavus Luke, - -	"	–	14	
Adam Murray, - -	"	–	14	
David Mason, - -	"	–	14	
William McEnery, - -	"	–	14	
James Madison, - -	"	–	9	Joined the blues Sep. 3.
Charles Melna, - -	"	–	3	
Robert Neilson, - -	"	–	14	
Robert Poore, - -	"	–	14	
Nath'l Perkins, - -	"	–	9	
James Roper, - -	"	–	10	
Geo. H. Stanback, - -	"	–	9	Flying artillery.
James S. Smithers, - -	"	–	14	
John H. Sublett, - -	"	–	9	
Joseph Todd, - -	"	–	14	
Lewis Webb, - -	Private,	–	14	
John Walden, - -	"	–	9	Flying artillery 3.
John Winston, - -	"	–	14	
James Winston, - -	"	–	14	
Thos. N. Walker, - -	"	–	9	Joined the blues Sep. 3.

MUSTER ROLL

Of Captain Anderson Miller's Company, from the Nineteenth Regiment, Virginia Militia, commanded by Lieutenant Colonel John Ambler, in the Service of the United States, from the 18th to 27th March, and from 28th June to 3d July, 1813, and from 26th August to 7th September, 1814.

NAMES.	RANK.	TIME OF SERVICE.		REMARKS.
		Months.	Days.	
Anderson Miller,	Captain,	–	28	
Michael B. Portiaux,	Brevet Lieut.	–	28	Promoted from corp'l.
Geo. E. Tiffin,	Lieutenant,	–	16	
William H. Hughes,	Ensign,	–	16	
Fred. M. McCraw,	"	–	12	
Geo Fisher,	Sergeant,	–	16	
Edward Bailey,	"	–	16	
Thomas Cushing,	"	–	16	
Dabney Eubank,	"	–	6	
Charles Carter,	"	–	10	
Gordon H. Backus,	"	–	12	
James Herron,	"	–	8	
Thomas Hatcher,	"	–	12	
John H. Norman,	"	–	12	
William R. Butler,	"	–	9	
William H. Prince,	Corporal,	–	16	
John Dryman,	"	–	6	
John Roberts,	"	–	28	
Edmund Banks,	"	–	10	
James Armstrong,	"	–	10	
John Crouch,	"	–	10	
William Burke,	"	–	12	
Geo. Bosher,	"	–	12	
Elias Carlton,	"	–	8	
Richard Davis,	"	–	8	
Robert Moreland,	"	–	8	
Robert Andrews,	Private,	–	18	
Thos. M. Ambler,	"	–	22	
Geo. Allen,	"	–	10	
Philip Aylett,	"	–	10	
Robert Atkinson,	"	–	10	
Thomas Baish,	"	–	12	
Daniel Baugh,	"	–	12	
Wilson Brackett,	"	–	12	
James Brook,	"	–	12	
Geo. Bosher,	"	–	12	
William Banks,	"	–	12	
Edmund Banks,	"	–	12	
Samuel D. Brame,	"	–	12	
William R. Butler,	"	–	12	
William Burke,	"	–	2	
John Brakenbrough,	"	–	16	
John H. Blair,	"	–	13	
William V. Butler,	"	–	16	
James Blair,	"	–	3	
Hickman Bachelor,	"	–	16	
Robert Bradford,	"	–	16	

NAMES.	RANK.	TIME OF SERVICE.		REMARKS.
		Months.	Days.	
John Banks, - -	Private,	–	6	
Lewin Blake, - -	"	–	10	Or Levin,
Washington Berry, - -	"	–	10	
Geo. R. Cocke, - -	"	–	3	
Lemuel Churchill, - -	"	–	12	
William Cook, - -	"	–	12	
John Campbell, - -	"	–	22	
Elias Carlton, - -	"	–	12	
Samuel N. Cardozo, - -	"	–	8	
Thomas Cook, - -	"	–	6	
Micajah Clarke, - -	"	–	10	
Josiah Cushing, - -	"	–	10	
John W. Dance, - -	"	–	12	
Richard Davis, - -	"	–	12	
John Day, - -	"	–	16	
Francis Dunington, - -	"	–	16	
Philip Duval, - -	"	–	6	
John Drinan, - -	"	–	6	
Johnson Eubank, - -	"	–	16	
Miles Egleston, - -	"	–	6	
John H. Eustace, - -	"	–	16	
Joseph Ellis, - -	"	–	6	
Theoderick Furguson, -	"	–	12	
Alexander Fulcher, - -	"	–	7	
James Fisher, - -	"	–	6	
Henry Frobus, - -	"	–	6	
Robert Fuller, - -	"	–	10	
Jesse Franklin, - -	"	–	10	
John Grantland, - -	"	–	12	
Gideon B. Green, - -	"	–	12	
Robert Gordon, - -	"	–	16	
Thomas Gibbs, - -	"	–	16	
Matthew Gentry, - -	"	–	6	
James Gunn, - -	"	–	6	
John P. Grantland, - -	"	–	6	
Wiltshur Golden, - -	"	–	6	
Martin Gentry, - -	"	–	10	
Geo. Greenhow, - -	"	–	10	
Richard Graves, - -	"	–	10	
Martin Holloway, - -	"	–	28	
Henry Hucksford, - -	"	–	12	
John Hays, - -	"	–	12	
John Holman, - -	"	–	12	
James Herron, - -	"	–	22	
Thomas G. Hull, - -	"	–	16	
John Hocady, - -	"	–	6	
John Holman, - -	"	–	6	
John Herrick, - -	"	–	10	
Daniel Higginbotham, -	"	–	10	
Christopher Hudson, - -	"	–	10	
Joseph Hill, - -	"	–	10	
Sterling R. Hood, - -	"	–	10	
Charles A. Jacobs, - -	"	–	22	
Joseph Jenkins, - -	"	–	16	
Thomas Jefferys, - -	"	–	6	
James Jefferys, - -	"	–	10	
William Johnston, . -	"	–	10	
John M. Key, - -	"	–	12	
Matthew Lacy, - -	"	–	12	
Alexander Lithgow, - -	"	–	16	
Fleming Lacy, - -	"	–	10	
Charles J. McMurdo, - -	"	–	28	
William McCabe, - -	"	–	12	
William Minor, - -	"	–	12	

NAMES.	RANK.	TIME OF SERVICE.		REMARKS.
		Months.	Days.	
Robert Moreland, - -	Private,	–	12	
William McCaw, - -	"	–	3	
William Mann, - -	"	–	6	
Robert McCullough, - -	"	–	6	
William McKenny, - -	"	–	10	
Edmund Mosby, - -	"	–	6	
Thomas Muir, - -	"	–	10	
William Neale, - -	"	–	10	
Norborne Norton, - -	"	–	16	
Lewell Osgood, - -	"	–	16	
Walter Porter, - -	"	–	12	
Henry Pettus, - -	"	–	10	
Kincheon Parker, - -	"	–	10	
William B. Price, - -	"	–	6	
William Perry, - -	"	–	16	
Edward Petticola, - -	"	–	12	
John Quarles, - -	"	–	12	
Richard Ross, - -	"	–	16	
Alexander Strother, - -	"	–	16	
Jacob Smith, - -	"	–	10	
Philip Sturdivant, - -	"	–	10	
Fendal J. Sebree, - -	"	–	16	
Philip Southall, - -	"	–	10	
Walter J. Steptoe, - -	"	–	10	
George Smith, - -	"	–	16	
William C. Shields, - -	"	–	12	
William Sadler, - -	"	–	12	
Isaac Sturdivant, - -	"	–	12	
Chiles Terrell, - -	"	–	16	
Thomas Terrell, - -	"	–	10	
Benjamin Thomas, - -	"	–	22	
James Taylor, - -	"	–	16	
Richard D. Taylor, - -	"	–	6	
Wilson Thomas, - -	"	–	12	
James Taylor, - -	"	–	12	
Rodney Walters, - -	"	–	16	
William Wickham, - -	"	–	16	
Charles Wade, - -	"	–	10	
Edmund Wade, - -	"	–	10	
John Wills, - -	"	–	10	
William C. Williams, - -	"	–	10	

PAY ROLL

Of Captain William Murphy's Company, of the First Corps D'Elite, in the Service of the United States, commanded by Colonel Thomas Mann Randolph, from 25th of August to 5th of October 1814.

NAMES.	RANK.	Time of Service.		REMARKS.
		Months.	Days.	
William Murphy, - -	Captain,	1	11	
John G. Gamble, - -	Lieutenant,	1	11	
John G. Smith, - -	"	1	11	
John G. Blair, - -	Ensign,	1	11	
William Finney, - -	"	1	11	
William Barrett, - -	Ord. Sergeant,	1	11	
Philip Duval, - -	Q. M. Serg't,	1	11	
Isaac B. Sixas, - -	1st Sergeant,	1	11	
Charles J. Shelton, - -	2d "	1	11	
John W. Cheadle, - -	3d "	1	11	
William H. Shields, - -	4th "	1	11	
Fleming B. Cross, - -	1st Corporal,	1	11	
George Nicholson, - -	2d "	1	11	
N. B. Kimbrough, - -	3d "	1	11	
George Stillman, - -	4th "	1	11	
Sam'l J. Bagby, - -	5th "	1	11	
Samuel Mordecai, - -	6th "	1	11	
William I. Cole, - -	7th "	1	11	
Richard Henderson, - -	8th "	1	11	
John Ewens, - -	P. Musician,	1	11	
Joseph Viglini, - -	Musician,	1	11	
John H. Strobia, - -	"	1	11	
Anthony Croaswell, - -	"	1	11	
E. V. Lachaise, - -	"	1	11	
Henry J. Arnhold, - -	"	1	11	
Henry Stanhope, - -	"	1	11	
George Christian, - -	"	1	11	
George M. Allen, - -	Private,	1	11	
John Anderson, - -	"	1	11	
Richard Archer, - -	"	1	11	
Alexander Brander, - -	"	1	11	
Beverly Blair. - -	"	1	11	
Samuel J. Blair, - -	"	1	11	
Albert Booker, - -	"	1	11	
Abram Block, - -	"	1	11	
A. G. Booker, - -	"	1	11	
James Bray, - -	"	1	11	
James Baily, - -	"	1	11	
James Brown, jr., - -	"	1	11	
Thomas Cowles, - -	"	1	11	
William Cowan, - -	"	1	11	
William Craig, - -	"	1	11	
Sterling I. Crump, - -	"	1	11	
L. V. Crandall, - -	"	1	11	
Turner Christian, - -	"	1	11	
Thomas T. Dickinson, - -	"	1	11	
Rivers Drake, - -	"	1	11	
Charles James Fox, - -	"	1	11	
John T. Fleming, - -	"	1	11	
William R. Geddy, - -	"	1	11	
Peter Hohn, - -	"	1	11	
William Hooper, - -	"	1	11	
William Howard, - -	"	1	11	
Charles H. Hyde, - -	"	1	11	

NAMES.	RANK.	Time of Service.		REMARKS.
		Months.	Days.	
Fleming James,	Private,	1	11	
John Jenks,	"	1	11	
John Jones,	"	1	11	
Ro. S. James,	"	1	11	
Richard Jeffries,	"	1	11	
Nevin Kearns,	"	1	11	
James Liggon,	"	1	11	
Edward Leneave,	"	1	11	
George H. Mitchell,	"	1	11	
Philip Mayo,	"	1	11	
B. S. Morrison,	"	1	11	
John Murphy, jr.,	"	1	11	
James Madison,	"	1	11	
Thomas Nash,	"	1	11	
Arch'd Pleasants,	"	1	11	
Thomas S. Pope,	"	1	11	
Munford Perks,	"	1	11	
Jacob Phillips,	"	1	11	
Samuel Parkhill,	"	1	11	
Robert Pleasants,	"	1	11	
Robert M. Pulliam,	"	1	11	
Theodorick Robertson,	"	1	11	
Jasper Robins,	"	1	11	
George Robertson,	"	1	11	
Geo. P. Richardson,	"	1	11	
James Sizer,	"	1	11	
Philip Turner Shelton,	"	1	11	
Randolph Snelson,	"	1	11	
John Shore,	"	1	11	
Robert Shapard,	"	1	11	
Saml. Scott,	"	1	11	
Harry Tompkins,	"	1	11	
Elisha Turpin,	"	1	11	
John L. Thomas,	"	1	11	
Henry Turpin,	"	1	11	
Philip M. Tabb,	"	1	11	
Ben. C. Tompkins,	"	1	11	
Robert Triplett,	"	1	11	
Abel Webster,	"	1	11	
Robert G. Williamson,	"	1	11	
George Wells,	"	1	11	
Charles Wortham,	"	1	11	
John Wilson,	"	1	11	
Richard Woolfolk,	"	1	11	
Charles Watson,	"	1	11	
Nelson Walker,	"	1	11	
William Warwick,	"	1	11	
John Yore,	"	1	11	

Captain William Murphy's Company—Nineteenth Regiment.

NAMES.	RANK.	TIME OF SERVICE.		REMARKS.
		Months.	Days.	
William Murphy, - -	Captain,	–	5	
David J. Burr, - -	Lieutenant,	–	5	
Thomas Diddep, - -	Ensign,	–	5	
John G. Blair, - -	Sergeant,	–	5	
William Finney, - -	"	–	5	
Edw. C. Cook, - -	"	–	5	
Philip Duval, - -	"	–	5	
James Rawlings, - -	Corporal,	–	5	
William J. Cole, - -	"	–	5	
Robert Lyman, - -	"	–	4	
John W. Cheadle, - -	"	–	5	
Henry J. Arnhold, - -	Private,	–		
Bentley Anderson, - -	"	–	3	
John M. Armistead, - -	"	–	3	
Charles Beck, - -	"	–	5	
Albert Booker, -	"	–	3	
William Barrett, - -	"	–	5	
James Brown, jr. - -	"	–	5	
Thomas Bendle, - -	"	–	5	
Alexander Brown, - -	"	–	3	
Beverly Blair, - -	"	–	5	
John Bootright, - -	"	–	5	
John H. Blair, - -	"	–	10	
Peter Copland, - -	"	–	5	
Benj. Cheigneau, - -	"	–	5	
William Cowan, - -	"	–	5	
Samuel Carey, - -	"	–	2	
Edward V. Crandall, - -	"	–	5	
Sterling I. Crump, - -	"	–	5	
Thomas Cheadle, - -	"	–	5	
William Craig, - -	"	–	5	
Flem. B. Cross, - -	"	–	4	
Thomas Cowles, - -	"	–	5	
Nat. Dick, - -	"	–	10	
Thos. S. Dickerson, - -	"	–	2	
Geo. Dabney, - -	"	–	2	
Rivers Drake, - -	"	–	5	
John Darrac, - -	"	–	5	
Simon Frazer, - -	"	–	3	
Charles J. Fox, - -	"	–	5	
John Fore, - -	"	–	5	
John G. Gamble, - -	"	–	2	
William R. Geddy, - -	"	–	5	
Robert Hughes, - -	"	–	3	
William Hooper, - -	"	–	4	
Peter Hohn, - -	"	–	5	
Manuel Judah, - -	"	–	5	
John Jones, - -	"	–	2	
Flem'g James, - -	"	–	3	
James Liggon, - -	"	–	5	
E. V. Lachaize, - -	"	–	5	
Thomas Morgan, - -	"	–	2	
William Minton, - -	"		5	

****

NAMES.	RANK.	TIME OF SERVICE.		REMARKS.
		Months.	Days.	
Fred. McCraw, - -	Private,	–	5	
Theo. Nash, - -	"	–	5	
Jacob Philips, - -	"	–	5	
Arch'd Pleasants, - -	"	–	5	
Thos. S. Pope, - -	"	–	5	
Walter Potter, - -	"	–	5	
Ro. M. Pulliam, - -	"	–	5	
Fred. Pleasants, - -	"	–	5	
Geo. Robertson, - -	"	–	3	
Joseph Robbins, - -	"	–	5	
Youell Rust, - -	"	–	5	
Henry Rodgers, - -	"	–	5	
T. Y. Roddy, - -	"	–	5	
Theo. Robertson, - -	"	–	4	
John H. Strobia, - -	"	–	5	
Isaac B. Seixas, - -	"	–	5	
John G. Smith, - -	"	–	5	
James Sizer, - -	"	–	1	
Philip T. Shelton, - -	"	–	5	
Frs. Strobia, - -	"	–	5	
E. Sandford, - -	"	–	5	
William H. Shields, - -	"	–	5	
Sam'l Scott, - -	"	–	5	
Elisha Turpin, - -	"	–	5	
Harry Tompkins, - -	"	–	5	
John L. Thomas, - -	"	–	3	
John Wilson, - -	"	–	5	
Charles Watson, - -	"	–	2	
Geo. Wells, - -	"	–	5	
Abel Webster, - -	"	–	5	
Robert Wilkins, - -	"	–	5	
Corbin Warwick, - -	"	–	5	
William Warwick, - -	"	–	5	

(For rest of this company, see publication of Pay Rolls.)

MUSTER ROLL

Of Cornet Richard Randolph's Troop of Cavalry, from the Nineteenth Regiment, Virginia Militia, commanded by Lieutenant Colonel J. Ambler, in the Service from the 17th of April to 2nd May, 1813.

NAMES.	RANK.	TIME OF SERVICE.		REMARKS.
		Months.	Days.	
Richard Randolph, - -	Cornet,	–	15	
William Randolph, - -	Sergeant,	–	15	
James Whitlocke, - -	Private,	–	15	
Jed'h Allen, - -	"	–	15	
Richard Brooke, - -	"	–	15	
T. Burton, - -	"	–	15	
William Bootwright, - -	"	–	15	
B. F. Cocke, - -	"	–	15	
Charles Childrey, - -	"	–	15	
Thos. Gay, - -	"	–	15	
Charles Hay, - -	"	–	15	
Lightfoot Janney, - -	"	–	15	
James Lynch, - -	"	–	15	
Nath'l Nelson, - -	"	–	15	
T. Redmond, - -	"	–	15	
William Richardson, - -	"	–	15	
—— Miller, - -	"	–	15	
John Stagg, - -	"	–	15	
James Gawthmey, - -	"	–	15	
William Preston, - -	"	–	15	
H. Tompkins, - -	"	–	15	
John Watson, - -	"	–	15	
J. Webster, - -	"	–	15	
John Woodfin, -	"	–	15	

MUSTER ROLL

Of Captain Andrew Stevenson's Company, of the Nineteenth Regiment, Virginia Militia, commanded by Lieutenant Colonel John Ambler, called into the Service of the United States, from 18th to 27th of March, in the year 1814.

NAMES.	RANK.	TIME OF SERVICE.		REMARKS.
		Months.	Days.	
Andrew Stevenson,	Captain,	–	10	
Charles Bosher,	Lieutenant,	–	10	
Ralph Allen,	"	–	10	
Chs. Z. Abrahams,	Sergeant,	–	10	
John P. Prentis,	"	–	10	
Nath. Charter,	"	–	10	
James Golding,	"	–	10	
Abner Allen,	Private,	–	10	
John Bath,	"	–	10	
Elias Bennett,	"	–	10	
James Bosher,	"	–	10	
John Bosher,	"	–	10	
Jonas Crane,	"	–	10	
Zach. Clarke,	"	–	10	
Joseph Danforth,	"	–	10	
James Edwards,	"	–	10	
Richard Finch,	"	–	10	
Jas. A. Grant,	"	–	10	
William Gardner,	"	–	10	
Felix Grant,	"	–	10	
Wm. Henderson,	"	–	10	
Alex'r Hare,	"	–	10	
Mitchum Hudgins,	"	–	10	
Bathford Irvine,	"	–	10	
G. F. Kohler,	"	–	10	
William Keesee,	"	–	10	
William Lee,	"	–	10	
Thomas Lane,	"	–	10	
Samuel Liggon,	"	–	10	
Peter Lemons,	"	–	10	
Barrett Moss,	"	–	10	
H. Mettert,	"	–	10	
Joseph Murdock,	"	–	10	
—— Miller,	"	–	10	
Richard Norris,	"	–	10	
William O. Nash,	"	–	10	
James Ogden,	"	–	10	
John Patton,	"	–	10	
H. Pickrill,	"	–	10	
Solomon Robins,	"	–	10	
William Talman,	"	–	10	
James Thompson,	"	–	10	
James Tounley,	"	–	10	
Charles Wills,	"	–	10	
Amiel Williams,	"	–	10	
John Walker,	"	–	10	

MUSTER ROLL

Of Lieutenant John S. Stubbs' Company, in the Nineteenth Regiment, Virginia Militia, commanded by Lieutenant Colonel John Ambler, called into the Service of the United States, from the 26th August to the 7th September, 1814.

NAMES.	RANK.	TIME OF SERVICE.		REMARKS.
		Months.	Days.	
John S. Stubbs, - -	Lieutenant,	–	13	Appointed adjutant.
Jacob Weisiger, - -	Ensign,	–	13	
Francis J Lewis, - -	Sergeant,	–	13	Appointed assistant F. master.
Edmund Redford, - -	"	–	13	Appointed assistant Q. master.
George Watt, - -	"	–	10	Appointed Qr. master.
Edmund S. Norvell, - -	"	–	13	
John Ormond, - -	Corporal,	–	13	
Reuben Nash, - -	"	–	13	
Jabez Parker, - -	"	–	13	
John A. Lancaster, - -	"	–	13	
Wiliam Armistead, - -	Private,	–	7	F. artillery.
James Asby, - -	"	–	13	
Wm. Archer, - -	"	–	7	" "
Alexander Auter, - -	"	–	7	" "
Charles Bennett, - -	'	–	13	
William Brasie, - -	"	–	13	
Royal Brown, - -	"	–	13	
Joshua Brotherhood, - -	"	–	13	
Leonard Bowers, - -	"	–	7	Union artillery.
Benj. W. Coleman, - -	"	–	13	
George Charter, - -	"	–	13	
Andrew Crew, - -	"	–	13	
John Drinkard, - -	"	–	13	
Christ. Drummond, - -	"	–	7	F. artillery.
Andrew Dunn, - -	"	–	13	
Charles Elliott, - -	"	–	7	" "
John Enders, - -	"	–	13	
Wm. Fleming, - -	"	–	7	" "
Robert Fagg, - -	"	–	7	" "
John Goode, - -	"	–	13	
William Garrow, - -	"	–	13	
Isaac Hamard, - -	"	–	13	
George P. Hadin, - -	"	–	7	" "
Daniel Jones, - -	"	–	13	
John Johnson, - -	"	–	13	
Uriah Johnson, - -	"	–	13	
William Loyall, - -	"	–	13	
Nathaniel Long, - -	"	–	13	
Thomas Lee, - -	"	–	13	
Isaac Leonard, - -	"	–	13	
Carter Mallory, - -	"	–	7	" "
George Mettert, - -	"	–	7	" "
James McAllister, - -	"	–	13	
William Masonberg, - -	"	–	13	
Richard Minor, -	"	–	7	" "

NAMES.	RANK.	TIME OF SERVICE.		REMARKS.
		Months.	Days.	
Alexander Morris, - -	Private,	–	7	F. artillery.
G. W. Pam, - -	"	–	7	" "
Thomas Pickerell, - -	"	–	13	
Samuel Quay, - -	"	–	13	
James H. Royster, - -	"	–	6	
Richard Redford, - -	"	–	13	
James Rudd, - -	"	–	7	" "
Jacob Smith, - -	"	–	13	
George Smith, - -	"	–	13	
William Sheran, - -	"	–	13	
James Shell, - -	"	–	13	
Reuben M. Sizer, - -	"	–	13	
George F. Shifter, - -	"	–	10	
Simon Solomon, - -	"	–	13	
Samuel Smith, - -	"	–	8	
Michael Tucker, - -	"	–	13	
Watson Tyler, - -	"	–	7	
Roddy Towers, - -	"	–	7	" "
Charles Word, - -	"	–	13	Appointed F. master.
Thomas Whitlow - -	"	–	7	F. artillery.
Edmund Warner - -	"	–	7	
John Warwick, - -	"	–	13	
Matthew Watts, - -	"	–	7	" "
Benjamin Waller, - -	"	–	13	
Samuel Winston, - -	"	–	13	
Hugh Warden, - -	"	–	13	
George Woodfin, - -	"	–	6	Sutler.

PAY ROLL

Of Capt. Edmund Taylor's Company of Riflemen of Virginia Militia, Richmond City, from Feb. 6 to March 3, and from June 28 to July 3, 1813.

NAMES.	RANK.	Time of Service.		REMARKS.
		Months.	Days.	
Edmund Taylor,	Captain,	1	2	
William H. Richardson,	Lieutenant,	1	2	
Samuel H. Ege,	Ensign,	1	2	
Daniel Trueheart,	Sergeant,	1	2	
Ben. C. Turner,	"	1	2	
Leonard H. Seaton,	"	1	2	
Paul Christian,	"	1	2	
William Saunders,	Corporal,	1	2	
Lawson Puckett,	"	1	2	
Daniel Taylor,	"	1	2	
Henry Widmeyer,	Musician,	1	2	
George Kelley,	"	1	2	Or Kinley.
Jacob Dorsheimer,	"	1	2	
James H. Mann,	"	1	2	
William Holman,	"	1	2	
J. T. West,	"	1	2	
Daniel Brown,	"	1	2	
Charles Horwell,	"	1	2	
William Adams,	Private,	1	2	
James Allen,	"	1	2	
Vincent Boswell,	"	1	2	
John H. Cosby,	"	1	2	
Joshua P. Crump,	"	1	2	
John Field,	"	1	2	
William Fulcher,	"	1	2	
Alexander Gerard,	"	1	2	
Wilson C. Jones,	"	1	2	
Robert Kirby,	"	1	2	
Thornton C. Lipscomb,	"	1	2	
Philip Larus,	"	1	2	
John Lawler,	"	1	2	
Thornton Norwood,	"	1	2	
Oakley Philpotts,	"	1	2	
Thomas Shields,	"	1	2	
Samuel C. Tyree,	"	1	2	
George Woodfin,	"	1	2	
Braxton Waller,	"	1	2	

PAY ROLL

Of a Company of Infantry, commanded by Captain Anthony Turner, of the Nineteenth Regiment of Virginia Militia, in the Service of the United States, from 28th June to 3d July 1813, *and from the 26th August to 30th September* 1814.

NAMES.	RANK.	Time of Service.		REMARKS.
		Months.	Days.	
Anthony Turner,	Captain,	1	11	
William Richardson,	Lieutenant,	1	11	
Richard Denny, jr.	Ensign,	1	11	
Samuel Bowers,	Sergeant,	1	11	
Henry V. Williams,	"	1	11	
H. Baker,	"	1	5	
William Rowlett,	Corporal,	1	11	
William Hawkins,	"	–	2	Joined flying artillery.
William Vines,	"	1	5	
John H. Foster,	"	1	5	
James McKildoe,	"	1	5	
Samuel Alexander,	Private,	1	5	
Mitchell Bradley,	"	1	5	
Williamson Brown,	"	–	5	Do. do.
George Beaty,	"	1	5	
Joseph Barlow,	"	1	5	
Samuel Billen,	"	1	5	
Burwell Brown,	"	–	3	Do. do.
Thomas Cooper,	"	–	2	Do. do.
Richard Clarke,	"	–	3	Do. do.
John Crump,	"	–	2	Do. do.
James Duval,	"	–	4	Do. do.
Thomas S. Dicken,	"	1	5	
Burkett Dowdall,	"	1	5	
Jesse Franklin,	"	1	7	
Jesse Franklin, jr.	"	–	3	Do. do.
Daniel Ford,	"	1	5	
Anderson K. Freeman,	"	1	11	
Joseph Gale,	"	1	5	
Isaac Gill,	"	1	5	
William Hewlett, jr.	"	1	11	
Richard Hughes,	"	1	11	
Nicholas Hewlett,	"	1	11	
John Haywood,	"	1	5	
Charles R. Hatcher,	"	1	5	
Winston Haley,	"	–	2	Do. do.
Dobson Hall,	"	1	5	
Jordan Jones,	"	1	5	
George Lester,	"	1	11	
Henry Ligon,	"	1	11	
William Lewis,	"	1	4	
John Lester,	"	–	3	Do. do.
Philip Mallory,	"	1	11	
George R. Myers,	"	1	5	
Turner Mountcastle,	"	1	11	
John Martin,	"	1	11	
Samuel Mitchell,	"	1	5	
John Morris,	"	–	4	Joined volunteer company.
Charles Palmer,	"	1	11	
Henry Petty,	"	–	2	Joined flying artillery.
Henry C. Redford,	"	1	11	
John Royal,	"	1	11	
David R. Ross,	"	1	5	

NAMES.	RANK.	*Time of Service.*		REMARKS.
		Months.	Days.	
Anthony Robinson, - -	Private,	–	2	Joined flying artillery.
Peter Stywald, - -	"	1	11	
John Slater, - -	"	1	5	
Robert Sloan, - -	"	–	3	Do. do.
William Steel, - -	"	1	5	
Thomas Turner, - -	"	1	11	
Nathaniel Taylor, - -	"	1	11	
Henry Turpin, - -	"	–	2	Joined infantry blues.
William Walker, - -	"	1	5	
William Warriner, - -	"	1	5	
John West, - -	"	1	5	
James Young, - -	"	1	5	

Captain Anthony Turner's Company—Nineteenth Regiment.

NAMES.	RANK.	TIME OF SERVICE.		REMARKS.
		Months.	Days.	
Anthony Turner, - -	Captain,	–	10	
William Richardson, - -	Lieutenant,	–	10	
Patrick Coutts, - -	"	–	23	
Richard Drury, jun'r, -	Ensign,	–	10	
George M. Carrington, -	"	–	23	
James M. Couling, - -	Sergeant,	–	23	
Bartholomew Graves, -	"	–	14	
Archibald Parten, - -	"	–	16	
Lewis Wray, - -	"	–	16	
Miles Turpin, - -	"	–	6	
Freeborn G. Grenshaw, -	"	–	23	
Daniel P. Organ, - -	"	–	23	
William Brown, - -	"	–	10	
James Couling, - -	Corporal,	–	13	
Josiah Poore, - -	"	–	23	
David Reat, - -	"	–	23	
Nath. M. Johnson, - -	"	–	23	
Nicholas Moore, - -	"	–	6	
William Hockins, - -	"	–	10	
Henry Williams, - -	"	–	10	
William Rowlett, - -	"	–	10	
Miles Turpin, - -	"	–	10	
Thomas Cook, - -	Drummer,	–	19	
Martin Austin, - -	Private,	–	16	
Joseph Addington, - -	"	–	6	
Richard Anderson, - -	"	–	23	
John Armistead, - -	"	–	23	
Stephen Aldridge, - -	"	–	23	
Charles Blunt, - -	"	–	10	Enlisted in U. S. army.
Jonathan Brown, - -	"	–	10	
Williamson Brown, - -	"	–	10	
Simon Block, - -	"	–	17	
Alexander Brown, - -	"	–	23	
John Bluford, - -	"	–	6	
Henry H. Bowles, - -	"	–	5	
David Chalmers, - -	"	–	10	
Richard Clarke, - -	"	–	10	
John Cook, - -	"	1		
Edwin J. Clopton, - -	"	–	16	
Henry Cusor, - -	"	–	10	
Joel Callis, - -	"	–	10	
Samuel Choat, - -	"	–	6	
Francis Childers, - -	"	–	6	
John Cline, - -	"	–	23	
William M. Chick, - -	"	–	23	
Thomas Cushing, - -	"	–	23	
James Duval, - -	"	–	10	
Joseph Danforth, - -	"	–	10	
Wm. Depriest, - -	"	–	10	
Benajah Denham, - -	"	–	10	
John Dames, - -	"	1	6	
William Dunn, - -	"	–	23	
Russell Dutton, - -	"	–	23	
Nathaniel Dutton, - -	"	–	23	

****

NAMES.	RANK.	TIME OF SERVICE.		REMARKS.
		Months.	Days.	
Henry Ensor,	Private,	–	6	
Anderson K. Freeman,	"	–	10	
Reuben Freeman,	"	–	16	
Jesse Franklin, sr.	"	–	10	
John Francis,	"	–	9	
John H. Foster,	"	–	10	
Royall Freeman,	"	–	4	
John Gentry,	"	–	10	
Benj. Grover,	"	–	10	
Joseph Gale,	"	–	10	
George W. Godwin,	"	–	19	
Parke Glynn,	"	–	23	
Archibald Gardner,	"	–	6	
Wm. Hewlett, jr.	"	–	10	
Wm. Hoskin,	"	–	10	
Richard Hughes,	"	–	10	
Nicholas Hewlett,	"	–	10	
William Harper,	"	–	16	
Samuel Haywood,	"	–	7	
George W. Hill,	"	–	23	
Eppes Hughes,	"	–	5	
Peter Hamel,	"	–	4	
Daniel Higginbotham,	"	–	23	
John Henderson,	"	–	19	
Edward Hallam,	"	–	23	
Nathaniel Ireson,	"	–	23	
Moses H. Judah,	"	–	16	
John James,	"	–	10	
Solomon Jacobs,	"	–	23	
Westwood W. James,	"	–	23	
William Jordan,	"	–	5	
Jesse G. Jones,	"	–	6	
Bennett Kirby,	"	–	23	
Read Keir,	"	–	–	Joined artificers.
David Kinney,	"	–	23	
George Lester,	"	–	10	
James H. Lynch,	"	–	23	
Gustavus Luke,	"	–	11	
John Morris,	"	–	10	
John Martin,	"	–	10	
Meny Maynard,	"	–	10	
Richard Muir,	"	–	10	
Nicholas Moore,	"	–	10	
William Maddox,	"	–	17	
Amzi Munson,	"	–	16	
William Montague,	"	–	10	
William Morris,	"	–	13	
Daniel Mitchell,	"	–	23	
John McMarra,	"	–	23	
Turner Mountcastle,	"	–	10	
Davis Minor,	"	–	23	
Elisha May,	"	–	23	
John Marques,	"	–	23	
Charles M. Mitchell,	"	–	15	
David Mason,	"	–	23	
Adam Murry,	"	–	11	
Leslie Mitchell,	"	–	6	
John D. Miller,	"	–	6	
Benjamin Mason,	"	–	2	
Reuben Nash,	"	–	16	
Robert Neilson,	"			
John B. Ogg,	"	–	23	
Henry O'Neal,	"	–	5	
William Phillips,	"	–	16	

NAMES.	RANK.	TIME OF SERVICE. Months.	Days.	REMARKS.
Henry Porter, - -	Private,	-	15	
Robert Poore, - -	"			
Elisha Penay, - -	"	-	9	
John Perkins, - -	"	-	23	
David D. Phillips, - -	"	-	1	
Henry E. Ratford, - -	"	-	10	
Anthony Robertson, - -	"	-	10	
Armstead Russell, - -	"	-	10	
David R. Ross, - -	"	-	10	
John Royall, - -	"	-	10	
George Roper, - -	"	-	16	
Elijah Roberts, - -	"	-	10	
Reuben Ragland, - -	"	-	23	
John Rowland, - -	"	-	23	
Edward W. Rootes, - -	"	-	23	
George Reid, - -	"	-	23	
David Roper, - -	"	-	23	
Abner Robinson, - -	"	-	20	
James Reat, - -	"	-	23	
Alexander Read, - -	"	-	6	
Matthew H. Rice, - -	"	-	23	
James Roper, - -	"	-	23	
Elias Roberts, - -	"	-	4	
Henry C. Redford, - -	"	-	6	
Abner Richardson, - -	"	-	6	
John P. Schermerhorn, -	"	-	10	
Peter Stywald, - -	"	-	10	
Robert Sloan, -	"	-	10	
B. Slaughter, - -	"	-	16	
Benjamin Spratley, - -	"			
John St. John, - -	"			
Robert Seayres, - -	"	-	4	
Seymour Scott, - -	"	-	23	
Larkin Smith, - -	"	-	23	
Alexander Sharp, - -	"	-	23	
Samuel Sheppard, - -	"	-	23	
James S. Smithers, - -	"	-	4	
George Smith, - -	"			
Nathan Taylor, - -	"	-	10	
Curtis Tignor, - -	"	-	16	
John E. Thurman, - -	"	-	16	
Henry Turpin, - -	"	-	10	
Richardson D. Taylor, -	"	-	20	
Edward W. Trent, - -	"	-	23	
Thomas Turner, - -	"			
Martin Turner, - -	"	-	6	
John Toler, - -	"			
John Tull, - -	"	-	5	
Joseph W. Vaughan, . -	"			
Hezekiah Veach, - -	"	-	23	
Wm. Williamson, - -	"	-	16	
Wm. Williams, - -	"	-	16	
Allison Winstone, - -	"	-	10	
Wm. Walker, - -	"	-	10	
John Walker, - -	"	-	10	
Caleb Walker, - -	"	-	10	
James Watson, - -	"	-	23	
Conquest Wyatt, - -	"	-	23	
Sylvester Walkley, - -	"	-	23	
John Winston, - -	"	-	8	
Lewis Webb, - -	"	-	23	
Isham Williams, - -	"	-	,5	
James Young, - -	"	-	10	

(For rest of this company, see publication of Pay Rolls.)

PAY ROLL

Of Captain Wm. Wirt's Company of Flying Artillery, of the Nineteenth Regiment of Virginia Militia.

NAMES.	RANK.	Time of Service.		REMARKS.
		Months.	Days.	
William Wirt, - -	Captain,	1	4	
William Lambert, - -	1st Lieutenant,	1	4	
John W. Ellis, - -	2d "	1	4	
Nathaniel Dick, - -	3d "	1	4	
John Campbell, - -	Serg. Major,	1	4	
Thomas Gilliam, - -	Ord. Serg't,	1		
Caleb T. Worrell, - -	Q. M. Serg't,	1	4	
John Turpin, - -	1st Sergeant,	1	4	
Jos. W. Campbell, - -	2d "	1	4	
Rich'd Minor, - -	3d "	1	4	
Arch'd McRobert, - -	4th "	1		
Isaac Sturdivant, - -	1st Corporal,	1	4	
John Holman, - -	2d "	1	4	
Wm. R. Boulware, - -	3d "	1		
David J. Poore, - -	4th "	1	4	
Wm. B. Armistead, - -	Private,	1	4	
Rich'd Allfin, - -	"	1		
Rich'd Booker, - -	"	1	4	
Joshua Beale, - -	"	1	4	
John J. Banks, - -	"	1	4	
Henry Bacchus, - -	"	1	4	
Robert Bullington, - -	"	1	4	
Burwell Brown, - -	"	1	4	
John Barnard, - -	"	1	4	
Wm. Brown, - -	"	1	4	
Chs. A. Cox, - -	"	1	4	
John Crump, - -	"	1	4	
G. W. Compton, - -	"	1	4	
Edward Colgin, - -	"	1	4	
Rich'd Clarke, - -	"	1		
Thomas Cooper, - -	"	1	4	
Ed. Clarke, - -	"	1		
Walker Childress, - -	"	1	4	
Armistead Coles, - -	"	1		
John Durham, - -	"	1		
Chris. Drummond, - -	"	1	4	
Ed. Eubank, - -	"	1	4	
Chs. Elliott, - -	"	1	4	
Thos. M. Everson, - -	"	1	4	
Robt. V. Fagg, - -	"	1	4	
Wm. Fleming, - -	"	1	4	
Jesse Franklin, - -	"	1	4	
Geo. Ferguson, - -	"	1	4	
Wm. Foster, - -	"	1	4	
Wm. Gay, - -	"	1		
Dudley Gilman, - -	"	1		
Matthew P. Godfrey, - -	"	1	4	
Joseph Godwin, - -	"	1	4	
Powell Huff, - -	"	1		
Wm. Hawkins, - -	"	1	4	
Isaac Harper, - -	"	1		
Geo. P. Haden, - -	"	1	4	
Tho. Herbert, - -	"	1	4	
Winston Haley, - -	"	1	4	

NAMES.	RANK.	Time of Service.		REMARKS.
		Months.	Days.	
Jno. Hill, - -	Private,	1		
Thomas Hill, - -	"	1		
Thompson Hawkins, - -	"	1	4	
Jacob King, - -	"	1	4	
John Lester, - -	"	1	4	
John Ludden, - -	"	1	4	
Matthew Lacey, - -	"	1	4	
Rich'd C. Mills, - -	"	1	4	
George Mettert, - -	"	1	4	
Wm. Minor, - -	"	1	4	
Carter A. Mallory, - -	"	1	4	
Joseph Nero, - -	"	1		
John H. Norman, - -	"	1	4	
Alex'r Otter, - -	"	1	4	
Geo. W. Payne, - -	"	1	4	
Rich'd Prince, - -	"	1	4	
Nathaniel Perkins, - -	"	1		
Henry Pettis, - -	"	1	4	
J. W. Perryman, - -	"	1	4	
Wm. Preston, - -	"	1	4	
James Rudd, - -	"	1	4	
Geo. H Stainback, - -	"	1		
Rob. Sloan, - -	"	1	4	
Bernard Skyren, - -	"	1	4	
Phil. Sturdivant, - -	"	1	4	
Wm. Saddler, - -	"	1	4	
Jno. H. Subblett, - -	"	1		
Harvey Shirley, - -	"	1	4	
Roger Towers, - -	"	1	4	
Thomas Whillow, - -	"	1	4	
Jno. B. Walden, - -	"	1		
Alonson Winston, - -	"	1	4	
Henry Walker, - -	"	1	4	
Matthew Watts, - -	"	1	4	

MUSTER ROLL

Of Captain William D. Wrenn's Company, from the Nineteenth Regiment, Virginia Militia, in the City of Richmond, called into actual Service under general orders, from 18th to 27th March, and from 28th June to 3d July, in the year 1813.

NAMES.	RANK.	TIME OF SERVICE.		REMARKS.
		Months.	Days.	
William D. Wrenn, - -	Captain,	–	11	
John H. Robinson, - -	Lieutenant,	–	11	
Thomas Burling, - -	Ensign,	–	11	
Henry Fore, - -	Sergeant,	–	11	
James C. Bradley, - -	"	–	11	
Hezekiah Eubank, - -	"	–	11	
Caleb Cook, - -	"	–	11	
James Bray, - -	Corporal,	–	11	
Daniel G. Hudnall, - -	"	–	11	
Josiah Hill, - -	"	–	11	
E. Stratton, - -	"	–	5	
George Pickett, - -	Drummer,	–	5	
Prosper H. Rogers, - -	"	–	6	
Robert Atkinson, - -	Private,	–	6	
Joseph Butler, - -	"	–	11	
Henry Blacgrove, - -	"	–	[illegible]1	
Robert Brooks, - -	"	–	6	
Arthur Booker, - -	"	–	4	
William Burke, - -	"	–	2	
William Cook, - -	"	–	11	
Philip Crump, - -	"	–	11	
Samuel Churchill, - -	"	–	11	
John C. Crockett, - -	"	–	11	
Charles A. Cox, - -	"	–	11	
Alexander S. Dandridge, -	"	–	11	
Richard Dunlavy, - -	"	–	11	
Wm. B. Ellis, - -	"	–	11	
Dabney Eubank, - -	"	–	3	
Herman Gentry, - -	"	–	4	
Christo. Gill, - -	"	–	6	
Jno. T. Hughes, - -	"	–	11	
Stanley F. Hudnall, - -	"	–	5	
Wm. B. Jordan, - -	"	–	11	
Jekyle Jones, - -	"	–	6	
Richard C. Johnston, - -	"	–	5	
Newin Keanns, - -	"	–	6	
Samuel M. Lewis, - -	"	–	5	
William McEnory, - -	"	–	11	
Jno. P. Morris, - -	"	–	11	
Richard C. Mills, - -	"	–	11	
Charles Norman, - -	"	–	8	
Thomas Nash, - -	"	–	5	
Benjamin Phillips, - -	"	–	11	
Richard Prince, - -	"	–	11	
Grief Price, - -		–	4	
John Quarles, - -	"	–	11	

NAMES.	RANK.	TIME OF SERVICE.		REMARKS.
		Months.	Days.	
Benoni Robins, - -	Private,	–	11	
Wm. Robins, - -	"	–	11	
Alex'r L. Robinson, - -	"	–	9	
Robert Ransom, - -	"	–	4	
Nath'l Ragland, - -	"	–	2	
Austin Talman, - -	"	–	5	
Seymour Vial, - -	"	–	4	
Claudias Vial, - -	"	–	4	
Drewry Wilkinson, - -	"	–	11	
Robert G. Williamson, -	"	–	11	
Walker Watkins, - -	"	–	4	
John Yare, - -	"	–	2	

MUSTER ROLL

Of Captain William Birchett's Company, of Virginia Militia, from the Twenty-second Regiment, Mecklenburg County, in the Service from the 30th August to the 13th September, 1814.

NAMES.	RANK.	TIME OF SERVICE.		REMARKS.
		Months.	Days.	
William Birchett,	Captain,	–	16	
John G. Baptist,	1st Lieutenant,	–	16	
Mathew L. Baptist,	2d Lieutenant,	–	16	
Hume R. Field,	Cornet,	–	16	
Thomas Blackborne,	1st Sergeant,	–	16	Transferred to Capt. Pryor's company.
William C. Wall,	2d "	–	16	
David Crenshaw,	3d "	–	16	
James A. M. P. Stewart,	4th "	–	16	Transferred to Capt. Pryor's company.
Richard P. Montgomery,	Q. M. Serg.	–	16	
Giles R. Norment,	Corporal,	–	16	
Osborn Crooke,	"	–	16	
John Nelson,	"	–	16	Transferred to Capt. Pryor's company.
Richard S. Jeffres,	"	–	16	
Thomas Atkins,	Private,	–	16	
Edward B. Brown,	"	–	16	
Pleasant Brommall,	"	–	16	
William Baptist,	"	–	16	
Francis Blackborne,	"	–	16	
John Bigger,	"	–	16	
Grey Blackborne,	"	–	16	
Francis B. Bailey,	"	–	16	
Alexander Boyden,	"	–	16	
Josiah Crews,	"	–	16	
Miles T. Crowder,	"	–	16	
Thomas Crow,	"	–	16	
Little B. Carter,	"	–	16	
John P. Carter,	"	–	16	
Geo. Doggett,	"	–	16	
John Farrar,	"	–	16	
John S. Field,	"	–	16	
Richard Field,	"	–	16	
Thomas Gregory,	"	–	16	
Barnett Gregory,	"	–	16	
Daniel Hudson,	"	–	16	
Stephen Hudson,	"	–	16	
William C. Hudson,	"	–	16	
Sam'l G. Hunt,	"	–	16	
Edward Jones,	"	–	16	
Paul C. Jeffers,	"	–	16	
William Keen,	"	–	16	
John Loafman,	"	–	16	
Nath'l McCann,	"	–	16	
Thomas Marshall,	"	–	16	
Champion C. Marrable,	"	–	16	
Green Moss,	"	–	16	
Abner Moody,	"	–	16	
Stephen Mayes,	"	–	16	

NAMES.	RANK.	TIME OF SERVICE.		REMARKS.
		Months.	Days.	
William Neal, - -	Private.	–	16	
John J. Norment, - -	"	–	16	
Achilles Norment, - -	"	–	16	
Thos. J. Norment, - -	"	–	16	
Thomas Norment, - -	"	–	16	
Lewis Nunn, - -	"	–	16	
Joseph Ogborne, - -	"	–	16	
Philip Poindexter, - -	"	–	16	
John Puryear, - -	"	–	16	
Thomas Puryear, - -	"	–	16	
Rich'd C. Puryear, - -	"	–	16	
Lewis Roffe, - -	"	–	16	
Robt. Richardson, - -	"	–	16	
John Tabb, - -	"	–	16	
Richard H. Walker, - -	"	–	16	
William Williamson, -	"	–	16	
Charles Yancey, - -	"	–	16	
John Young, - -	"	–	16	
James L. Summervill, -	"	–	16	
Philip Lackett, - -	"	–	16	
Shearwood Colley, - -	"	–	16	
William Nelson, - -	"	–	16	Transferred to Capt.
William Towns, - -	"	–	16	Pryor's company.
Erasmus Kennon, - -	"	–	16	
Alexander Clansel, - -	"	–	16	
Farley Wade, - -	"	–	16	

MUSTER ROLL

Of the Field and Staff of a detachment of the Virginia Militia from the County of Chesterfield, composing the Twenty-third Regiment, commanded by Colonel William Brown, in the Service of the State from 13th March to the 2nd of July, in the year 1813.

NAMES.	RANK.	TIME OF SERVICE.		REMARKS.
		Months.	Days.	
William Brown, - -	Colonel,	–	14	
Archer Ball, - -	Major,	–	12	
Tom N. Traylor, - -	"	–	12	
Bev. C. Stanard, - -	Adjutant,	–	13	
Abner Crump, - -	Surgeon,	–	13	
Wm. A. O. Brown, - -	Sergt. Major,	–	13	
John R. Walk, - -	Pay Master,	–	9	
Thomas Vaden, - -	Qr. Master,	–	11	
Marley Walthall, - -	Q. M. Sergt.	–	12	
Samuel Flournoy, - -	Sergt. Major,	–	12	
Nath'l Childers, - -	Qr. Master,	–	12	

MUSTER ROLL

Of Lieutenant Robert Allen's Company of Artillery of Virginia Militia, from the Twenty-third Regiment, in the Service from the 18th day of March 1813, to the 30th of March 1813.

NAMES.	RANK.	TIME OF SERVICE.		REMARKS.
		Months.	Days.	
Robert Allen, - -	Lieutenant,	–	12	
W. A. Martin, - -	Sergeant,	–	12	
Jas. Cunningham, - -	"	–	12	
Jas. Adkins, - -	Private,	–	12	
Woodford Alvis, - -	"	–	12	
W. E. Gales, - -	"	–	12	
W. Shell, - -	"	–	12	
John Whillock, - -	"	–	12	
Jas. Branch, - -	"	–	12	
Jesse Russell, - -	"	–	12	
John Rancock, - -	"	–	12	
Dav. Brodel, - -	"	–	12	
W. Cary, - -	"	–	12	

Captain Samuel V. Allen's Company—First Regiment.

NAMES.	RANK.	TIME OF SERVICE.		REMARKS.
		Months.	Days.	
Samuel V. Allen,	Captain,	-	13	
William L. Venable,	Lieutenant,	-	13	
Henry E. Watkins,	"	-	13	
Samuel L. Lockett,	Cornet,	-	13	
Archer Fuqua,	Sergeant,	-	13	
Peyton Randolph,	"	-	13	
Pugh W. Price,	"	-	13	
Booker Foster,	"	-	13	
James J. Foster,	Corporal,	-	13	
Henry N. Watkins,	"	-	13	
Obadiah Marton,	"	-	13	
James D. Wood,	Musician,	-	13	
Leonard Anderson,	Private.			
James R. Allen,	"	-	13	Appointed Sword Master Sept. 7, 1814.
Merit B. Allen,	"	-	13	
Cary C. Allen,	"	-	13	
Samuel Anderson,	"	-	13	
William B. Booker,	"	-	13	
Richard Booker,	"	3	18	
Archer Brown,	"	3	18	
Patrick Boothe,	"	-	13	
Thomas Ellington,	"	-	13	
Paschal Foulkes,	"	-	13	
Peter Foster,	"	-	13	
Jennings Foulkes,	"	-	13	
William Foulkes,	"			
William Fleming,	"	-	13	
Francis Flippin,	"	-	13	
Thos. Goode,	"	-	13	
Joseph Goode,	"	-	13	
John Holcombe,	"	-	13	
Simon Hughs,	"	-	13	
Theodorick C. Haskins,	"	-	13	
Henry W. Holland,	"	-	13	
Thomas Jackson,	"	-	13	
Nathan G. McGehee,	"	-	13	
Nath. Morris,	"	-	13	
Charles Morris,	"	3	5	
Samuel Morris,	"	-	13	
William Martin,	"	-	13	
John F. Nash,	"	-	13	
Edwin Price,	"	-	13	
Daney Purman,	"	-	13	
Hastin Poe,	"	-	13	
James Price,	"	-	13	
Benjamin H. Price,	"	-	13	
William Price,	"	-	13	
William G. Price,	"	-	13	
Charles W. Price,	"	-	13	
William Phillips,	"	-	13	
John Redford,	"	-	13	
Josiah M. Rice,	"	-	13	
Stephen C. Richardson,	"	-	13	

NAMES.	RANK.	TIME OF SERVICE.		REMARKS.
		Months.	Days.	
John Rice, - -	Private,	–	13	
James S. Smith, - -	"	–	13	
Lion F. Spencer, - -	"	–	13	
Jos. H. Thurston, - -	"	–	13	
Henry H. Vaughan, - -	"	–	13	
John H. Venable, - -	"	–	13	
Nath. Venable, - -	"	–	13	
William Venable, - -	"	–	13	
Thomas Wilbourne, - -	"	–	13	
Wm. H. Walthall, - -	"	–	13	
Francis Walthall, - -	Saddler,	–	13	
Samuel Worsham, - -	Private,	–	13	
Richard Woodson, - -	"	–	13	
Augustus Watkins, - -	"	–	13	
John Williams, - -	"	–	13	
John A. Watson, - -	"	–	13	

(For rest of this company, see publication of Pay Rolls.)

MUSTER ROLL

Of Captain Edward Archer's Company of Virginia Militia, from Twenty-third Regiment, commanded by Colonel William Brown, in the Service from 17th to the 29th of March, from 27th to 28th of June, and from 30th day of June to the 20th day of July, 1813.

NAMES.	RANK.	TIME OF SERVICE.		REMARKS
		Months.	Days.	
Edward Archer, - -	Captain,	–	18	
Thomas Stratton, - -	Lieutenant,	–	18	
Samuel Clay, - -	Ensign,	–	18	
Henry Cox, - -	1st Sergeant,	–	18	
Charles E. Featherton, -	2d "	–	18	
John Walthall, - -	3d "	–	13	
Frank Walthall, - -	4th "	–	13	
Thomas Lambert, - -	Private,	–	15	
Joseph Dillon, - -	"	–	18	
William Stewart, - -	"	–	18	
James Hall, - -	"	–	18	
George Cox, - -	"	–	18	
Thomas Cousin, - -	"	–	18	
Armstead Hill, - -	"	–	15	
Thomas Hare, - -	"	–	18	
Thomas Wilson, - -	"	–	18	
David Johnston, - -	"	–	18	
John Stewart, - -	"	–	18	
John Varner, - -	"	–	18	
Benjamin Walthall, - -	"	–	18	
Thomas Howlett, - -	"	–	18	
John Covington, - -	"	–	18	
Robert Royall, - -	"	–	18	
Rich'd Warwick, - -	"	–	18	
Peter F. Edwards, - -	"	–	18	
Jacob Brentt, - -	"	–	18	
Henry Varner, - -	"	–	18	
Peter Varner, - -	"	–	18	
Thomas Hatchet, - -	"	–	18	
William Munk, - -	"	–	18	
Erby Fuqua, - -	"	–	18	
William Moody, - -	"	–	18	
Anthony K. Erby, - -	"	–	18	
Theo. F. Strachen, - -	"	–	18	
William Covington, - -	"	–	18	
Joseph Whiteford, - -	"	–	15	
Alexander Biggleston, -	"	–	18	
Solomon Baugh, - -	"	–	15	
Thomas Batte, - -	"	–	18	
Edw'd A. May, - -	"	–	18	
Bur. O. Descar, - -	"	–	13	
Simon Fraserx, - -	"	–	13	
James Stuart, - -	"	–	13	
John Jackson, - -	"	–	13	
John Nobes, - -	"	–	13	
Samuel Goode, - -	"	–	13	

NAMES.	RANK.	TIME OF SERVICE.		REMARKS.
		Months.	Days.	
Joseph Dudley,	Private,	–	13	
Peyton Fuqua,	"	–	13	
Thomas Marsh,	"	–	13	
Emanuel Blankenship,	"	–	13	
John Childers,	"	–	13	

MUSTER ROLL

Of Captain Thomas Burfoot's Company of Virginia Militia, from the 23d Regiment, commanded by Col. William Brown, in Service from 18th to 30th March, from 27th to 28th June, and from 30th June to 2d day of July, 1813.

NAMES.	RANK.	TIME OF SERVICE.		REMARKS.
		Months.	Days.	
Thomas Burfoot,	Captain,	–	19	
Francis Lockett,	1st Lieutenant,	–	16	
Henry Winfree,	2d "	–	19	
John Harley,	Cornet,	–	19	
William Gates,	Sergeant,	–	19	
Robert Aiken,	"	–	19	
Robert Wood,	"	–	19	
Robert Haskins,	"	–	19	
Peter Morisett,	Private,	–	19	
Henry Branch,	"	–	19	
William Walthall,	"	–	19	
Pleas't Taylor,	"	–	19	
Richard C. Hudson,	"	–	19	
Joseph Stewart,	"	–	19	
John Jennings,	"	–	19	
Newby Hancock,	"	–	19	
Mark Turner,	"	–	19	
Pleas't Aikin,	"	–	19	
John Andrews,	"	–	16	
William Bragg,	"	–	16	
James Alvis,	"	–	16	
William Jackson,	"	–	19	
Marvell Winfree,	"	–	19	
Thomas Vaden,	"	–	16	
Spencer B. Andrews,	"	–	16	
Joseph T. Hudson,	"	–	16	
Claiborne Conway,	"	–	3	
William Hancock,	"	–	16	

MUSTER ROLL

Of Captain Lawson Burfoot's Company of Virginia Militia, from the Twenty-third Regiment, Chesterfield County, under the command of Lieutenant Colonel William Brown, in Service from the 18th to 30th March, from 26th to 28th June, and from the 30th June to the 2d July, 1813.

NAMES.	RANK.	TIME OF SERVICE.		REMARKS.
		Months.	Days.	
Lawson Burfoot, - -	Captain,	—	18	
William G. Elam, - -	Lieutenant,	—	18	
James Elam, - -	Ensign,	—	18	
Thomas H. Bass, - -	Sergeant,	—	15	In the requisition one of these tours.
Richard Cheatham, - -	"	—	15	With Capt. Graves one of these tours.
Pleasant Cheatham, - -	"	—	18	
William Blankenship, -	Fifer,	—	18	
Thomas Godsay, - -	Private,	—	18	
Mackness Blankinship, -	"	—	6	
Obediah Bailey, - -	"	—	18	
Ezekiel Blankenship, -	"	—	18	
William Bailey, - -	"	—	18	
Geo. Blankenship, - -	"	—	18	
Henry Bailey, - -	"	—	18	
William Brown, - -	"	—	18	
Richard Bass, - -	"	—	18	
King Bailey, - - -	"	—	18	
Benjamin Bowles, - -	"	—	18	
Elisha Bailey, - -	"	—	18	
James Baker, - -	"	—	12	
Mark Blankenship, - -	"	—	12	
Abijah Cheatham, - -	"	—	18	
James Clairbone, - -	"	—	18	
Young Condrey, - -	"	—	18	
Geo. Crump, - -	"	—	18	
Francis Dunnevant, - -	"	—	18	
Noah Elam, - -	"	—	18	
William B. Elam, - -	"	—	18	
Ammon Elam, - -	"	—	18	
Joshua Elam, - -	"	—	18	
Robert Elam, - -	"	—	18	
Peter Elam, - -	"	—	18	
Benja. Farmer, - -	"	—	15	
John Farrell, - -	"	—	3	
Thomas Flournoy, - -	"	—	18	
Mark Flournoy, - -	"	—	18	
John Farell, - -	"	—	15	
Joseph Goode, - -	"	—	18	
John Gates, - -	"	—	18	
Robert Haskins, - -	"	—	15	
James Hubbard, - -	"	—	12	
Benjamin James, - -	"	—	3	
William Lockett, - -	"	—	6	
King Lockett, - -	"	—	18	
Joshua Lacy, - -	"	—	18	

NAMES.	RANK.	TIME OF SERVICE.		REMARKS.
		Months.	Days.	
Joshua Lacy, - -	Private,	–	18	
Alexander Moore, - -	"	–	18	
William Martin, - -	"	–	18	
Barnett Moore, - -	"	–	18	
William Moody, - -	"	–	18	
James Parker, - -	"	–	6	
John Purdie, - -	"	–	18	
Isaac D. Parker, - -	"	–	6	
Jeremiah Parker, - -	"	–	6	
Frederick Rudd, - -	"	–	18	
Henry Robertson, - -	"	–	6	
Henry Roberts, - -	"	–	18	
John Sims, - -	"	–	15	
Thomas Turpin, - -	"	–	18	
William Turpin, - -	"	–	18	
William Trent, - -	"	–	18	
Henry Turpin, - -	"	–	18	
John Winfree, - -	"	–	18	

MUSTER ROLL

Of Captain Samuel Clarke's Company of Infantry of the Twenty-third Regiment, Virginia Militia, in the County of Chesterfield, called into actual Service from 18th to 29th March, from the 27th to the 28th June, and from the 30th June to 2d July, in the year 1813.

NAMES.	RANK.	TIME OF SERVICE.		REMARKS.
		Months.	Days.	
Samuel Clarke, - -	Captain,	–	18	
Peter Clarke, - -	Lieutenant,	–	16	
Archibald Newby, - -	Ensign,	–	15	
Jeremiah Clarke, - -	Sergeant,	–	17	
Josiah Baugh, - -	"	–	17	
Thomas Belcher, - -	"	–	17	
John Woodfin, - -	"	–	17	
John Andrews, - -	Private,	–	17	
Peter Ashbrook, - -	"	–	5	
Admiral Brooks, - -	"	–	17	
William Baugh, - -	"	–	13	
Jeremiah Baugh, - -	"	–	13	
Martin Brooks, - -	"	–	17	
Peter Baugh, - -	"	–	17	
Abner Baugh, - -	"	–	17	
Henry Blankenship, - -	"	–	17	
Hatcher Clarke, - -	"	–	17	
Gardner Clarke, - -	"	–	17	
Charles Clarke, - -	"	–	17	
Ezekiel Davis, - -	"	–	17	
Pleasant Ellett, - -	"	–	13	
Moses Fergusson, - -	"	–	17	
John Fergusson, - -	"	–	17	
Thomas Fergusson, - -	"	–	17	
Gardner Fowler, - -	"	–	17	
Jesse Fergusson, - -	"	–	2	
Jesse Gill, - -	"	–	17	
Robert Lockett, - -	"	–	17	
Richard Loving, - -	"	–	17	
Andrew Laprade, - -	"	–	17	
Walthall Lockett, - -	"	–	12	
James Maxley, - -	"	–	12	
William Newby, sen'r, -	"	–	17	
John Newby, - -	"	–	17	
William Newby, jr. - -	"	–	17	
Claibourne Nunnally, - -	"	–	17	
Nelson Newby, - -	"	–	17	
James Newby, - -	"	–	3	
Levi Puckett, - -	"	–	17	
John Perdue, - -	"	–	17	
Thomas Perdue, - -	"	–	17	
Labourn Puckett, - -	"	–	17	
Isham Puckett, - -	"	–	11	
Rowlett Patram, - -	"	–	17	
Shadrack Perdue, - -	"	–	11	
Rowling Puckett, - -	"	–	11	
Littleberry Perdue, - -	"	–	11	
Enoch Roberts. - -	"	–	17	
Bedford Traylor, - -	Private,	–	17	
Henry Vest, - -	"	–	17	
Obadiah Vest, - -	"	–	13	
John Wyatt, - -	"	–	17	
Peter Winfree, - -	"	–	14	
Ransom Wyatt, - -	"	–	11	

MUSTER ROLL

Of Lieutenant James Clarke's Company of the Twenty-third Regiment, Virginia Militia, in the County of Chesterfield, called into actual Service under general orders, from the 18th to the 24th March, and from the 26th June to the 2d July, in the year 1813.

NAMES.	RANK.	TIME OF SERVICE.		REMARKS.
		Months.	Days.	
James Clarke, jun'r, -	Lieutenant,	–	14	
Isaac Davis, - -	Ensign,	–	14	
Young Pomroy, - -	Sergeant,	–	12	
Robt. R. Miller, - -	"	–	13	
Thomas Winfree, - -	"	–	14	
Wash. Weisiger, - -	"	–	7	
James Caskie, - -	Corporal,	–	14	
Thomas Smith, - -	"	–	7	
William Bradshaw, - -	"	–	7	
Ro. Dainsworth, - -	"	–	7	
James Long, - -	"	–	7	
James Gray, - -	"	–	3	
James B. Hooper, - -	"	–	7	
Ro. Ainsworth, - -	Private,	–	3	
Thomas Brackett, - -	"	–	7	
W. Brackett, - -	"	–	7	
Isaac Burnard, - -	"	–	14	
John Bunoff, - -	"	–	7	
W. B. Clarke, - -	"	–	10	
Ro. Clarke, - -	"	–	14	
M. Elam, - -	"	–	7	
And. Fare, - -	"	–	12	
Jno. Gilchrist, - -	"	–	14	
Nich. Garden, - -	"	–	10	
P. E. Graves, - -	"	–	7	
James Gray, - -	"	–	7	
John Hobson, - -	"	–	10	
J. B. Hooper, - -	"	–	7	
Jno. Jenkins, - -	"	–	7	
Edw'd Johnston, - -	"	–	9	
Stephen Johnston, - -	"	–	12	
James Long, - -	"	–	7	
Wm. Long, - -	"	–	7	
C. McRae, - -	"	–	7	
H. Moody, - -	"	–	14	
B. S. Morrison, - -	"	–	10	
Nicholas Mills, - -	"	–	14	
P. Michaels, - -	"	–	9	
Hugh M. Miller, - -	"	–	6	
Ro. D. Murchie, - -	"	–	14	
Daniel McLeod, - -	"	–	3	
Stephen Pankey, - -	"	–	14	
Wm. A. Patterson, - -	"	–	7	
Bev. Randolph, - -	"	–	14	
Edm'd Radford, - -	"	–	7	
Tarlton Saunders, - -	"	–	8	
Jno. Scott, - -	"	–	14	

NAMES.	RANK.	TIME OF SERVICE.		REMARKS.
		Months.	Days.	
Sam'l Sizer, - -	Private,	–	13	
John Spencer, - -	"	–	14	
Sam'l Taylor, - -	"	–	14	
Thos. Vaden, - -	"	–	10	
J. Winfree, - -	"	–	9	
Ro. Warren, - -	"	–	14	
W. Weisiger, - -	"	–	7	
Ro. Weisiger, - -	"	–	7	
Jno. Weisiger, - -	"	–	14	
Daniel Weisiger, - -	"	–	12	
Mansfield Watkins, - -	"	–	12	
James Willet, - -	"	–	14	
James W. Winfree, - -	"	–	3	
Hailey Cole, - -	Captain,	–	13	
Thomas Finney, - -	Lieutenant,	–	13	
William Ellis, - -	Ensign,	–	13	
Isham Cheatham, - -	Sergeant,	–	13	
Robert Baugh, - -	"	–	13	
James Folks, - -	"	–	13	
Geo. W. Cole, - -	"	–	13	
Daniel Cheatham, - -	Corporal,	–	16	
Matthew Anderson, - -	Fifer,	–	13	
Peter Archer, - -	Private,	–	9	
William Beasley, - -	"	1		
Richard Bass, - -	"	–	13	
Edward Bass, - -	"	–	13	
Archibald Bass, - -	"	–	9	
Young Beasley, - -	"	–	11	
Thomas Barnes, - -	"	–	11	
Daniel Blankinship, - -	"	–	11	
Henry Beasley, - -	"	–	11	
Richard Beasley, - -	"	–	11	
Henry Bridgwater, - -	"	–	11	
Samuel Cheatham, - -	"	–	13	
Samuel Cashon, - -	"	–	13	
Elam Cheatham, - -	"	–	13	
Joseph Cole, jr. - -	"	–	13	
Joseph Cole, - -	"	1		
John H. Cole, - -	"	–	13	
Jackson Cashon, - -	"	–	9	
Pleasant Cole, - -	"	–	9	
Obadiah Cox, - -	"	–	13	
Francis Cashon, - -	"	–	11	
Josiah Cendry, - -	"	–	29	
Henry Cox, - -	"	–	11	
Fountain Cheatham, - -	"	1	9	
Henry Cheatham, - -	"	1	9	
Charles Elam, - -	"	–	13	
Joel Folks, - - -	"	–	13	
John Folks, - - -	"	–	9	
William Hill, - -	"	–	11	
Edward Hill, - -	"	–	9	
John Hill, - - -	"	–	11	
James Lockett, - -	"	–	11	
Everett Moore, - -	"	–	13	
Haley Moore, - -	"	–	13	
Edward Nunnally, - -	"	–	13	
Elijah Nunnally, - -	"	–	9	
Lewis Puckett, - -	"	–	9	
John Pringle, - -	"	–	11	
Phineas Puckett, - -	"	–	11	

****

NAMES.	RANK.	TIME OF SERVICE.		REMARKS.
		Months.	Days.	
Elijah Rudd, - -	"	–	13	
John W. Rudd, - -	"	–	13	
Jabez Rucks, - -	"	–	9	
John Rudd, sr. - -	"	–	13	
Leonard Rudd, - -	"	–	13	
Hezekiah Rudd, - -	"	–	13	
Robert Rudd, - -	Private,	–	13	
John Robertson, - -	"	–	13	
Archibald Rudd, - -	"	–	13	
Thomas Roberts, - -	"	–	13	
James H. Spears, - -	"	–	9	
William Talbot, - -	"	–	9	
John Wilkerson, sr. - -	"	–	9	
John Womack, - -	"	–	13	
Mark Wilkerson, - -	"	–	13	
Joseph Wilkerson, - -	"	–	13	
James Wilkerson, - -	"	–	23	
Peter Wilkerson, sr. -	"	–	9	
Peter Wilkerson, jr. -	"	–	9	
John Ware, - - -	"	–	9	
Edward Worsham, - -	"	–	11	

(For rest of this company, see publication of Pay Rolls.)

PAY ROLL

Of Captain Haley Cole's Company, of Virginia Militia, Chesterfield County, at Camp Holly, under Col. Jno. H. Cocke, from 27th June to 26th July 1813.

NAMES.	RANK.	Time of Service.		REMARKS.
		Months.	Days.	
Haley Cole, - -	Captain,	1		Capt. Cole also served
Thomas Finney, - -	Lieutenant,	1		under Col. Ambler at
William Ellis, - -	Ensign,	1		Camp Holly in 1814.
Isham Cheatham, - -	Sergeant,	1		See pay roll of his
James Fulks, - -	"	1		company.
Geo. W. Cole, - -	"	1		
Pleasant Cole, - -	"	1		
John Ware, - -	Corporal,	1		
Jno. H. Cheatham, - -	"	1		
James Lockett, - -	"	1		
Matthew Anderson, - -	Fifer,	1		
John Pringle, - -	Drummer,	1		
Peter Archer, - -	Private,	1		
Pleasant Aiken, - -	"	1		
Samuel Bowles, - -	"	1		
Arch'd Bass, - -	"	1		
Edward Bass, - -	"	1		
William Bragg, - -	"	1		
Henry Bridgwater, - -	"	1		
Archer Bridgwater, - -	"	1		
Henry Beasley, - -	"	1		
Richard Beasley, - -	"	1		
Young Beasley, - -	"	1		
Arch'd Bass, - -	"	1		
Thomas Barnes, - -	"	1		
Thomas Cheatham, - -	"	1		
Elam Cheatham, - -	"	1		
Jackson Cashion, - -	"	1		
Zachariah Cheatham, - -	"	1		
Obed Cox, - -	"	1		
Joseph Condry, - -	"	1		
Henry Cox, - -	"	1		
Charles Elam, - -	"	1		
Joel Fulkes, - -	"	1		
John Fulkes, - -	"	1		
King Fowler, - -	"	1		
William Farguson, - -	"	1		
Edward Hill, - -	"	1		
William Hill, - -	"	1		
John Hill, - -	"	1		
Holt Lacy, - -	"	1		
Everett Moore, - -	"	1		
Haley Moore, - -	"	1		
Edw'd Nunnally, - -	"	1		
Eli Nunnally, - -	"	1		
Daniel Nunnally, - -		1		
Lewis Puckett, - -	"	1		
Phineas Puckett, - -	"	1		
Jabez Rucks, - -	"	1		
Thomas Roberts, - -	"	1		
Jno. A. Rudd, - -	"	1		
Elijah Rudd, - -	"	1		
John Rudd, - -	"	1		
Leonard Rudd, - -	"	1		

NAMES.	RANK.	Time of Service.		REMARKS.
		Months.	Days.	
Hezekiah Rudd, - -	Private,	1		
Robert Rudd, - -	"	1		
Archer Rudd, - -	"	1		
James H. Spear, - -	"	1		
William Talbott, - -	"	1		
John Wilkinson, - -	"	1		
John Womack, - -	"	1		
Mark Wilkinson, - -	"	1		
Joseph Wilkinson, - -	"	1		
Peter Wilkinson, jr. - -	"	1		
Peter Wilkinson, sen. - -	"	1		
Edward Worsham, - -	"	1		

MUSTER ROLL

Of Captain Daniel Flournoy's Company of Virginia Militia, from the Twenty-third Regiment, Chesterfield County, commanded by Colonel William Brown, in the Service from the 18th to the 30th March, from 26th to 28th June, and from 30th June to 2d July, 1813.

NAMES.	RANK.	TIME OF SERVICE.		REMARKS.
		Months.	Days.	
Daniel Flournoy,	Captain,	–	18	
Abram S. Woodridge,	Lieutenant,	–	18	Or Wooldridge.
Edward H. Mosley,	Ensign,	–	18	
Francis Watkins,	Sergeant,	–	18	
John Crump,	"	–	18	
John Roper,	"	–	18	
Berkley Elam,	"	–	18	
Anderson Johnson,	Private,	–	18	
Ephraim Miles,	"	–	18	
Bartholomew Kidds,	"	–	18	
John Stainford,	"	–	18	
Phineas Clay,	"	–	18	
Solomon Godsey,	"	–	18	
Carrington Simpson,	"	–	18	
Richard W. Michaux,	"	–	18	
Langhorn Simpson,	"	–	18	
Joseph Flournoy,	"	–	18	
Joshua Powell,	"	–	18	
Hezekiah Thurman,	"	–	18	
Spencer Hancock,	"	–	18	
James Alsop,	"	–	18	
Wade McGruder,	"	–	18	
Cheatham Lockett,	"	–	18	
James Adkinson,	"	–	18	
Jesse Snelling,	"	–	18	
Jacob A. Flournoy,	"	–	18	
John Elliott,	"	–	18	
Joseph H. Walker,	"	–	18	
Jeremiah Fowler,	"	–	18	
Milton Cary,	"	–	18	
William Howard,	"	–	18	
Landa Hopkins,	"	–	18	
Royal Martin,	"	–	18	
Forest Flournoy,	"	–	18	
Daniel Taylor,	"	–	18	
Nelson Flournoy,	"	–	18	
Elisha Keen,	"	–	18	
Peter F. Farrow,	"	–	18	
Anthony Taylor,	"	–	18	
Benjamin Burton,	"	–	18	
Thomas Taylor,	"	–	18	
Seth W. Flournoy,	"	–	18	
Jacob Alpine,	"	–	18	
Hickerson Hancock,	"	–	18	
John Baugh,	"	–	18	
James Hubbard,	Private,	–	18	
Robert Hoskins,	"	–	18	
Cyrus Powell,	"	–	2	
Obadiah Lockett,	"	–	2	
Arch'd. L. Wooldridge,	"	–	2	
Jeremiah Wooldridge,	"	–	2	
William T. Johnson,	"	–	13	

Captain Alexander Gibbs' Company—Twenty-third Regiment.

NAMES.	RANK.	TIME OF SERVICE.		REMARKS.
		Months.	Days.	
Alexander Gibbs, - -	Captain,	–	17	
Peter Gill, - -	Lieutenant,	–	17	
William H. Vaden, - -	Ensign,	–	17	
John H. Cole, - -	Q. S.	–	29	
Daniel Brown, - -	Sergeant,	–	17	
Thomas Rowlett, - -	"	–	17	
Abner Tolley, - -	"	–	17	
Aaron Marsh, - -	"	–	17	
Edmund Belcher, - -	Private,	–	3	
William Andress, - -	"	–	17	
Adam Andress, - -	"	–	17	
William Allen, - -	"	–	17	
Joseph Andress, - -	"	–	17	
Bullard Andress, - -	"	–	17	
Erasmus Andress, - -	"	–	17	
Peter Archer, - -	"	–	13	
Ephraim Blankenship, -	"	–	17	
Isham Belcher, jr. - -	"	–	17	
Alexander Brown, - -	"	–	17	
Daniel P. Berry, - -	"	–	17	
Abel Browman, - -	"	–	2	
Edmund Belcher, - -	"	–	17	
Archer Bott, - -	"	–	12	
Gabriel Broodie, - -	"	–	14	
James Blankenship, - -	"	–	15	
Jacob Bennette, - -	"	–	14	Substituted by P. T. Farrar.
William Beasly, - -	"	–	13	
William Bragg, - -	"	–	13	
Fleming Bowles, - -	"	–	13	
Francis Cashon, - -	"	–	13	
Francis Chatham, - -	"	–	13	
Joshua Coudre, - -	"	–	13	
John Davis, - -	"	–	17	
Robert Davis, - -	"	–	17	
James Deaton, - -	"	–	17	
John Dyre, - -	"	–	14	
John Dishman, - -	"	–	17	
Daniel Dishman, - -	"	–	17	
William Drummond, -	"	–	5	
Isham Evans, - -	"	–	17	
David Evans, - -	"	–	17	
George B. Greenhow, -	"	–	17	
Good Gill, - -	"	–	17	
Allen Granger, - -	"	–	17	
Daniel Gill, - -	"	–	17	
Benjamin Gates, - -	"	–	5	
William Gill, - -	"	–	5	
Temple Gates, - -	"	–	17	
James Howlett, - -	"	–	17	
John G. Hayes, - -	"	–	15	
Jeremiah Holby, - -	"	–	27	Substituted by David T. Butler.
James Lynch, - -	"	–	2	

NAMES.	RANK.	TIME OF SERVICE.		REMARKS.
		Months.	Days.	
Claiborne Loyal, - -	Private,	–	2	
Robert Mall, - -	"	–	17	
Cain Mann, - -	"	–	17	
Tary Mate, - -	"	–	17	Or Irby.
James McGee, - -	"	–	24	Substituted by Claiborne Royal.
Isham Male, - -	"			
Isham Mall, - -	"	–	15	
David Nunney, - -	"	–	17	
Robert Partin, - -	"	–	17	
Mufford Perkinson, - -	"	–	17	
Dennis Parten, - -	"	–	2	
Perkinson Peter, - -	"	–	2	
William Rowlett, jr. - -	"	–	17	
William Rowlett, - -	"	–	17	
Claiborne Royal, - -	"	2	12	
Richard Spain, - -	"	–	17	
Austin Spears, - -	"	–	13	
John Styles, - -	"	–	8	Sub. Wm. Traylor.
James B. Simms, - -	"	–	13	
Ewin Traylor, - -	"	–	17	
Thomas Traylor, - -	"	1	17	Sub. by John Drummond.
Archer Traylor, - -	"	–	24	Sub. by Geo. Greenhow.
Joseph Traylor, - -	"	–	5	
William Traylor, - -	"	–	28	
Archer Totley, - -	"	–	17	
William Vaden, - -	"	–	17	
Isham Vaden, - -	"	–	5	
Randal Wyatt, - -	"	–	17	
Dickerson Wells, - -	"	–	17	
Lodick Wilson, - -	"	–	17	
William Wyatt, - -	"	–	17	

(For rest of this company, see publication of Pay Rolls.)

MUSTER ROLL

Of Captain John W. Gill's Company, from the Twenty-third Regiment, Virginia Militia, Chesterfield County, commanded by Lieutenant Colonel William Brown, in the Service from the 17th to 29th March, from 26th to 28th June, and from 1st to 2d July, 1813.

NAMES.	RANK.	TIME OF SERVICE.		REMARKS.
		Months.	Days.	
John W. Gill, - -	Captain,	–	7	
William Dyson, - -	Lieutenant,	–	7	
Thomas J. Bragg, - -	Ensign,	–	7	
Samuel D. Davis, - -	1st Sergeant,	–	7	No. 1, and under Capt. Weisiger 3 days.
Robert V. Fogg, - -	"	–	7	
William Evans, - -	"	–	7	
John Evans, - -	"	–	7	
Fielding Archer, - -	Private,	–	7	
William Archer, - -	"	–	7	
Mark Andrews, - -	"	–	5	
Bartlett Andrews, - -	"	–	3	
William Berry, - -	"	–	7	
Arthur Burton, - -	"	–	7	
Abram Blankenship, - -	"	–	5	
Abraham Burton, - -	"	–	4	
William Britton, - -	"	–	7	
Henry Britton, - -	"	–	7	
Gabriel Bocciard, - -	"	–	7	
Jessee Brown, - -	"	–	7	
Charles Burton, - -	"	–	7	
Daniel Blankenship, - -	"	–	7	
Robert Bashall, - -	"	–	2	
John Burton, - -	"	–	4	
Thomas Britton, - -	"	–	5	
John Britton, - -	"	–	3	
James Clardy, - -	"	–	7	
Lodwick Covington, - -	"	–	7	
John Cozins, - -	"	–	7	
William Cozins, - -	"	–	3	
John Dance, - -	"	–	7	
Edward Dance, - -	"	–	7	
William Dance, jr. - -	"	–	7	
Thomas Dance, - -	"	–	7	
William Dance, sr. - -	"	–	5	
John W. Davis, - -	"	–	3	
Thomas Eanes, - -	"	–	4	
Parker G. Ervin, - -	"	–	7	
James Franklin, - -	"	–	7	
Jessee Franklin, - -	"	–	7	
Robert Gill, - -	"	–	7	
John Gill, - -	"	–	7	
Alexander Gibbs, - -	"	–	7	
Peter Gill, - -	"	–	7	
Edward Griffin, - -	"	–	7	
Thomas Gill, - -	"	–	7	
Peter D. Gibbs, - -	"	–	3	

NAMES.	RANK.	TIME OF SERVICE.		REMARKS.
		Months.	Days.	
Henry Haxall, - -	Private,	–	3	
John Mann, - -	"	–	5	
William McKean, - -	"	–	7	
Fielding Purkinson, - -	"	–	7	
Wilson Purkinson, - -	"	–	7	
Thomas Purkinson, - -	"	–	7	
Worsham Purkinson, - -	"	–	7	
John A. Pride, - -	"	–	7	
William Reams, - -	"	–	7	
Daniel Reams, - -	"	–	7	
Benjamin Smith, - -	"	–	7	
John Stiles, - -	"	–	7	
William Stiles, - -	"	–	5	
Geo. Traylor, - -	"	–	7	
Arch'd. Traylor, - -	"	–	7	
Thomas Tolly, - -	"	–	7	
William B. Tunstill, - -	"	–	3	
Thomas Varner, - -	"	–	7	
Ephraim Wilson, - -	"	–	7	
John Whiteford, - -	"	–	7	
Thomas Wyatt, - -	"	–	5	
Edmund Wells, - -	"	–	5	
Joseph Whiteford, - -	"	–	3	
Thomas Jones, - -	"	–	7	

MUSTER ROLL

Of Captain William Goff's Company, from the Twenty-third Regiment, Virginia Militia, commanded by Lieutenant Colonel William Brown, in the Service from the 24th to 30th March, from 26th to 28th June, and from 30th June to 2d July, 1813.

NAMES.	RANK.	TIME OF SERVICE.		REMARKS.
		Months.	Days.	
William Goff,	Captain,	–	11	
John Lera,	Lieutenant,	–	11	Or Lara.
James Ford,	Ensign,	–	11	
Thomas Ball,	Sergeant,	–	6	
G. N. Brichan,	"	–	6	
Thomas Drake,	"	–	11	
Bennet Goode,	"	–	11	
Branch Turner,	"	–	5	
Thomas A. Brookin,	"	–	11	
Robert H. Adams,	"	–	11	
Joseph C. Adkins,	"	–	11	
Robert Adams,	"	–	11	
John Anderson,	"	–	5	
John Anderson,	"	–	2	
Samuel Brooks,	"	–	6	
G. W. Branch,	"	–	11	
William Britervill,	"	–	6	Or Britewell.
John Brooks,	"	–	11	
Levin H. Boles,	"	–	5	
John Benereff,	"	–	5	
Charles Buckan,	"	–	5	
John Banony,	"	–	3	
Charles Cunleff,	"	–	11	
Frs. Cheatham,	"	–	11	
John W. Dandridge,	"	–	11	
Henry Hobson,	"	–	5	
John Handcock,	"	–	5	
Lewis Jeffries,	"	–	11	
Jacob Lora,	"	–	11	
William Lora,	"	–	6	
Wilson Lane,	"	–	6	
Drury L. Luckadoe,	"	–	11	
David Luckadoe,	"	–	5	
Riley Moore,	"	–	6	
John McCollum,	"	–	11	
John Norman,	"	–	6	
Samuel Nelson,	"	–	11	
John L. Pleasants,	"	–	11	
William Paul,	"	–	11	
Austin Pourtor,	"	–	6	
Austin Paul,	"	–	5	
John Rozell,	"	–	5	
John Rockp'd,	"	–	5	
Turner Sharp,	"	–	11	
Samuel Short,	"	–	11	
John Simpson,	"	–	11	
James Short,	"	–	11	

NAMES.	RANK.	TIME OF SERVICE.		REMARKS.
		Months.	Days.	
John Simpson, - -	Private,	–	6	
William Simpson, - -	"	–	5	
Henry Sumpter, - -	"	–	5	
Josiah Taylor, - -	"	–	11	
John S. Vauhan, - -	"	–	11	Or Vaughan.
Walter S. Winfree, - -	"	–	11	
Frs. Watkins, - -	"	–	5	
John Fowler, - -	"	–	5	
John R. Olders, - -	"	–	5	

Captain Benjamin Goode's Company—Twenty-third Regiment.

NAMES.	RANK.	TIME OF SERVICE.		REMARKS.
		Months.	Days.	
Benjamin Goode,	Captain,		17	
William Blankenship,	Lieutenant,	–	17	
Henry Cox,	Ensign,	–	17	
John Cheatham,	Sergeant,	–	17	
John Robertson,	"	–	17	
Joseph Wilkerson,	"	–	17	
Spencer Wooldridge,	"	–	17	
Thomas Anderson,	Private,	–	17	
William Anderson,	"	–	17	
Jacob Andrews,	"	–	17	
John Ashborne,	"	–	17	
Edward Anderson,	"	–	15	
Thomas Branch,	"	–	17	
Benjamin Branch,	"	–	17	
Geo. Bailey,	"	–	17	
Thomas Branch, jr.	"	–	17	
Thomas Bass,	"	–	17	
Lenevas Bass,	"	–	17	
Miles Branch,	"	–	15	
Matthew H. Branch,	"	–	17	
Robert F. Branch,	"	–	17	
Henry Beazley,	"	–	13	
Robert Bass,	"	–	2	
Henry Branch,	"	–	2	
William Dunevant,	"	–	17	
Haley Dunevant,	"	–	17	
Henry Dillon,	"	–	17	
Buckner Eans,	"	–	12	
Forrest Flournoy,	"	–	15	
John Fuqua,	"	–	17	
King Fowler,	"	–	17	
Murck Goode,	"	–	17	
Tapley Goode,	"	–	17	
Isham Graves,	"	–	17	
Thomas Gibbs,	"	–	17	
John Goode,	"	–	17	
Francis Goode,	"	–	17	
Pleasant Gordon,	"	–	17	
Elijah Gresham,	"	–	17	
Edward Goode,	"	–	15	
John Hill,	"	–	17	
Thomas Hix,	"	–	26	
James Moore,	"	–	3	
Thomas Morriss,	"	–	17	
Pleasant H. Mann,	"	–	17	
James McDowell,	"	–	17	
Zachariah Puckett,	"	–	17	
John Pinchback,	"	–	17	
Bartholomew Perdue,	"	–	17	
Francis Patram,	"	–	17	
Benjamin Patram,	"	–	15	
John Rison,	"	–	17	

NAMES.	RANK.	TIME OF SERVICE.		REMARKS.
		Months.	Days.	
Henry W. Robertson, -	Private,	–	17	
John Rowlett, - -	"	–	17	
William Rowlett, - -	"	–	17	
Daniel Stringer, - -	"	–	17	
Elijah Smith, - -	"	–	17	
Robert Stokes, - -	"	–	15	
William Sadler, - -	"	–	17	
Thomas B. Thweatt, - -	"	–	17	
John Turpin, - -	"	–	17	
Benjamin Watkins, - -	"	–	17	
Samuel Wilkerson, - -	"	–	17	
Edward Wanderson, - -	"	–	2	
Jessee Cashion, - -	"	–	17	
William Coats, - -	"	–	17	
Thomas Cheatham, - -	"	–	17	
Shadrack Clarke, - -	"	–	15	

(For rest of this company, see publication of Pay Rolls.)

Captain Benjamin Graves' Company—Twenty-third Regiment.

NAMES.	RANK.	TIME OF SERVICE. Months.	Days.	REMARKS.
Benjamin Graves,	Captain,	1	14	
Edward Nunnalley,	Lieutenant,	1	14	
Henry Waltham,	Ensign,	1	14	
Edward Anderson,	Sergeant,	1	14	
John Lafon,	"	–	11	
Jessee Coghill,	"	1	14	
William Chapple,	"	1	3	
Henry Farmer,	"	–	11	
Henry Elliott,	Corporal,	1	14	
Henry Winfree,	"	1	3	
Willi. Jackson,	"	1	14	
Thomas Gregory,	"	–	11	
Archbold Blankenship,	"	1	14	
Edward B. Archer,	Private,	1	14	
Richard H. Archer,	"	–	11	
William Bragg, jr.	"	1	14	
John Bowman,	"	1	14	
Jessee W. Busten,	"	1	14	
Thos. Brintle,	"	1	3	
Edmond Burton,	"	1	14	
Matthew H. Branch,	"	1	3	
Edw'd W. Bass,	"	–	11	
Christopher M. Bass,	"	1	3	
Thomas Clayton,	"	1	14	
John Clayton,	"	–	11	
Reubin Cole,	"	1	14	
Sherard Crostick,	"	2	4	
William Chappel,	"	–	11	
William Crostick,	"	–	11	
Philip Coghill,	"	–	11	
Ellison Clarke,	"	1	14	
Spencer Chalkley,	"	1	3	
Richard W. Crouch,	"	1	3	
Willi. Q. Dunevant,	"	1	14	
Asa Drereal,	"	1	3	
John W. Edwards,	"	1	14	
John Evans,	"	–	11	
Pleasant Elliott,	"	1	3	
Thomas Evans,	"	1	3	
Daniel Furguson,	"	1	14	
Newby Furguson,	"	–	11	
Thomas Franklin,	"	1	14	
Asa Furguson,	"	1	14	
Abner Farmer,	"	1	14	
James Furgason,	"	–	11	
Pleasant Farmer,	"	1	10	
Eben Farmer,	"	1	14	
John Freeman,	"	–	11	
Daniel Ford,	"	–	11	
Stephen Farmer,	"	1	14	
John Fuqua,	"	1	3	
Joseph Gill,	"	1	14	
Thos. Gregory,	"	1	3	
Thos. J. Gordon,	"	–	27	

NAMES.	RANK.	TIME OF SERVICE.		REMARKS.
		Months.	Days.	
Geo. Harrison,	Private,	1	14	
Christopher Hudson,	"	1	3	
William Jackson,	"	1	14	
Atwell Lafon,	"	1	3	
John Martin,	"	1	14	
Francis O. Markham,	"	1	3	
Thomas H. Mann,	"	–	11	
Baker Miles,	"	–	11	
Abner Mewby,	"	–	11	
David Moore,	"	–	7	
Benjamin Moody,	"	–	11	
Abraham Newby,	"	1	14	
John Nunnally,	"	1	14	
Edward Nunnally,	"	–	11	
Thomas Pride,	"	1	14	
Littleby Perdue,	"	1	3	
Sylvester Plumb,	"	1	3	
John Perdue, sen.	"	–	11	
John Ratteff,	"	1	14	
Thomas Shell,	"	1	14	
Geo. Soller,	"	1	3	
John Smith,	"	1	14	
Thomas Saddler,	"	–	11	
Lewis Senan,	"	–	11	
Isham Traylor,	"	1	14	
John Truman,	"	1	3	
Thomas T. Totty,	"	1	3	
Thomas W. Traylor,	"	1	3	
Bedford Traylor,	"	1	3	
Daniel Vaden,	"	1	3	
Martial Vaden,	"	1	3	
Michael Wells,	"	1	14	
Daniel Wilkerson,	"	1	3	
Thomas Wilkins,	"	1	3	
Baker Wells,	"	1	3	
Miles Watkins,	"	1	3	
Daniel Wilkerson,	"	–	11	
Henry Walthall,	"	–	11	
Thomas Wilkerson,	"	–	11	
Nelson Winfree,	"	–	11	

(For rest of this company, see publication of Pay Rolls.)

MUSTER ROLL

Of Captain John Gregory's Company, from the Twenty-third Regiment, Virginia Militia, commanded by Lieutenant Colonel William Brown, in the Service from 18th to 29th March, from 27th to 28th June, and from 1st to 2d July, 1813.

NAMES.	RANK.	TIME OF SERVICE.		REMARKS.
		Months.	Days.	
John Gregory, - -	Captain,	–	15	
Arch'd Franklin, - -	Lieutenant,	–	15	
Thomas Graves, - -	Ensign,	–	15	
Martin Newby, - -	Sergeant,	–	15	
James Newby, - -	"	–	11	
Thomas Fendley, - -	"	–	15	
Reuben Bottoms, - -	"	–	15	
Nath'l Newby, - -	"	–	11	
Robert Belcher, - -	"	–	14	
Benj. V. Jackson, - -	"	–	14	
Martin Adkins, - -	Private,	–	15	
Edmond Adkins, - -	"	–	15	
Geo. Adkins, - -	"	–	15	
William Adkins, - -	"	–	15	
David Adkins, - -	"	–	15	
Robert P. Archer, - -	"	–	15	
Geo. S. Anthony, - -	"	–	15	
John Beasley, - -	"	–	15	
Wilson Branch, - -	"	–	15	
Ezekiel Bowman, - -	"	–	15	
Branch Blankinship, - -	"	–	15	
Martin Costley, - -	"	–	15	
John P. Crump, - -	"	–	15	
Charles Graves, - -	"	–	15	
Wm. Haden, - -	"	–	2	
Zach. Hatcher, - -	"	–	15	
Edward Hatcher, - -	"	–	15	
David Hancock, - -	"	–	4	
Jeremiah Jackson, - -	"	–	15	
Henry Newby, - -	"	–	15	
Matthew Newby, - -	"	–	15	
Stephen Perdue, - -	"	–	15	
John Perry, jr. - -	"	–	15	
Hezekiah Smith, - -	"	–	15	
William Smith, - -	"	–	15	
Alexander Smith, - -	"	–	15	
Thomas Smith, - -	"	–	15	
Isham Smith, - -	"	–	15	
Granvill Smith, - -	"	–	15	
Valentine Smith, - -	"	–	15	
John Smith, - -	"	–	15	
John Taylor, sr. - -	"	–	15	
Stephen Turner, - -	"	–	15	
William Vaden, - -	"	–	15	
Clem. Watkins, - -	"	–	15	
Joshua White, - -	"	–	15	
Henry Woodcock, - -	"	–	15	
Marvil Winfree, - -	"	–	15	
Haley Ferguson, - -	"	–	15	
Felix Ferguson, - -	"	–	15	
David Franklin, - -	"	–	15	

MUSTER ROLL

Of Captain John Hix's Company, from the Twenty-third Regiment, Virginia Militia, Chesterfield County, commanded by Colonel William Brown, in the Service from 18th to 30th March, and from 27th to 28th June, in the year 1813.

NAMES.	RANK.	TIME OF SERVICE.		REMARKS.
		Months.	Days.	
John Hix, - - -	Captain,	–	14	
William Elliott, - -	Lieutenant,	–	14	
Green Hancock, - -	Ensign,	–	14	
Samuel Hancock, - -	Sergeant,	–	14	
John Snelling, - -	"	–	14	
John B. Morrissett, -	"	–	14	
Charles Lockett, - -	"	–	14	
John Ashland, - -	Private,	–	2	
John Brummatt, - -	"	–	14	
Thomas Bottoms, - -	"	–	14	
Samuel Bowels, - -	"	–	14	
Elias Brooks, - -	"	–	14	
Anderson Bowles, - -	"	–	2	
Lewing Bowles, - -	"	–	12	
Higgason Cox, - -	"	–	14	
Charles Cunliff, - -	"	–	14	
William Ellison, - -	"	–	2	
James Ellison, - -	"	–	12	
Daniel Furcrum, - -	"	–	14	
Cornelius Furcrum, - -	"	–	14	
Josiah Flournoy, - -	"	–	14	
John Furgason, - -	"	–	14	
Obediah Hix, - -	"	–	14	
Thomas Hix, - -	"	–	14	
William Hix, - -	"	–	2	
Francis Hix, - -	"	–	12	
John Hopkins, - -	"	–	12	
James Harding, - -	"	–	12	
John Johnson, - -	"	–	14	
William Johnson, - -	"	–	12	
Samuel Lockett, - -	"	–	14	
James Moore, - -	"	–	14	
Neal McLane, - -	"	–	14	
Robt. McClure, - -	"	–	12	
Peter Perdure, - -	"		14	
Barnard Roberts, - -	"	–	14	
Oliver Roberts, - -	"	–	12	
Richard Sowell, - -	"	–	14	
Thomas Snellings, - -	"	–	14	
William Swhatt, - -	"	–	14	
Edmond Saprad, - -	"	–	14	
Samuel Short, - -	"	–	14	
John Strange, - -	"	–	2	
John Sabarrear, - -	"	–	12	
Richard Sizer, - -	"	–	12	
James O. Sandrum, -	"	–	12	
Robert M. Tyre, - -	"	–	2	
John B. Taylor, - -	Private,	–	14	
Josiah Taylor, - -	"	–	12	
James Trasher, - -	"	–	12	
Hudson Thomas, - -	"	–	12	
James Williams, - -	"	–	14	
Edmond Wooldridge, -	"	–	14	
Henry Williams, - -	"	–	14	
Thomas Williams, - -	"	–	14	
Martin Wooldridge, -	"	–	2	

MUSTER ROLL

Of Ensign John Lare's Company of Infantry, from the Twenty-third Regiment, Virginia Militia, Chesterfield County, commanded by Lieutenant Colonel William Brown, in the Service from the 18th to 21st March, 1813.

NAMES.	RANK.	TIME OF SERVICE.		REMARKS.
		Months.	Days.	
John Lare, - - -	Ensign,	–	3	Lara or Lore.
Thomas Ball, - -	Sergeant,	–	3	
Geo. N. Brichan, - -	"	–	3	
Thomas Drake, - -	"	–	3	
Bennet Goode, - -	"	–	3	
Robert H. Adkins, - -	Private,	–	3	
Joseph C. Adams, - -	"	–	3	
Andrew Adkins, - -	"	–	3	
Andrew Adkinson, - -	"	–	3	
John Brooks, - -	"	–	3	
William Brightwell, - -	"	–	3	
Geo. W. Branch, - -	"	–	3	
Thomas A. Brookin, -	"	–	3	
Thomas A. Bookin, - -	"	–	3	
Charles Cuntiff, - -	"	–	3	Or Cunliff.
John W. Dandridge, -	"	–	3	
Bal'a Furnia, - -	"	–	3	
James Fore, - -	"	–	3	
William Goff, - -	"	–	3	
Wilson Lain, - -	"	–	3	
Lewis Jeffers - -	"	–	3	
Drewry L. Lockadoe, -	"	–	3	
Jacob Lora, - -	"	–	3	
John McColum, - -	"	–	3	
Riley Moore, - -	"	–	3	
John Norman, - -	"	–	3	
Samuel Nelson, - -	"	–	3	
Samuel Nelson, - -	"	–	3	
Josiah Olds, - -	"	–	3	
William Paul, - -	"	–	3	
John L. Pleasants, - -	"	–	3	
John Rozell, - -	"	–	3	
Henry Sumpler, - -	"	–	3	
Samuel Short, - -	"	–	3	
John Simpson, - -	"	–	3	
James Short, - -	"	–	3	
John L. Vaughan, - -	"	–	3	
Waller T. Winfree, - -	"	–	3	

MUSTER ROLL

Of Captain Geo. Markham's Company, from the Twenty-third Regiment, Virginia Militia, commanded by Lieutenant Colonel William Brown, in the Service from the 13th to 30th March, from 27th to 28th June, and from 1st to 2d July, 1813.

NAMES.	RANK.	TIME OF SERVICE.		REMARKS.
		Months.	Days.	
Geo. Markham, - -	Captain,	–	21	
John L. Morgan, - -	Lieutenant,	–	21	
James Martin, - -	Ensign,	–	21	
Lewis Neal, - -	Sergeant,	–	21	
Reuben Cross, - -	"	–	21	
James Burrute, - -	"	–	21	
Leroy Branch, - -	"	–	21	
Willey Andrews, - -	Private,	–	21	
William Adkins, - -	"	–	21	
Ambrose Alexander, - -	"	–	21	
John Andrews, - -	"	–	2	
James Adkins, - -	"	–	2	
Woodford Alvis, - -	"	–	2	
John Anderson, - -	"	–	17	
Zephaniah Alvis, - -	"	–	1	
Eleazer Bennet, - -	"	–	21	
William Burton, - -	"	–	21	
Samuel Bridgewater, - -	"	–	21	
John Burton, - -	"	–	21	
Thomas Branch, - -	"	–	21	
Caleb Bradley, - -	"	–	21	
John Branch, - -	"	–	5	
Matthew Branch, - -	"	–	3	
Samuel B. Collin, - -	"	–	19	
John W. Cardwell, - -	"	–	21	
William Cary, - -	"	–	2	
Francis Cheatham, - -	"	–	17	
Darius H. Furgison, - -	"	–	21	
Nathaniel Foster, - -	"	–	21	
Owen Franklin, - -	"	–	17	
Edmond George, - -	"		19	
Radford C. Gooding, - -	"	–	21	
William Good, - -	"	–	2	
Jeremiah Huccoe, - -	"	–	19	
Benjamin Horace, - -	"	–	21	
Samuel Horace, - -	"	–	21	
Caleb Hartgrove, - -	"	–	21	
James Holman, - -	"	–	21	
Benjamin Hatcher, - -	"	–	19	
Edward Henry, - -	"	–	2	
John Johnson, - -	"	–	21	
Leonard Jones, - -	"	–	21	
Watson Johnson, - -	"	–	21	
John Murrinder, - -	"	–	21	
James Miles, - -	"	–	21	
Nathaniel Mason, - -	"	–	21	
Overton Mason, - -	"	–	19	

NAMES.	RANK.	TIME OF SERVICE.		REMARKS.
		Months.	Days.	
John Moore, - -	Private,	–	3	
Peter Mason, - -	"	–	17	
William Nash, - -	"	–	17	
Claiborne Nash, - -	"	–	21	
Francis Patram, - -	"	–	20	
Stephen Russell, - -	"	–	17	
John Sorrell, - -	"	–	19	
William Shell, - -	"	–	2	
Richard Sassue, - -	"	–	21	
Moses Stanley, - -	"	–	19	
Thomas Winfrey, - -	"	–	21	
Samuel Winfrey, - -	"	–	21	
Abner Winfrey, - -	"	–	21	
Green Wood, - -	"	–	21	
Francis O. Watkins, - -	"	–	17	
Christopher Thomas, - -	"	–	21	
Matthew Winfrey, - -	"	–	17	
Joseph Smith, - -	"	–	17	
John Vickers, - -	"	–	21	
Philip H. Vest, - -	"	–	21	
Charles Zebmme, - -	"	–	4	Or Zebmure.

PAY ROLL

Of Captain David Weisiger's Company, belonging to the First Battalion of the Detachment under the command of Col. John H. Cocke, from the 26th June to 27th July 1813.

NAMES.	RANK.	Time of Service. Months.	Days.	REMARKS.
David Weisiger,	Captain,	1		
William Elliott,	Lieutenant,	1		
Green Hancock,	Ensign,	1		
John Ennis,	Sergeant,	–	15	Sub. by John Whiteford.
Thomas H. Bass,	"	1		
A. S. Wooldridge,	"	1		
William Hatchett,	Corporal,	1		
Matthew Branch,	"	1		
Ed. Redford,	"	1		
Thomas Bates,	"	1		
Jacob Alpin,	Private,	1		
John Branch,	"	1		
E. Blankinship,	"	1		
John Bragg,	"	1		
Abel Bowman,	"	1		
M. H. Branch,	"	1		
N. B. Burton,	"	1		
Thomas Cheatham,	"	1		
John Childers,	"	1		
Thomas Eanes,	"	1		
Seth W. Flournoy,	"	1		
Mark T. Flournoy,	"	1		
John Fuqua,	"	1		
H. Hancock,	"	1		
Robert Haskins,	"	1		
C. R. Hatcher,	"	1		
James Howard,	"	1		
William Lang,	"	1		
James Lynch,	"	1		
Walthall Lockett,	"	1		
Edward Laprade,	"	1		
Thomas Marsh,	"	1		
James McDowell,	"	1		
James Moxley,	"	1		
John Moore,	"	1		
W. S. McGruder,	"	1		
James Newby,	"	1		
Bar. Perdue,	"	1		
Shadrach Perdue,	"	1		
Peter Purkinson,	"	1		
L. Perdue,	"	1		
Rollin Puckett,	"	1		
Dennis Parten,	"	1		
John Rowlett,	"	1		
Bernard Roberts,	"	1		
Claiborne Royal,	"	1		
William Rowlett,	"	1		
Obed Short,	"	1		
Samuel Short,	"	1		
Richard Thompson,	"	1		
John Turpin,	"	1		
William Turpin,	"	1		
Daniel Traylor,	"	1		
H. Thurman,	"	1		

NAMES	RANK.	Time of Service.		REMARKS.
		Months.	Days.	
William Vaden, - -	"	1		
Mar. Vaden, - -	"	1		
James Vest, - -	"	1		
Obed Vest, - -	"	1		
Jeremiah Wooldridge, - -	"	1		
Peter Winfree, - -	"	1		
John Whiteford, - -	"	–	15	Sub. for John Ennis.

Captain David Weisiger's Company—Twenty-third Regiment.

NAMES.	RANK.	TIME OF SERVICE.		REMARKS.
		Months.	Days.	
David Weisiger, - -	Captain,	–	11	
James Clarke, - -	Lieutenant,	–	1	
Isaac Davis, - -	Ensign,	–	4	
Young Pankey, - -	Sergeant,	–	4	
Robert Miller, - -	"	–	4	
Thomas Winfree, - -	"	–	4	
Thomas Smith, - -	"	–	4	
Fred'k Patram, - -	"	–	7	
Jno. Fuqua, - -	"	–	7	
Jno. Emses, - -	"	–	7	
Thos. H. Bass, - -	"	–	7	
Thomas Smith, - -	Corporal,	–	4	
Wm. Bradshaw, - -	"	–	4	
Ro. Dinsworth, - -	"	–	1	
James Caskie, - -	"	–	4	
Wm. Hutchett, - -	"	–	7	
Matt. Branch, - -	"	–	7	
Edward A. May, - -	"	–	7	
Zach. Rowlett, - -	"	–	7	
Jacob Alpin, - -	Private,	–	7	
T. Brackett, - -	"	–	1	
Wm. Brackett, - -	"	–	1	
Isaac Burnard, - -	"	–	1	
John Banoff, - -	"	–	4	
Rob't F. Branch, - -	"	–	7	
Chas. Burton, - -	"	–	7	
Thomas Butts, - -	"	–	4	
James S. Bass, - -	"	–	29	
John Branch, - -	"	–	7	
E. Blankinship, - -	"	–	7	
Jno. L. Berry, - -	"	–	7	
John Bragg, - -	"	–	7	
Abel Bowman, - -	"	–	7	
Matthew H. Branch, - -	"	–	7	
William B. Clarke, - -	"	–	4	
Robert Clarke, - -	"	–	4	
Thomas Cheatham, - -	"	–	7	
John Childer, - -	"	–	1	
Miles Elam, - -	"	–	1	
Jno. Evans, - -	"	–	7	
William Elam, - -	"	–	7	
Andrew Fore, - -	"	–	4	
Mark F. Flournoy, - -	"	–	7	
Seth W. Flournoy, - -	"	–	7	
John Gilchrist, - -	"	–	4	
Nich. Garden, - -	"	–	1	
P. E. Graves, - -	"	–	4	
James Gray, - -	"	–	1	
Rand. Hatchett, - -	"	–	4	
Josiah Hobson, - -	"	–	1	
Rob't Haskins, - -	"	–	7	
J. B. Hooper, - -	"	–	4	
H. Hancock, - -	"	–	7	
Jno. Jenkins, - -	"	–	4	

NAMES.	RANK.	TIME OF SERVICE.		REMARKS.
		Months.	Days.	
Edward Johnston, - -	Private,	–	4	
Stephen Johnson, - -	"	–	4	
Wm. Long, - -	"	–	11	
James Long, - -	"	–	4	
James Lynch, - -	"	–	7	
Wastus Lockett, - -	"	–	7	
Nich. Mills, - -	"	–	4	
C. McKae, - -	"	–	1	
Henry Moody, - -	"	–	1	
B. B. Morrison, - -	"	–	4	
Philip Michaels, - -	"	–	4	
Hugh M. Miller, - -	"	–	4	
Ro. D. Murchie, - -	"	–	4	
John Moore, - -	"	–	7	
James Moyley, - -	"	–	7	
Jas. McDowell, - -	"	–	7	
Stephen Pankey, - -	"	–	4	
Wm. A. Patterson, - -	"	–	4	
Little'n Perdue, - -	"	–	7	
Peter Perkins, - -	"	–	7	
Robin Packett, - -	"	–	4	
Dennis Pastin, - -	"	–	7	
Shad. Perdue, - -	"	–	7	
Bernard Perdue, - -	"	–	7	
Cole Powell, - -	"	–	7	
Bev. Randolph, - -	"	–	4	
Edward Redford, - -	"	–	4	
William Rowlett, - -	"	–	7	
Clab. Royall, - -	"	–	7	
Bernard Roberts, - -	"	–	7	
John Rowlett, - -	"	–	7	
Richard Sizer, - -	"	–	28	
Tarlton Saunders, - -	"	–	1	
John Scott, - -	"	–	4	
Samuel Sizer, - -	"	–	4	
Joseph Spencer, - -	"	–	1	
Oba'h Short, - -	"	–	7	
Richard Tomaston, - -	"	–	7	
John Turpin, - -	"	–	7	
Thomas Turpin, - -	"	–	7	
Daniel Traylor, - -	"	–	7	
Samuel Traylor, - -	"	–	4	
T. Vaden, - -	"	–	4	
William Vaden, - -	"	–	7	
James Vast, - -	"	–	7	
Samuel Wilson, - -	"	–	7	
John Willet, - -	"	–	4	
Mans'n Watkins, - -	"	–	4	
Richard Weisiger, - -	"	–	4	
John Weisiger, - -	"	–	4	
Daniel Weisiger, - -	"	–	4	
H. Weisiger, - -	"	–	4	
Robert Warren, - -	"	–	4	
John W. Winfree, - -	"	–	1	

(For rest of this company, see publication of Pay Rolls.)

MUSTER ROLL

Of Captain Littleberry West's Company, from the Twenty-third Regiment, Virginia Militia, in the County of Chesterfield, called into actual Service under general orders, from 18th to 29th March, from 27th to 28th June, and from 1st to 2d of July, in the year 1813.

NAMES.	RANK.	TIME OF SERVICE.		REMARKS.
		Months.	Days.	
Littleberry West, - -	Captain,	–	18	
Burwell Parkinson, - -	Lieutenant,	–	19	
Henry P. Eanes, - -	Ensign,	–	19	
Archer Taylor, - -	Sergeant,	–	19	
John Rowlett, - -	"	–	19	
Vaden Moore, - -	"	–	19	
William Wilson, - -	"	–	19	
Benj. Andrews, - -	Private,	–	19	
Ledwick Andrews, - -	"	–	19	
Daniel Andrews, - -	"	–	19	
Erasmus Andrews, - -	"	–	12	
Hugh Bragg, - -	"	–	19	
Laban Blankenship, - -	"	–	19	
John Bragg, - -	"	–	12	
John L. Bany, - -	"	–	12	
Andrew Costley, - -	"	–	19	
Isaac Caulfield, - -	"	–	19	
Jordan R. Davis, - -	"	–	19	
Joseph Dunavant, - -	"	–	19	
Martin Davis, - -	"	–	15	
John Deaton, - -	"	–	19	
Buckner Eanes, - -	"	–	19	
Daniel Eanes, - -	"	–	19	
Isham Eanes, - -	"	–	19	
Thomas Eanes, - -	"	–	12	
Arthur Fraylor, - -	"	–	3	
Rob't Gill, - -	"	–	7	
Will. Goodwin, - -	"	–	12	
Will. Hatchett, - -	"	–	12	
Alexander Moore, - -	"	–	19	
Edward Moore, - -	"	–	19	
Francis Mann, - -	"	–	19	
Thomas R. Mann, - -	"	–	19	
Charles Mann, - -	"	–	19	
Jos. G. Mann, - -	"	–	19	
Chastain Mann, - -	"	–	19	
Drury Moore, - -	"	–	19	
Cain Mann, - -	"	–	19	
Spencer Moore, - -	"	–	19	
Peter Moody, - -	"	–	14	
Will. Mann, jr. - -	"	–	19	
John Perkinson, - -	"	–	19	
James Perdue, - -	"	–	19	
Daniel Patram, - -	"	–	19	
Nelson Phillips, - -	"	–	19	
George Patram, - -	"	–	7	

NAMES.	RANK.	TIME OF SERVICE.		REMARKS.
		Months.	Days.	
John Phillips, - -	Private,	–	16	
Peter Perdue, - -	"	–	12	
Nelson Rurtin, (or Burton,) -	"	–	12	
Daniel Rowlett, - -	"	–	19	
Joseph Ross, - -	"	–	12	
Zachariah Rowlett, - -	"	–	12	
Josiah Stringer, - -	"	–	19	
Thomas Stone, - -	"	–	19	
Michael Traylor, - -	"	–	19	
Herbert Traylor, - -	"	–	19	
John Traylor, - -	"	–	19	
Arthur Traylor, - -	"	–	19	
Matthew Traylor, - -	"	–	16	
Terray Talley, - -	"	–	16	
Daniel Traylor, - -	"	–	12	
Marshall Vaden, - -	"	–	15	
Stamander Vaden, - -	"	–	12	
Willi. Vaden, - -	"	–	12	
George Wilson, - -	"	–	19	
Ledwick Wilson, - -	"	–	19	
Willi. Wilson, - -	"	–	19	
Littleton Wilson, - -	"	–	19	
Creed Wilson, - -	"	–	19	
Henry Wilson, - -	"	–	19	
Thomas Wilson, - -	"	–	16	
John Wilkinson, - -	"	–	12	

Captain John Wilson's Company—Twenty-sixth Regiment.

NAMES.	RANK.	TIME OF SERVICE.		REMARKS.
		Months.	Days.	
John Wilson, - -	Captain,	–	14	
Robert Wilson, - -	Lieutenant,	–	14	
Wm. C. Wilson, - -	Ensign,	–	14	
Thomas Matthews, - -	Sergeant,	–	14	
Isham Bagby, - -	"	–	14	
Dabney Jones, - -	"	–	14	
James Sisson, - -	"	–	14	
Chisholme Ellis, - -	Corporal,	–	14	
Henry Cartmill, - -	"	–	14	
Hiram Cobbs, - -	"	–	14	
John Donnally, - -	"	–	14	
John Fisher, - -	Fifer,	–	14	
Isham Bayley, - -	Private,	–	14	
Moses Brown, - -	"	–	14	
Thomas Cobbs, - -	"	–	14	
Thomas Casdrop, - -	"	–	14	
Jacob Casdrop, - -	"	–	14	
Alexander Cartwright, -	"	–	14	
John Campbell, - -	"	–	14	
Solomon Casdrop, - -	"	–	14	
John Cooper, - -	"	–	14	
Leonard Cooper, - -	"	–	14	
Joseph Dawson, - -	"	–	14	
Gutrell Dawson, - -	"	–	14	
William Fowler, - -	"	–	14	
Asa Fowler, - -	"	–	14	
Joshua Fowler, - -	"	–	14	
Leonard Fisher, - -	"	–	14	
John Guthrie, - -	"	–	14	
Thomas Hensley, - -	"	–	14	
Thomas Lowe, - -	"	–	14	
John Medley, - -	"	–	14	
Thomas Milam, - -	"	–	14	
Moses Milam, - -	"	–	14	
Malcom McCown, - -	"	–	14	
Simeon Milam, - -	"	–	14	
Henry McLaughlin, - -	"	–	14	
James McCown, - -	"	–	14	
James Newport, - -	"	–	14	
Thomas Parrish, - -	"	–	14	
Nimrod Paul, - -	"	–	14	
Edmund Price, - -	"	–	14	
Arch'd Price, - -	"	–	14	
Samuel Presley, - -	"	–	14	
Joel Rucker, - -	"	–	14	
John Ray, - -	"	–	14	
Andrew Slaughter, - -	"	–	14	
John Smith, , -	"	–	14	
Joseph Still, - -	"	–	14	
Elisha Smith, - -	"	–	14	
Luke Shiverdecker, - -	"	–	14	
Alexander Taylor, - -	"	–	14	
George Weldy, - -	"	–	14	
Longston Ward, - -	"	–	14	

MUSTER ROLL

Of Captain David Jacobs' Troop of Cavalry, of the Twenty-eighth Regiment, Virginia Militia, in the County of Nelson, called into actual Service under the general orders of the 26th August, 1814, *from the 2d to the 12th of September,* 1814.

NAMES.	RANK.	TIME OF SERVICE.		REMARKS.
		Months.	Days.	
David Jacobs,	Captain,	–	12	
Richard Phillips,	Lieutenant,	–	12	
Peter C. Jacobs,	"	–	12	
Alexander Roberts,	Cornet,	–	12	
Nathaniel Harlow, jr.	Sergeant,	–	12	
John P. Scruggs,	"	–	12	
Nath'l H. Ragland,	"	–	12	
William Miggison,	"	–	12	
Chapel Deveanport,	Corporal,	–	12	
Nicholas Fortune,	"	–	12	
William Crisp,	"	–	12	
Patterson Scruggs,	"	–	12	
Kendol Brent,	Private,	–	12	
James Bibb,	"	–	12	
Benjamin Bradshaw,	"	–	12	
Peter Clarkeson,	"	–	12	
James Campbell,	"	–	12	
John Carr,	"	–	12	
William Campbell,	"	–	12	
Samuel Denny,	"	–	12	
William Davis,	"	–	12	
John Demastus,	"	–	12	
James Demastus,	"	–	12	
Jordan Edmunds,	"	–	12	
Thomas Fortune,	"	–	12	
John W. Green,	"	–	12	
Henry M. Green,	"	–	12	
Elias Hamlet,	"	–	12	
John Hamlet,	"	–	12	
Nathaniel Hill,	"	–	12	
Wyatt Hare,	"	–	12	
Robert Hunter,	"	–	12	
John Hensley,	"	–	12	
Augustin Henlow,	"	–	12	
Robert Johnson,	"	–	12	
Holeman Jopling,	"	–	12	
William C. Kidd,	"	–	12	
William J. Kidd,	"	–	12	
Lavender London,	"	–	12	
Richard Ligon,	"	–	12	
Samuel P. Lane,	"	–	12	
Charles Langford,	"	–	12	
Edmund T. Lively,	"	–	12	
James B. Lane,	"	–	12	
John Lavender,	"	–	12	
Reuben T. Mitchell,	"	–	12	
Aaron H. Morrison,	"	–	12	

NAMES.	RANK.	TIME OF SERVICE.		REMARKS.
		Months.	Days.	
James McAlexander, -	Private,	-	12	
Vincent Marks, - -	"	-	12	
Davis R. Patterson, - -	"	-	12	
Charles Philips, - -	"	-	12	
James Panock, - -	"	-	12	
Lucas Powell, - -	"	-	12	
Nelson Philips, - -	"	-	12	
Richard C. Pollard, - -	"	-	12	
Lymore Powell, - -	"	-	12	
Conyers Philips, - -	"	-	12	
Nathaniel Powell, - -	"	-	12	
William Reppetoe, - -	"	-	12	
Giles Richardson, - -	"	-	12	
Joseph Seay, - -	"	-	12	
John Scruggs, - -	"	-	12	
Richard Saunders, - -	"	-	12	
David Shields, - -	"	-	12	
John Statham, - -	"	-	12	
James Smith, - -	"	-	12	
George Shields, - -	"	-	12	
Lemuel Turner, - -	"	-	12	
James S. Thomas, - -	"	-	12	
James Thomas, - -	"	-	12	
Henry Turner, - -	"	-	12	
Lewis White, - -	"	-	12	
William Watkins, - -	"	-	12	
John Willoughby, - -	"	-	12	
Nelson Wanick, - -	"	-	12	
Hudson Watkins, - -	"	-	12	
Milliner Wilkinson, - -	"	-	12	
Augustin Wright, - -	"	-	12	
Robert Woody, - -	"	-	12	
Nelson Wright, - -	"	-	12	
James Wright, - -	"	-	12	

PAY ROLL

Of Captain William C. Scott's Company, from the Twenty-eighth Regiment of Virginia Militia, Nelson County, attached to the Eighth Regiment, Fourth Brigade, in the Service of the United States, at Camp Carter, commanded by Brigadier General Cocke, from the 30th August 1814 to 22d February 1815.

NAMES.	RANK.	Time of Service.		REMARKS.
		Months.	Days.	
William C. Scott,	Captain,	5	25	
Henry Dawson,	Lieutenant,	6		
Joseph Hopkins,	"	5	3	
William Tomlinson,	Ensign,	6	3	
William H. Shelton,	"	1	10	
Nath'l Anderson,	"	3	28	
Jno. B. Rawlings,	Sergeant,	5	9	
Moses Fitzpatrick,	"	1	19	Jos. Trusler his sub.
Ben. Harris,	"	3	28	Walter Cannon "
Sam. Edmonds,	"	4	23	Wm. Hudson "
William Witt,	"	6	1	A. Wright, "
James Christian,	"	5	5	
Thomas Fitzpatrick,	"	6		
John Housewright,	"	5	29	
Thomas Carter, Sr.,	"	5	7	
Thos. Fitzpatrick, (saddler,)	Corporal,	6		
Joel Bethel,	"	5	28	
Thomas Rhodes,	"	4	11	D. Rhodes his sub.
Ben. Wright,	"	5		
Megginson Loving,	"	6	1	
Thomas Woodson,	"	5	9	A. Pollock his sub.
William Johnson,	"	4	2	Ro. Watkins "
Joel Hight,	"	5	14	
John Massicap,	"	5	7	
Henry Niece,	"	5	29	
William Hamlet,	"	5	28	
Abram Seay,	"	5	29	
Richardson Alphine,	Private,	4	16	
John Anderson,	"	4	21	
John Bonds,	"	4	5	F. Miller his sub.
Richard Ball,	"	1	29	
John Bethel,	"	5	27	
William Bailey,	"	5	26	
Jacob Baker,	"	2	12	
Williamson Burke,	"	4	22	Sub. for W. Thompson.
William Bryant,	"	2	15	
Nelson Bridgewater,	"	6	1	
Nat. Bridgewater,	"	5	12	
Jesse Burks,	"	3	28	
Zenith Baber,	"	5	6	
Geo. Campbell,	"	4	16	S. Kendrick his sub.
Jesse Carter,	"	6	2	
Thomas Carter, Jr.,	"	6	2	
Nath'l Clarke,	"	5	16	
Thomas Catlin,	"	4	12	Jno. Hunter his sub.
William Caler,	"	3	22	
Sam. Crawford,	"	6	2	
Walter Cannon,	"	2	1	Sub. for Ben. Harris.
William Dennis,	"	4	25	
Claiborne Derrett,	"	5	10	

****

NAMES.	RANK.	Time of Service.		REMARKS.
		Months.	Days.	
William Deguise, - -	Private,	–	–	Deserted.
John Dixon, - -	"	6	1	
William Fowles, - -	"	3	27	
Richard Fox, - -	"	6	1	
Isaac Grey, - -	"	6	2	
Richard Harvey, - -	"	6	2	
William Henderson, - -	"	6	2	
George Hight, - -	"	5	7	
Robert Henderson, - -	"	5	6	
William Henderson, jr., -	"	6	2	
James Housewright, - -	"	6	1	
William Hill, - -	"	6	2	
John Hunter, - -	"	1	17	
Robert Hunter, - -	"	1	17	
Joshua Jones, - -	"	4	20	Wm. Rippeto his sub.
Samuel Johnson, - -	"	6	1	
Stephen Johnson, - -	"	6	1	
Coleman W. Kidd, - -	"	6	1	
Ben. Kesterson, - -	"	5	16	
Sam'l Kendrick, - -	"	1	7	
James Lobin, - -	"	4	12	R. Hunter his sub.
John Langford, - -	"	6	1	
James Lively, - -	"	5	10	
William Lanham, - -	"	5	6	
Lewis F. Lanham, - -	"	6		
William Lanham, jr., - -	"	6		
William Lively, - -	"	6	2	
John Massacup, - -	"	1	29	
Geo. Morris, - -	"	6	2	
William Moses, - -	"	–	–	Deserted.
C. C. McMullin, - -	"	6		
William McLain, - -	"	6	2	
Leonard Moyer, - -	"	5	7	
Archibald Mitchell, - -	"	5	23	
Thos. C. McMullen, - -	"	6	2	
Dabney Madison, - -	"	3	18	
Fleming Miller, - -	"	1	24	
William Melton, - -	"	1	8	Sub. for Jos. Trusler.
Randolph Newton, - -	"	1	8	
Thomas Offlighter, - -	"	6	2	
David Oglesby, - -	"	4	14	
Jacob Pucket, - -	"	5	18	
Emanuel Phillips, - -	"	5	10	
Jno. S. Phillips, - -	"	6	2	
John Paxton, - -	"	2	3	
Absalom Pugh, - -	"	1	20	
John Rippeto, - -	"	6	2	
William Rippeto, - -	"	1	9	
David Rhodes, - -	"	1	17	
Abram Seay, - -	"	5	9	
Ben. Scruggs, - -	"	4	24	
James Swinney, - -	"	6	2	
John Spears, - -	"	6	1	
Charles Toms, - -	"	6	2	
Clifton Toms, - -	"	2	5	
William Tyree, - -	"	5	16	
Hezekiah Tyree, - -	"	5	7	
Joseph Tyree, - -	"	6	2	
Charles Thompson, - -	"	6	2	
William Trusler, - -	"	5	6	
Joseph Trusler, - -	"	3	1	Sub. for M. Fitzpatrick, and W. Melton his sub,
William Thompson, - -	"	1	10	Wm. Burke his sub.
Thomas Wright, - -	"	4	9	
Landon Wright, - -	"	1	11	

NAMES.	RANK.	Time of Service.		REMARKS.
		Months.	Days.	
Thomas Ware, - -	Private,	4	20	R. Newton his sub.
John Wood, - -	"	6	2	
Rich'd Witt, - -	"	6	2	
James Wood, - -	"	6	2	
John H. Wingfield, - -	"	1	29	
Thomas Wilson, - -	"	5	8	
Ro. Watkins, - -	"	1	27	

Captain William C. Scott's Company—Twenty-eighth Regiment.

NAMES.	RANK.	TIME OF SERVICE.		REMARKS.
		Months.	Days.	
Mathew Lanford, - -	Lieutenant,	–	15	
James Edmonds, - -	Sergeant,	–	9	
Jesse Becknal, - -	Private,			
Woodson Fitzgerald, - -	"			
Alexander Fitzpatrick, -	"	–	29	
John Harris, jr. - -	"			
John Henderson, - -	"	–	16	
William Hudson, - -	"	–	26	
Larkin Miller, - -	"			
Walker Nicholas, - -	"			
Abram Polack, - -	"	–	20	
Alexander B. Rose, - -	"			
William Settles, - -	"			

(For rest of this company, see publication of Pay Rolls.)

MONTHLY PAY ROLL

Of Captain William Allen's Company of Infantry, from Thirty-third Regiment of Virginia Militia, in the Service from the 19th to the 29th March, 1813.

NAMES.	RANK.	TIME OF SERVICE.		REMARKS.
		Months.	Days.	
William Allen, - -	Captain,	–	5	
John Pemberton, - -	Lieutenant,	–	4	
John Carter, - -	Ensign,	–	5	
Christian Allen, - -	Sergeant,	–	5	
Claiborne Bethell, - -	"	–	5	
William Baker, - -	"	–	5	
John Morris, - -	"	–	5	
William Eacho, - -	Private,	–	5	
Hazlewood Bottom, -	"	–	5	
James Smith, - -	"	–	5	
Terry Hill, - - -	"	–	5	
Geo. Leach, - - -	"	–	5	
Daniel Tucker, - -	"	–	5	
Ishmael Lawrence, - -	"	–	5	
Therwood Binford, - -	"	–	5	
John Eacho, - -	"	–	5	
John Warriner, - -	"	–	5	
Thomas Wade, - -	"	–	5	
Ansel Gathright, - -	"	–	5	
Reuben Matthews, - -	"	–	5	
William Austin, - -	"	–	5	
Thomas Johnson, - -	"	–	4	
Jonathan Brackett, - -	"	–	5	
John Turner, - -	"	–	5	
Littlebery Allen, - -	"	–	5	
William Gathright, - -	"	–	5	
John Valentine, - -	"	–	5	
John Childreys, - -	"	–	5	
Thomas Bethel, - -	"	–	5	
Carter Bethel, - -	"	–	5	
James Matthews, - -	"	–	5	
Moses Woodfin, - -	"	–	5	
Thomas Goodman, - -	"	–	5	
John Dunn, - -	"	–	5	
Robt. Bethell, - -	"	–	5	
Samuel Barker, - -	"	–	5	
William Carter, - -	"	–	5	
Samuel Gathright, - -	"	–	5	
William Barker, - -	"	–	5	
Samuel Lawrance, - -	"	–	5	
George Savage, - -	"	–	5	
Joseph Wade, - -	"	–	5	
Carter Gathright, - -	"	–	5	
Richard Allen, - -	"	–	5	
Fleming Pollard, - -	"	–	5	
Thomas Holmes, - -	"	–	5	
John Hailes, - -	"	–	5	
Winston Harwood, - -	"	–	5	
Moses Carter, - -	"	–	5	

NAMES.	RANK.	TIME OF SERVICE.		REMARKS.
		Months.	Days.	
William Matthews, - -	Private,	–	5	
John Clark, - -	"	–	5	
Pleasant Smith, - -	"	–	5	
Thomas Gathright, - -	"	–	5	
William Ferress, - -	"	–	5	
Edward Gathright, - -	"	–	5	
John Francis, - -	"	–	5	
Edward Morriss, - -	"	–	5	
John W. Royster, - -	"	–	3	
Hobson Warriner, - -	"	–	5	
Jacob Truman, - -	"	–	5	
Dandridge Carter, - -	"	–	5	
Stephen Warriner, - -	"	–	2	
James Austin, - -	"	–	5	
Thomas Hamblett, - -	"	–	5	
Matthews Carter, - -	"	–	5	
John W. Lawrence, - -	"	–	5	
Joseph Goodman, - -	"	–	5	

****

RECEIPT ROLL

Of Captain Samuel Brown's Company of Virginia Militia, from the Thirty-third Regiment, in the Service from the 19th to 29th March, 1814.

NAMES.	RANK.	TIME OF SERVICE.		REMARKS.
		Months.	Days.	
Samuel Brown, - -	Captain,	–	5	On duty every other day.
Josiah Peck, - -	Lieutenant,	–	5	
William B. Ellis, - -	Ensign,	–	5	
William Ellis, - -	Sergeant,	–	5	
Cabil David, - -	"	–	5	
Martin Pait, - -	"	–	5	
Machichi Feniley, - -	"	–	5	Or Tinsley.
Richard Clarke, - -	Corporal,	–	5	
Reubin Allen, - -	"	–	5	
Daniel Brown, - -	"	–	5	
William Cottrell, - -	"	–	5	
William Hutcherson, -	Private,	–	5	
Richard Sampson, - -	"	–	5	
William Brown, - -	"	–	5	
Anderson Taylor, - -	"	–	5	
John Miller, - -	"	–	5	
John Ellis, - - -	"	–	5	
Stephen Duval, - -	"	–	5	
Wilson Price, - -	"	–	5	
Charles Woodward, -	"	–	5	
Joseph Blackbourn, - -	"	–	5	
William Baughan, - -	"	–	5	
Henry Willis, - -	"	–	5	
John Baughan, - -	"	–	5	
Samuel Cottrell, - -	"	–	5	
David Powers, - -	"	–	5	
Ellis Brown, - -	"	–	5	
Samuel Conway, - -	"	–	5	
William Blackborne, -	"	–	5	
Reaves Tinsley, - -	"	–	5	
John Thomas, - -	"	–	8	
Alexander Gordan, - -	"	–	5	
Nathaniel Tinsley, - -	"	–	5	
John Blackborne, - -	"	–	5	
Geo. Montgurmery, - -	"	–	5	
John Montgomery, -	"	–	5	
James Ellis, - - -	"	–	5	
Wilson Coats, - -	"	–	5	
Overton B. Pettit, - -	"	–	5	
Joseph W. Campbell, -	"	–	5	
Stephen Stone, - -	"	–	5	
John R. Whome, - -	"	–	5	
John Fanant, - -	Private,	–	5	
James Jones, - -	"	–	5	
Joseph Ellis, - -	"	–	5	
Thomas Duke, - -	"	–	5	

PAY ROLL

Of Captain William Childrey's Company of Infantry, Virginia Militia, from the Second Battalion, Thirty-third Regiment, called into Service the 19th and discharged the 29th of March, 1813.

NAMES.	RANK.	TIME OF SERVICE.		REMARKS.
		Months.	Days.	
William Childrey,	Captain,	–	5	
John Lindsay,	Lieutenant,	–	5	
John Hobson,	Ensign,	–	4	
Thomas Goode,	Sergeant,	–	5	
Samuel Norment,	"	–	5	
Jno. R. Pierce,	"	–	5	
Lewis Throgmorton,	"	–	5	
Billard Ammens,	Private,	–	5	
Joseph Bailey,	"	–	5	
Stanhope Bradley,	"	–	5	
Enes Bottoms,	"	–	1	
William Crittenden,	"	–	5	
Samuel Crenshaw,	"	–	5	
Edward Coghill,	"	–	5	
William Dandridge,	"	–	5	
Abay Duke,	"	–	5	
Edward Eppes, jr.	"	–	5	
Edward Eppes, sr.	"	–	5	
Benj. A. Foster,	"	–	5	
Edward Goode,	"	–	1	
Benjamin Goode,	"	–	5	
Isaac Goode,	"	–	5	
Arch'd Goode,	"	–	5	
Hobson Goode,	"	–	5	
Jno. Goode,	"	–	5	
Robert Goode,	"	–	5	
Turner Hutchings,	"	–	5	
Henry G. Heath,	"	–	4	
James E. Hardyman,	"	–	5	
Robert Jolley,	"	–	5	
William Keepell,	"	–	5	
Francis Lewis,	"	–	5	
Moses Lindsay,	"	–	5	
Elijah Lindsay,	"	–	5	
Jonathan M. Laine,	"	–	5	
Benjamin Mosby,	"	–	3	
Jno. G. Mosby,	"	–	5	
William H. Minson,	"	–	5	
Hartwell M. Manners,	"	–	2	
William Profer,	"		5	
William Pierce,	"	–	5	
Samuel Robinson,	"	–	3	
Nathaniel S. Robinson,	"	–	5	
Peter Robinson,	"	–	5	
John Roper,	"	–	5	
Milner Redford,	"	–	5	
James Robertson,	Private,	–	5	
—— Sharps,	"	–	5	
John Sanrenie,	"	–	5	
Jesse Throgmorton,	"	–	5	
Robert Throgmorton,	"	–	5	
Arch'd Taylor,	"	–	2	
Jno. Vaughan,	"	–	5	
Thomas J. West,	"	–	5	
James Whitlock,	"	–	5	
Peter West,	"	–	5	

PAY ROLL

Of Captain Abraham Cowley's Company of Infantry, from the Second Battalion of the Thirty-third Regiment of Virginia Militia, called into Service the 19*th and discharged* 29*th March*, 1813.

NAMES.	RANK.	TIME OF SERVICE.		REMARKS.
		Months.	Days.	
Abraham Cowley, - -	Captain,	–	5	
Josiah Gathright, - -	Lieutenant,	–	5	
Philip Faloher, - -	Ensign,	–	5	
Samuel Henry, - -	Sergeant,	–	5	
Henry Negby, - -	"	–	5	
Henry Vaughan, - -	"	–	5	
Bartholomew Martin, -	"	–	5	
James V. Thompson, -	Corporal,	–	5	
William King, - -	"	–	5	
William Beverage, - -	"	–	4	
William Straus, - -	"	–	5	
Robert Anderson, - -	Private,	–	5	
John W. Allen, - -	"	–	5	
Nelson Anderson, - -	"	–	5	
John Beverage, - -	"	–	5	
William Banks, - -	"	–	5	
Jesse Britain, - -	"	–	5	
Gideon Bosher, - -	"	–	1	
Elisha Bethell, - -	"	–	5	
Charles Barker, - -	"	–	4	
Nimrod Chience, - -	"	–	3	
Samuel Cowley, - -	"	–	5	
Pery Clark, - -	"	–	1	
Peter Franklin, - -	"	–	4	
Dudley Gillman, - -	"	–	3	
Jno. A. Grant, - -	"	–	5	
Elisha Harwood, - -	"	–	5	
John Harlin, - -	"	–	5	
Benjamin Haley, - -	"	–	5	
Gabriel C. Higgason, -	"	–	5	
Joseph C. Haley, - -	"	–	4	
Mitchem Hadkins, - -	"	–	1	
William Johnson, - -	"	–	5	
John Kemp, - -	"	–	4	
David Knight, - -	"	–	1	
Mordecai Marks, - -	"	–	2	
William New, - -	"	–	5	
John Philips, - -	"	–	5	
Francis R. Price, - -	"	–	5	
Joseph C. Pleasants, -	"	–	5	
John Paul, - - -	"	–	5	
Robert Price, - -	"	–	3	
Jonathan Quisall, - -	"	–	5	
Jno. H. Saunders, - -	"	–	4	
William Williams, - -	"	–	1	

PAY ROLL

Of Captain Thomas Friend's Company, from Thirty-third Regiment, Virginia Militia, in the Service from 19th to 29th March, 1813.

NAMES.	RANK.	TIME OF SERVICE.		REMARKS.
		Months.	Days.	
Thomas Friend, - -	Captain,	–	5	
Francis Pearil, - -	Lieutenant,	–	4	
Edward Marable, - -	Ensign,	–	3	
Richard Turpin, - -	Sergeant,	–	5	
Collin Adams, - -	Private,	–	5	
John Williams, - -	"	–	5	
James Jourdan, - -	"	–	5	
Rowland Hampton, - -	"	–	4	
Archer Johnson, - -	"	–	5	
Samuel Williams, - -	"	–	4	
Braxton Redford, - -	"	–	5	
William Clarke, - -	"	–	5	
Spotswood Bradey, - -	"	–	4	
William Giles, - -	"	–	3	
Morgan Pearce - -	"	–	5	
Edward Enroughty, - -	"	–	4	
Major Johnson, - -	"	–	5	
Bernard Redford, - -	"	–	4	
Thomas Berry, - -	"	–	5	
William Carter, - -	"	–	5	
Josiah Bulington, - -	"	–	5	
John Breeding, - -	"	–	5	
Richard Williams, - -	"	–	4	
William Hampton, - -	"	–	4	
Charles Breeding, - -	"	–	5	
Robert Bradley, - -	"	–	5	
William B. Crumpton, -	"	–	5	
Josiah Throgmorton, - -	"	–	3	
Sam'l Ball, - -	"	–	5	
William Hix, - -	"	–	5	
Andrew Redford, - -	"	–	3	
Edward Cox, - -	"	–	4	
Pleasant Jourdan, - -	"	–	4	
Edward Moody, - -	"	–	4	
Edward Marable, - -	"	–	2	

MUSTER ROLL

Of Captain William Henley's Company, from the Thirty-third Regiment, Virginia Militia, Henrico County, commanded by Lieutenant Colonel John Mayo, in the Service from the 19th to 29th March, 1813.

NAMES.	RANK.	TIME OF SERVICE.		REMARKS.
		Months.	Days.	
William Henley, - -	Captain,	–	10	
John Thomasson, - -	Lieutenant,	–	10	
Thomas Willis, - -	Ensign,	–	10	
Peter Cottrell, jr. - -	Sergeant,	–	10	
Jesse Harlow, - -	"	–	10	
Reuben Cottrell, - -	"	–	10	
John Jude, - -	"	–	10	
John Harlow, - -	Drummer,	–	10	
Dabney Cawthorn, - -	Fifer,	–	10	
Benjamin Duvall, - -	Private,	–	10	
Leon'd Henly, - -	"	–	10	
John Lacey, - -	"	–	10	
Jones Tyler, - -	"	–	10	
James Haweton, - -	"	–	10	
John Miller, - -	"	–	10	
John Harlow, - -	"	–	10	
Joseph Holman, - -	"	–	10	
John Alley, - -	"	–	10	
Allen Tyler. - -	"	–	10	
Zachariah McGruder, - -	"	–	10	
John Guine, - -	"	–	10	
Thomas Wade, - -	"	–	10	
Daniel H. Thacker, - -	"	–	10	
Zachariah Ford, - -	"	–	10	
Richard Wade, - -	"	–	10	
Fleming Ford, - -	"	–	10	
Richard C. Gilliam, - -	"	–	10	
Elisha Wade, - -	"	–	10	
Henry Baughan, - -	"	–	10	
David Hughes, - -	"	–	1	
Ambrose Hutcherson, - -	"	–	10	
James Lawrence, - -	"	–	10	
Peter Flesher, - -	"	–	10	
Austin Ford, - -	"	–	10	
John Flesher, - -	"	–	10	
Joseph Webber, - -	"	–	7	
Tilman Tacker, - -	"	–	10	
Elijah Miller, - -	"	–	10	
William Miller, - -	"	–	10	
Joseph Bowles, - -	"	–	10	
William M. Burton, - -	"	–	10	
Robert Jennings, - -	"	–	10	
John Fandry, - -	"	–	5	
Richard Butler, - -	"	–	10	
Joseph Baughan, - -	"	–	10	
Michael Johnson, - -	"	–	10	
Miles Wade, - -	"	–	10	
Nathl. Harlow, - -	"	–	10	

MUSTER ROLL

Of Captain Isaiah Johnson's Company of Infantry of the Thirty-third Regiment, Virginia Militia, commanded by Lieutenant Colonel Charles Bagwell, in the Service of the United States, from the 28th to the 30th May, 1813.

NAMES.	RANK.	TIME OF SERVICE.		REMARKS.
		Months.	Days.	
Isaiah Johnson, - -	Captain,	–	3	
Thorogood Taylor, - -	Lieutenant,	–	3	
John S. Johnson, - -	Ensign,	–	3	
David Mears, - -	Qr. M. Serg't,	–	3	
John Bird, - -	Sergeant,	–	3	
Geo. Russell, - -	"	–	3	
Southey Northam, - -	"	–	3	
John F. Fisher, - -	Corporal,	–	3	
Joseph Gladding, - -	"	–	3	
Thomas Hinmond, - -	"	–	3	
Gilbert M. Leatherbury, -	"	–	3	
Isaac Marshall, - -	Drummer,	–	3	
James Stant, - -	Fifer,	–	3	
Jacob Andrews, - -	Private,	–	2	
Henry Ayres, - -	"	–	3	
James Bayly, - -	"	–	3	
William Bell, - -	"	–	3	
Johannas Bird, - -	"	–	3	
Selby Bloxom, - -	"	–	3	
Elisha Bayley, - -	"	–	3	
James Bloxom, - -	"	–	3	
Major Bird, - -	"	–	3	
Eli Bloxom, - -	"	–	3	
Upshur Bailey, - -	"	–	3	
John Bailey, (of Robert,) -	"	–	3	
William Bloxom, - -	"	–	3	
Robert P. Brodwater, - -	"	–	2	
John Bayly, (of Southy,) -	"	–	2	
Richard Bloxom, - -	"	–	2	
Daniel T. Bird, - -	"	–	1	
William Christopher, - -	"	–	3	
John Christopher, - -	"	–	3	
Ephraim Chessee, - -	"	–	1	
Eli Chesson, - -	"	–	1	
Jesse Dickerson, - -	"	–	3	
Edmund Duncan, - -	"	–	3	
Zadock Davis, - -	"	–	3	
William Davis, - -	"	–	2	
Henry Fletcher, - -	"	–	3	
William Hutson, - -	"	–	3	
John Harmon, - -	"	–	3	
Galen Hindmand, - -	"	–	3	
Levin Harmon, - -	"	–	1	
James Hoffman, - -	"	–	1	
Richard Hart, - -	"	–	1	
John Jester, - -	"	–	3	
Isaiah Johnson, jr. - -	"	–	3	
Major Kelly, - -	"	–	3	
Thomas Kelley, - -	"	–	3	

NAMES.	RANK.	TIME OF SERVICE.		REMARKS.
		Months.	Days.	
James Kelley, - -	Private,	–	3	
Elijah Lucas, - -	"	–	2	
Selby Lankford, - -	"	–	3	
Sampson Marshall, - -	"	–	3	
John Marshall, - -	"	–	3	
George Mears, - -	"	–	3	
William Mears, - -	"	–	3	
Henry Marshall, - -	"	–	3	
John Russell, - -	"	–	3	
James Russell, - -	"	–	3	
Noah Riggin, - -	"	–	3	
John Rew, - -	"	–	2	
William Riley, - -	"	–	2	
William Silvertherer, - -	"	–	3	
William Tatham, - -	"	–	3	
Abbott Trader, - -	"	–	3	
William Trader, - -	"	–	3	
Nathaniel Taylor, - -	"	–	3	
Nathaniel Taylor, jr. - -	"	–	1	
Levi Trader, - -	"	–	3	
Southey Walker, - -	"	–	3	
George Wilson, - -	"	–	2	
Henry Young, - -	"	–	3	

MUSTER ROLL

Of Captain Morris L. Miller's Company of Riflemen, from the Thirty-third Regiment, Virginia Militia, Henrico County, in the Service from the 19th to 29th March, 1813.

NAMES.	RANK	TIME OF SERVICE.		REMARKS.
		Months.	Days.	
Morris L. Miller,	Captain,	–	5	
Samuel Gathright,	Lieutenant,	–	5	
Richard H. Frazer,	Ensign,	–	5	
Robert Redford,	Sergeant,	–	5	
David W. Robinson,	"	–	5	
Anthony Matthews,	"	–	5	
William Tussle,	Corporal,	–	5	
Geo. Whitten,	"	–	5	
Thomas Epperson,	"	–	5	
Reuben George,	"	–	5	
George V. Angle,	Private,	–	5	
Thomas Barbour,	"	–	5	
Charles Breeding,	"	–	5	
James Bridgwater,	"	–	5	
James Brightwell,	"	–	5	
Benjamin Cotten,	"	–	5	
Thomas Childrey,	"	–	5	
Rolling Childress,	"	–	5	
Reuben Childress,	"	–	5	
Charles G. Carter,	"	–	4	
Theodrick Carter,	"	–	5	
Charles Childress,	"	–	5	
Joseph G. Carter,	"	–	5	
William H. Childress,	"	–	5	
Nathaniel Enroughty,	"	–	5	
Richard Enroughty,	"	–	5	
Peter Francis,	"	–	4	
Charles Fussle,	"	–	5	
John Fussle,	"	–	5	
Martin Farrell,	"	–	5	
Anderson Gathwright,	"	–	5	
Thomas Goode,	"	–	5	
Jackson Hampton,	"	–	5	
Henry Johnson,	"	–	5	
William M. Laster,	"	–	5	
Hartwell M. Manners,	"	–	5	
Benjamin Morriss,	"	–	5	
Robert Sharp,	"	–	5	
Price Sharpe,	"	–	4	
Thomas Salmon,	"	–	5	
Eaton Tyler,	"	–	4	
Isaac Truman,	"	–	5	
Matthew Vaughan,	"	–	5	
Wyatt Wade,	"	–	5	
John Wade,	"	–	5	
Elisha Williams,	"	–	5	
Samuel Warriner,	"	–	5	

MUSTER ROLL

Of Captain Thomas H. Prosser's Troop of Cavalry, in the Thirty-third Regiment, Virginia Militia, in the County of Henrico, called into the Service of the United States, under the general order of the 26th August, from 27th August to 10th September, 1814.

NAMES.	RANK.	TIME OF SERVICE.		REMARKS.
		Months.	Days.	
Thomas H. Prosser, - -	Captain,	–	15	
John M. Radford, - -	Lieutenant,	–	15	
Richard C. Gilliam, - -	"	–	15	
Reuben Burton, - -	Cornet,	–	15	
Spotswood Austin, - -	Private,	–	15	
Lyddell Bowles, - -	"	–	15	
Thomas O. Burton, - -	"	–	15	
Samuel Burton, - -	"	–	11	
John Burton, - -	"	–	11	
Josiah Blackburn, - -	"	–	11	
Wm. M. Burton, - -	"	–	11	
Samuel Carlisle, - -	"	–	11	
Samuel Conway, - -	"	–	11	
Reuben Cottrell, - -	"	–	11	
Wm. Jas. Cawthorn, - -	"	–	11	
Wm. Cottrell, - -	"	–	11	
Jos. Cottrell, - -	"	–	11	
Peter Coutts, - -	"	–	11	
Frank R. Ellis, - -	"	–	11	
Bartholomew Ellis, - -	"	–	11	
John Goode, - -	"	–	11	
William Gentry, - -	"	–	11	
Matthew Jordan, - -	"	–	11	
William Hooker, - -	"	–	11	
David Hughes, - -	"	–	11	
Nathaniel Holman, - -	"	–	11	
William Layne, - -	"	–	11	
Benj. Mann, - -	"	–	11	
John Mann, - -	"	–	11	
Thomas Mallory, - -	"	–	11	
Reuben Meredith, - -	"	–	11	
James Nuckolds, - -	"	–	11	
Robert Priddy, - -	"	–	11	
Overton Pettit, - -	"	–	11	
John C. Pleasants, - -	"	–	11	
Smith Puryear, - -	"	–	11	
Jacob Smith, - -	"	–	11	
David Sheet, - -	"	–	11	
Andrew Todd, - -	"	–	11	
James Todd, - -	"	–	11	
Malachi Tinsley, - -	"	–	11	
Christopher Taliaferro, -	"	–	11	
Jacob Woodrum, - -	"	–	11	
Frederick Woodson, - -	"	–	11	
Joseph Webber, - -	"	–	11	

MUSTER ROLL

Of Captain Martin Smith's Company, of the Thirty-third Regiment, in the County of Henrico, called into actual Service under the general orders of the 13th March, 1813, from 19th to 29th March, in the same year.

NAMES.	RANK.	TIME OF SERVICE.		REMARKS.
		Months.	Days.	
Martin Smith, - -	Captain,	–	5	
Wm. Shepperson, - -	Lieutenant,	–	5	
James Whitelaw, - -	Ensign,	–	5	
Wm. S. Blackburn, - -	Sergeant,	–	5	
Matt. H. Owen, - -	"	–	5	
John Burton, - -	"	–	5	
Lyddall Cornet, - -	"	–	5	
Joseph V. Owen, - -	Corporal,	–	5	
Granvill Ford, - -	"	–	5	
Isham Lucas, - -	"	–	5	
Samuel Blackbron, - -	"	–	5	
William Alley, - -	Private,	–	5	
Edmund Bowles, - -	"	–	5	
Royall Blackburn, - -	"	–	5	
Thomas Blackburn, - -	"	–	5	
William Blackburn, - -	"	–	5	
Claiborne Boone, - -	"	–	5	
Lyddall Bowles, - -	"	–	5	
Wm. B. Chamberlain, -	"	–	5	
Thomas Courtney, - -	"	–	5	
Allen Cornet, - -	"	–	5	
Thomas Cawthorn, - -	"	–	5	
Ephraim Clark, - -	"	–	5	
Patrick Daniel, - -	"	–	5	
Lewis S. Edwards, - -	"	–	5	
David Elmore, - -	"	–	5	
Robert England, - -	"	–	5	
Dabney Eubank, - -	"	–	5	
Dabney Ford, - -	"	–	5	
Daniel Ford, - -	"	–	5	
Martin Ford, - -	"	–	5	
Gilley Ford, - -	"	–	5	
Zachariah Francis, - -	"	–	5	
James Griffin, - -	"	–	5	
Charles Griffin, - -	"	–	5	
Benj. Gromes, - -	"	–	5	
Daniel Horner, - -	"	–	5	
Austin Hill, - -	"	–	5	
Samuel Jennings, - -	"	–	5	
Allen Jennings, - -	"	–	5	
Jesse Jennings, - -	"	–	5	
David Jennings, - -	"	–	5	
William Jennings, - -	"	–	5	
Hezekiah Jennings, - -	"	–	5	
George King, - -	"	–	5	
Benjamin Lay, - -	"	–	5	
George Miller, - -	"	–	5	
Thomas Mallory, - -	"	–	5	

NAMES.	RANK.	TIME OF SERVICE.		REMARKS.
		Months.	Days.	
John Melton, - -	Private,	–	5	
David Melton, - -	"	–	5	
John G. Nelson, - -	"	–	5	
Henry Owen, - -	"	–	5	
Thomas Owen, - -	"	–	5	
Samuel Owen, - -	"	–	5	
William Owen, - -	"	–	5	
Thomas Phillips, - -	"	–	5	
Isaac Phillips, - -	"	–	5	
Smith Puryear, - -	"	–	5	
Mosby Sheppard, - -	"	–	5	
Benj. Sheppard, - -	"	–	5	
Thomas Smith, - -	"	–	5	
Wilson Staples, - -	"	–	5	
Charles A. Stanley, - -	"	–	5	
Walter Thacker, - -	"	–	5	
John Toler, - -	"	–	5	
Eleazer Vest, - -	"	–	5	
Isaac Winston, - -	"	–	5	
Wm. Warbleton, - -	"	–	5	
Wm. Winston, - -	"	–	5	
John Walton, - -	"	–	5	
Edmund West, - -	"	–	5	

PAY ROLL

Of Captain Francis Wicker's Company of Infantry, from the Thirty-third Regiment, in the County of Henrico, called into Service from 19th to 29th March, 1813.

NAMES.	RANK.	TIME OF SERVICE.		REMARKS.
		Months.	Days.	
Francis Wicker,	Captain,	–	5	
John S. West,	Lieutenant,	–	4	
John Jourdan,	Sergeant,	–	5	
Nathaniel Whitelaw,	"	–	5	
William Robinson,	"	–	5	
Francis Smith,	"	–	5	
Jacob Bowes,	Private,	–	5	
John Bridgewater,	"	–	5	
George Blakey,	"	–	5	
John Banks,	"	–	5	
Jas. M. Franklin,	"	–	5	
Joseph Francis,	"	–	5	
James Frost,	"	–	5	
Zachariah Franklin,	"	–	5	
John Gum,	"	–	5	
Dandridge Garratt,	"	–	5	
John Hardin,	"	–	5	
Geo. N. Hopkins,	"	–	5	
Reuben Hamlett,	"	–	2	
William Harwood,	"	–	5	
Dobson Hull,	"	–	2	
Herbert Haynes,	"	–	5	
Huddleston Jourdan,	"	–	5	
Henry Johnson,	"	–	5	
Benjamin Jones,	"	–	5	
John Lyle,	"	–	5	
John Mims,	"	–	5	
Thomas Miller,	"	–	5	
William Oakley,	"	–	5	
Edward Roush,	"	–	4	
James Roush,	"	–	4	
Littleberry Roundtree,	"	–	5	
Simeon Rowland,	"	–	5	
James Roundtree,	"	–	4	
Adam Shrum,	"	–	5	
William Shrum,	"	–	5	
William Silam,	"	–	3	
Wm. Tenson,	"	–	5	
Charles Turner,	"	–	4	
And. Tenson,	"	–	5	
James Valentine,	"	–	5	
Josiah Via,	"	–	5	
Arcelm Walker,	"	–	5	
William Warriner,	"	–	5	
Brylon Waide,	"	–	5	
Bartlett Woodward,	"	–	5	
Samuel Whitelaw,	Private,	–	5	
John Whitlock,	"	–	5	
J. Whites,	"	–	4	
James Yarborough,	"	–	5	

MUSTER ROLL

Of Captain Dabney Williamson's Company, from the Thirty-third Regiment, Virginia Militia, in the County of Henrico, called into actual Service under the general orders of the 13*th March,* 1813, *from* 19*th to* 29*th March, in the year* 1813.

NAMES.	RANK.	TIME OF SERVICE.		REMARKS.
		Months.	Days.	
Dabney Williamson, - -	Captain,	–	11	
Jesse Smith, - -	Lieutenant,	–	11	
Edwin Burton, - -	Ensign,	–	11	
George Matthews, - -	Sergeant,	–	11	
George Eubank, - -	"	–	11	
George A. Kelley, - -	"	–	11	
Absalom Blackburn, - -	"	–	11	
Thomas Alley, - -	Private,	–	11	
John Alvis, - -	"	–	11	
John Brown, - -	"	–	11	
Lewis H. Brown, - -	"	–	11	
Joseph Brown, - -	"	–	11	
Robert Bigart, - -	"	–	11	
Thos. Burnett, - -	"	–	11	
Robt. Browning, - -	"	–	11	
Francis Cornett, - -	"	–	11	
James Currie, - -	"	–	11	
Henry Duke, - -	"	–	11	
Thos. Eubank, - -	"	–	11	
Daniel Edwards, - -	"	–	11	
Enoch Ford, - -	"	–	11	
Tarlton Ford, - -	"	–	11	
Reuben Ford, - -	"	–	11	
John Ford, - -	"	–	11	
Gilley Franklin, - -	"	–	11	
Abner Griffin, - -	"	–	11	
Neley Glenn, - -	"	–	11	
Joseph Green, - -	"	–	11	
James Grimstead, - -	"	–	11	
James Glenn, - -	"	–	11	
Fleming Gentry, - -	"	–	11	
Thomas W. Hill, - -	"	–	11	
Richard Harris, - -	"	–	11	
Ambrose Hutchison, - -	"	–	11	
Aaron Howard, - -	"	–	11	
Thomas Jennings, - -	"	–	11	
Woody Jennings, - -	"	–	11	
William Jentry, - -	"	–	11	
Thomas Johnson, - -	"	–	11	
William Jennings, - -	"	–	11	
Claiborn Jennings, - -	"	–	11	
Isham Jennings, - -	"	–	11	
Wilson Kelley, - -	"	–	11	
John Lawrence, - -	"	–	11	
William Lankaster, - -	"	–	11	
John McGraugh, - -	"	–	11	
James Nicholas, - -	"	–	11	

NAMES.	RANK.	TIME OF SERVICE.		REMARKS.
		Months.	Days.	
Daniel Night, - -	Private,	–	11	
David Nicholas, - -	"	–	11	
Robt. Priddy, - -	"	–	11	
Spencer Padget, - -	"	–	11	
Henry Phillips, - -	"	–	11	
Robt. Potter, - -	"	–	11	
Solomon Pursley, - -	"	–	11	
Valentine Quorrye, - -	"	–	11	
Charles Rice, - -	"	–	11	
Randolph Rice, - -	"	–	11	
William Rigdon, - -	"	–	11	
William Roach, - -	"	–	11	
Robt. Steward, - -	"	–	11	
Price Shoemaker, - -	"	–	11	
Wm. Snead, - -	"	–	11	
Jacob Smith, - -	"	–	11	
John Thorps, - -	"	–	11	
Christopher Taliaferro, -	"	–	11	
John Williamson, - -	"	–	11	
Robt. Whealey, - -	"	–	11	
James Whealey, - -	"	–	11	
Burnard Whealey, - -	"	–	11	
William Whealey, - -	"	–	11	
Saml. Whitis, - -	"	–	11	
Peter Wilkinson, - -	"	–	11	
Henry Winfree, - -	"	–	11	
John Whitis, - -	"	–	11	

MUSTER ROLL

Of Captain William Bolling's Troop of Cavalry, Thirty-eighth Regiment, Virginia Militia, in the Service of the State of Virginia, from September 4th to September 13th, 1814.

NAMES.	RANK.	TIME OF SERVICE.		REMARKS.
		Months.	Days.	
William Bolling, - -	Captain,	–	10	
James B. Furguson, - -	1st Lieutenant,	–	10	
Charles J. Eins, - -	"	–	10	
John Royster, - -	"	–	10	
Warner Lewis, - -	Cornet,	–	10	
John Philpots, - -	1st Sergeant,	–	10	
Granvill Smith, - -	"	–	10	
William George, - -	"	–	10	
Thomas H. Crouch, - -	"	–	10	
Joseph S. Clarke, - -	"	–	10	
Alexander S. Dandridge, -	Corporal,	–	10	
William Humber, - -	"	–	10	
Francis W. Royster, -	"	–	10	
Neil B. Gay, - -	"	–	10	
Richard Garrett, - -	"	–	10	
Anthony Cabiness, - -	"	–	10	
Moses Overton, - -	"	–	10	
Edward Bruce, - -	"	–	10	
Jessee Bother, - -	"	–	10	
Anderson Jackson, - -	"	–	10	
John R. Bell, - -	"	–	10	
Robert Oliver, - -	"	–	10	
Paulin Anderson, - -	Private,	–	10	
Dandridge Bradshaw, -	"	–	10	
Peyton Bailey, - -	"	–	10	
Russel B. Belcher, - -	"	–	10	
Ambos Brooks, - -	"	–	10	
Peyton Baughan, - -	"	–	10	
James Burton, - -	"	–	10	
Henry D. Carver, - -	"	–	10	
Alex'r A. Cambell, - -	"	–	10	
James L. Cocke, - -	"	–	10	
Kenner Cralle, - -	"	–	10	
Moses Collier, - -	"	–	10	
Francis Carter, - -	"	–	10	
Asa Cabiness, - -	"	–	10	
Pleasant Clark, - -	"	–	10	
William Crittenten, - -	"	–	10	
Thomas Dunevant, - -	"	–	10	
John Dunevant, - -	"	–	10	
James W. Druprey, - -	"	–	10	
Joshua Davis, - -	"	–	10	
John Dickerson, - -	"	–	10	
Jessee Ellis, - -	"	–	10	
John Foster, - -	"	–	10	
Pascal Foster, - -	"	–	10	
Gideon Foster, - -	"	–	10	
Gabriel Fowlkes, - -	"	–	10	
Cradock Fowlkes, - -	"	–	10	

NAMES.	RANK.	TIME OF SERVICE.		REMARKS.
		Months.	Days.	
Tarlton Fleming,	Private,	–	10	
Wyatt Fleming,	"	–	10	
Edward Gay,	"	–	10	
Edmund George,	"	–	10	
Reuben George,	"	–	10	
William Gill,	"	–	10	
Anderson Gill,	"	–	10	
James Goodwin,	"	–	10	
Edward Humber,	"	–	10	
Daniel Hardaway,	"	–	10	
Younger Hardaway,	"	–	10	
Thomas L. Holiday,	"	–	10	
William Hardaway,	"	–	10	
John Holoway,	"	–	10	
John B. Humbers,	"	–	10	
Isaiah Humphries,	"	–	10	
Spicer Humphries,	"	–	10	
William Hicks,	"	–	10	
David Jarret,	"	–	10	
Freeman Jordan,	"	–	10	
Thomas P. Jackson,	"	–	10	
Asa Jeffries,	"	–	10	
John W. Jennings,	"	–	10	
Leweling Jones,	"	–	10	
Benj'n Jackson,	"	–	10	
Simon C. Jackson,	"	–	10	
Robert Key,	"	–	10	
Tiscamer Knight,	"	–	10	
William Leeds,	"	–	10	
Arch'd B. Lewis,	"	–	10	
Charles May,	"	–	10	
Kenneth McRae,	"	–	10	
Thomas Miller,	"	–	10	
David Mines,	"	–	10	
John Morrison,	"	–	10	
John Mullins,	"	–	10	
Sygnal Moore,	"	–	10	
Edward Morriss,	"	–	10	
Pauncey Nuckols,	"	–	10	
Thomas Nelson,	"	–	10	
Daniel Nelson,	"	–	10	
Rice Newman,	"	–	10	
John B. Oliver,	"	–	10	
Alex'r P. Payne,	"	–	10	
Thomas Payne,	"	–	10	
Sam'l H. Pankey,	"	–	10	
Thompson Penick,	"	–	10	
James Reynolds,	"	–	10	
Thomas Richardson,	"	–	10	
Samuel D. Rawlins,	"	–	10	
John Stanley,	"	–	10	
Shederick Saidsbury,	"	–	10	
William Smith, (son of Hall,)	"	–	10	
Thomas Salmons,	"	–	10	
William Smith,	"	–	10	
Ezekiel Saidsbury,	"	–	10	
John P. Samson,	"	–	10	
William Tourman,	"	–	10	
Samuel Thomas,	"	–	10	
Thos. C. Vaughan,	"	–	10	
John P. Woodson,	"	–	10	
George W. Watkins,	"	–	10	
Ambrose Wade,	"	–	10	
Daniel Wade,	"	–	11	
Bassett Watson,	"	–	10	
William Wright,	"	–	10	

MUSTER ROLL

Of the Field and Staff Officers of the Thirty-ninth Regiment of Virginia Militia, commanded by Lieutenant Colonel James Byrne, in Service from 30th June to 12th July 1813.

NAMES.	RANK.	TIME OF SERVICE.		REMARKS.
		Months.	Days.	
James Byrne, - -	Lieut. Col.	–	–	Absent.
Joseph G. Wilder, - -	Major,	–	13	
John Hamlin, - -	"	–	6	
William B. Branch, - -	Adjutant.			
Arch'd Baugh, - -	Pay Master,	–	6	
Charles Cowling, - -	Qr. Master,	–	6	
David Walker, - -	Surgeon,	–	6	
John Gilliam, - -	S. Mate,	–	6	
Joseph Caldwell, - -	Serg't Major,	–	13	

MUSTER ROLL

Of Captain Edwin Beasley's Company from Thirty-ninth Regiment, Virginia Militia, commanded by Major Jo. G. Wilder, in the Service from the 30th day of June, 1813, *to the* 12*th of July*, 1813.

NAMES.	RANK.	TIME OF SERVICE.		REMARKS.
		Months.	Days.	
Edwin Beasley,	Captain,	–	13	
John Hanserd,	Lieutenant,	–	13	
Rob't Ritchie,	1st Sergeant,	–	13	
Henry Marks,	2d "	–	13	
William Robertson,	3d "	–	13	
John L. Merten,	4th "	–	13	
James Boisseau,	1st Corporal,	–	13	
William Hawthorn,	2d "	–	13	
John Batley,	3d "	–	13	
Clement Hawks,	4th "	–	13	
Benj'n B. Anderson,	Private,	–	13	
Hezekiah B. Anderson,	"	–	13	
Daniel Baugh,	"	–	13	
John Baird,	"	–	13	
Herbert Baird,	"	–	13	
Peter Baird,	"	–	13	
Thos. C. Batte,	"	–	13	
William Berry,	"	–	13	
Eli Bennett,	"	–	13	
Lewellen R. Cain,	"	–	13	
James Cole,	"	–	13	
William Couch,	"	–	13	
William Cathbert,	"	–	13	
John R. Daniel,	"	–	13	
William P. Daniel,	"	–	13	
Marvil Dunivant,	"	–	13	
Ira A. Ester,	"	–	13	
Belfield Fauntleroy,	"	–	13	
Bailey Gee,	"	–	13	
Nath'l Harris,	"	–	13	
Moses Jeffres,	"	–	13	
Robert K. Jones,	"	–	13	
William H. Jones,	"	–	13	
Thomas E. Lacy,	"	–	13	
Samuel Leech,	"	–	13	
Eaton Lamb,	"	–	13	
Charles Mann,	"	–	13	
Hector McMillen,	"	–	13	
William Mottley,	"	–	13	
William Meikle,	"	–	13	
James Merrow,	"	–	13	
William Old,	"	–	13	
James Orr,	"	–	13	
Peter Peterson,	"	–	13	
Sylvester Plumb,	"	–	13	
Samuel Peniston,	"	–	13	
William Russell,	"	–	13	
William B. Ritchie,	"	–	13	

NAMES.	RANK.	TIME OF SERVICE.		REMARKS.
		Months.	Days.	
Beverly H. Randolph, -	Private,	–	13	
Richard Richards, - -	"	–	13	
John Roper, - -	"	–	13	
Jabez Smith, - -	"	–	13	
John Somerville, - -	"	–	13	
James Selby, - -	"	–	13	
Lewis G. Simmons, - -	"	–	13	
William Stevenson, - -	"	–	13	
Sceva Thayer, - -	"	–	13	
Henry Tharp, - -	"	–	13	
Carter Wells, - -	"	–	13	
Ebenezer Watts, - -	"	–	13	
Wyllie Wells, - -	"	–	13	
Henry Wright, - -	"	–	13	
Baker Woodward, - -	"	–	13	
John Zimmerman, - -	"	–	13	
Jonathan Zimmerman, -	"	–	13	

MUSTER ROLL

Of Captain Joseph Bragg's Company of Virginia Militia, (Infantry,) from Thirty-ninth Regiment, commanded by Major Jo. G. Wilder, in the Service from 30th June to the 12th July, 1813.

NAMES.	RANK.	TIME OF SERVICE.		REMARKS.
		Months.	Days.	
Joseph Bragg,	Captain,	–	13	
Richard F. Hannon,	Lieutenant,	–	13	
Thomas Wilcox,	Ensign,	–	13	
Solomon High,	Sergeant,	–	13	
James B. Coggbill,	"	–	13	
Steven Aldridge,	"	–	13	
David A. Rawlings,	Corporal,	–	13	
Thomas Rosser,	"	–	13	
Joseph Bacon,	"	–	13	
Joel Aldridge,	Private,	–	13	
James D. M. Anderson,	"	–	13	
William Branch,	"	–	13	
Armistead O. Butler,	"	–	13	
William Clarke, jr.	"	–	13	
William Cain,	"	–	13	
William Clarke,	"	–	13	
Richard Cotton,	"	–	13	
Silas Canterbury,	"	–	13	
Andrew Cross,	"	–	13	
James Cain,	"	–	13	
George J. Cain,	"	–	13	
Nathan Dunphe,	"	–	13	
Herbert Elder,	"	–	13	
Pleasant Elam,	"	–	13	
Francis R. Farlamb,	"	–	13	
William H. Gent,	"	–	13	
Dinwiddie Goodwyn,	"	–	13	
James Harriss,	"	–	7	
Cary Hobbs,	"	–	13	
Hartwell P. Heath,	"	–	13	
Robert Harris,	"	–	13	
George King,	"	–	13	
Peter Kendall,	"	–	13	
Peyton Lynch,	"	–	13	
William Leavy,	"	–	13	
James Lea,	"	–	13	
John McKetrich,	"	–	13	
Allen Mitchell,	"	–	13	
Elijah Mitchell,	"	–	13	
John McLean,	"	–	13	
Robert McLean,	"	–	13	
Edward Powell,	"	–	13	
John Powell,	"	–	13	
Ezra Pride,	"	–	13	
Robert P. Potts,	"	–	13	
George Patterson,	"	–	13	
Elgin Russell,	"	–	13	

NAMES.	RANK.	TIME OF SERVICE.		REMARKS.
		Months.	Days.	
Joseph Rowlett, - -	Private,	–	8	
William Robertson, - -	"	–	13	
Daniel Stringer, - -	"	–	13	
Isaac Sharp, - -	"	–	13	
John B. Smith, - -	"	–	13	
Alba Sexton, - -	"	–	13	
Theodore Trezvant, - -	"	–	13	
William E. Turner, - -	"	–	13	
Hartwell Webb, - -	"	–	13	
John H. Warwich, - -	"	–	13	
Edward Williams, - -	"	–	13	
Duncan Watts, - -	"	–	13	

MUSTER ROLL

Of Captain Thomas S. Booth's Company of Virginia Militia, from the 39*th Regiment, under the command of Major John G. Wilden, from the* 1*st to* 6*th July*, 1813.

NAMES.	RANK.	TIME OF SERVICE.		
		Months.	Days.	
Thomas S. Booth,	Captain,	–	7	
Edward Watkins,	Lieutenant,	–	7	
Peter Vaden,	Ensign,	–	7	
Vivant Quimchet,	Sergeant,	–	7	
John Lee,	"	–	7	
Nathaniel Gray,	"	–	7	
David Thacker,	"	–	7	
Frederick B. Overby,	Corporal,	–	7	
Nelson Crowder,	"	–	7	
Peter Bedlock,	"	–	7	
Westley Crowder,	"	–	7	
Atkinson, Robert	Private,	–	7	Sub. by Geo. Day.
Atkinson, Thomas	"	–	7	Do Ananias Crowder.
Aldridge, Littleberry	"	–	7	
Andrews, Robert	"	–	7	
Andrews, Joseph	"	–	7	
Brown, Archer	"	–	7	
Branton, William	"	–	7	
Butler, Jonathan	"	–	7	
Butler, Micajah	"	–	7	
Butler, Joseph	"	–	7	
Butler, Samuel	"	–	7	
Butler, Robt. H.	"	–	7	
Binford, Bobert	"	–	7	
Crowder, Wiley	"	–	7	
Crowder, Joseph	"	–	7	
Clements, Nicholas	"	–	7	
Dabney, Nathaniel	"	–	7	
Fiby, Henry	"	–	7	
Gresham, Henry	"	–	7	
Gray, Frederick	"	–	7	
Harwell, Batte	"	–	7	
Jolley, Daniel	"	–	7	
Jones, Henry	"	–	7	
Jones, Edmond	"	–	7	
King, Wiley	"	–	7	
Lewis, Thompson	"	–	7	
Lewis, William	"	–	7	
Moody, Kerby	"	–	7	
Moody, David	"	–	7	
McCulloch, Cad.	"	–	7	
Pillion, Thomas	"	–	7	
Pillsborough, Moses B.	"	–	7	
Stowe, Wiley	"	–	7	
Sandifer, Joshua	"	–	7	
Stonton, John	"	–	7	
Tudor, Richard	"	–	7	
Thomas, Ebenezer	"	–	7	
Vaughan, Berayman	"	–	7	
Williams, Thomas	"	–	7	
Wells, Jessee	"	–	7	
Whitehead, Jeremiah	"	–	7	
Wells, Adam	"	–	7	
Yates, Benjamin P.	"	–	7	

PAY ROLL

Of Captain Cadwallader J. Claiborne's Company, of the Thirty-ninth Regiment, in Service from 1st to 10th July 1813; and of the First Regiment, in Service from 27th August to 30th November 1814.

NAMES.	RANK.	Time of Service.		REMARKS.
		Months.	Days.	
Cadr. J. Claiborne,	Captain,	3	15	
William B. Branch,	Lieutenant,	3	15	
Augustine Claiborne,	"	3	15	
Russell Dance,	Ensign,	3	15	
John E. Dance,	Q. M. Serg't,	3	15	
Stephen Spain,	Sergeant,	3	15	
Edwin Lewis,	"	3	15	
William Watkins,	"	3	15	
Henry Vaden,	"	3	15	
Henry Tudor,	Corporal,	3	5	
Edward Worsham,	"	3	5	
William H. Jones,	"	3	5	
William T. Shackleford,	"	3	5	
Thomas D. Phillips,	Drummer,	3	5	
James Phillips,	Fifer,	3	5	
Frederick Adams,	Private,	3	5	
Frederick Andrews,	"	3	15	
Henry Andrews,	"	3	15	
James Andrews,	"	3	15	
Jacob Andrews,	"	3	5	
Simon Andrews,	"	3	5	
William Anderson,	"	3	15	
Archer Brown,	"	3	5	
Archer Butler,	"	3	5	
Edward Birchet,	"	3	5	
Richard Booth,	"	3	5	
William Barrow,	"	3	5	
Coleman Burge,		3	5	
Thomas Browder,	"	3	5	
Archer Crowder,	"	3	5	
Henry Chandler,	"	3	5	
John Coleman,	"	3	5	
Nelson Crowder,	"	3	5	
Wesley Crowder,	"	3	5	
William T. Cole,	"	3	15	
William Chandler,	"	3	5	
James Cole,	"	3	5	
Benjamin Dabney,	"	3	15	
Edwin Ellyson,	"	3	5	
Elisha Eanes,	"	3	5	
William Ford,	"	3	15	
Jeremiah Ford,	"	1	25	
David Grimes,	"	3	15	
Henry P. Guthrie,	"	3	5	
John Grant,	"	3	5	
Andrew Hardy,	"	3	5	
Armstead Hawkins,	"	3	5	
Edmond Hitchcock,	"	3	15	
William T. Hancil,	"	3	5	
Henry Jones,	"	3	5	
Peyton Kirkland,	"	3	15	
Samuel H. Kirks,	"	3	5	
Thomas B. King,	"	3	5	
John King,	"	3	5	

NAMES.	RANK.	Time of Service.		REMARKS.
		Months.	Days.	
David Keys, - - .	Private,	3	5	
Joshua Lunsford, - -	"	3	5	
John Lee, - - -	"	3	5	
John Moody, - - -	"	3	15	
Thomas Murrell, - -	"	3	5	
Drury Mayes, - - -	"	3	5	
Frederick B. Overby, - -	"	3	5	
John Overby, - - -	"	3	5	
John R. Overby, - -	"	3	5	
Joseph Owen, - - -	"	3	5	
Nicholas Overby, - -	"	3	5	
David Phillips, - -	"	3	15	
Daniel Patrum, - -	"	3	5	
Abel T. Pucket, - -	"	3	5	
Samuel Peniston, - -	"	3	5	
William Prosire, - -	"	3	5	
Hartwell Rawlings, - -	"	3	5	
William F. Rather, - -	"	3	5	
Jesse Reames, - -	"	3	5	
Thomas Roberts, - -	"	2	21	
Herbert Reese, - -	"	3	5	
George W. Spain, - -	"	3	15	
John Spain, - - -	"	3	5	
John Stanfield, - -	"	3	15	
William Spain, sen., - -	"	3	15	
William Spain, jr., - -	"	3	5	
Jeremiah Still, - -	"	3	5	
John F. Shearman, - -	"	3	5	
Abner B. Tye, - -	"	3	15	
Joel Traylor, - -	"	3	15	
James Turner, - -	"	3	5	
Thomas Tally, - -	"	3	5	
Benjamin Verell, - -	"	3	5	
Peter Verell, - -	"	3	15	
Peter Vaughan, - -	"	3	5	
Baker Wells, - -	"	3	15	
Benjamin Wells, - -	"	3	15	
Charles Williamson, - -	"	3	15	
George Williamson, - -	"	3	15	
Hartwell Wells, - -	"	3	15	
Claiborne Wells, - -	"	3	5	
Denis Whealhouse, - -	"	3	5	
Drury Wells, - - -	"	3	5	
Frederick Wall, - -	"	3	5	
John Wood, - - -	"	3	5	
Manson Wells, - -	"	3	5	
Nelson Wells, - -	"	3	5	
Wiley Wells, - -	"	3	5	
Nicholas Wilkerson, - -	"	3	5	
Robert Williams, - -	"	3	5	
Thomas Wilborne, - -	"	3	5	
William Wynn, - -	"	3	5	
Daniel Wall, - -	"	3	5	
James Young, - -	"	3	5	

Captain Cadwallader J. Claibourne's Company—Thirty-ninth Regiment.

NAMES.	RANK.	TIME OF SERVICE.		REMARKS.
		Months.	Days.	
Mathew B. Dyer,	Ensign,	–	10	
Nelson Wells,	Corporal,	–	10	
Henry Pegram,	"	–	10	
Benjamin Andrews,	Private,	–	10	
Lynder Andrews,	"	–	10	
George Crowder,	"	–	10	
Peterson Crowder,	"	–	10	
Samuel Chandler,	"	–	10	
Edmund Dance,	"	–	10	
Benjamin George,	"	–	10	
Chesley Hardy,	"	–	10	
Joseph Hardy,	"	–	10	
Thomas James,	"	–	10	
Hamlin E. Spain,	"	–	10	
Thomas Trewhatt,	"	–	10	
Bedford Wills,	"	–	10	
Benjamin Walter,	"	–	10	
Edmund Wells,	"	–	10	
Edward Washam,	"	–	10	
John Watts,	"	–	10	
Jerrell Wills,	"	–	10	
Thomas Wilbar,	"	–	10	

(For rest of this company, see publication of Pay Rolls.)

MUSTER ROLL

Of Captain Thomas Claiborne's Company of Infantry of the Thirty-ninth Regiment, Virginia Militia, in the County of Dinwiddie, called into actual Service under the general orders of the 30th of June 1813, from the 30th June to the 12th July, inclusive, in the year 1813.

NAMES.	RANK.	TIME OF SERVICE.		REMARKS.
		Months.	Days.	
Thomas Claiborne, - -	Captain,	–	8	
Drewry Burge, - -	Lieutenant,	–	11	
Allen Archer, - -	Ensign,	–	11	
Arthur Leath, - -	Sergeant,	–	11	
Edward Lee, jr. - -	"	–	12	
A. B. Venable, - -	"	–	10	
John Gordon, - -	"	–	10	
Anthony Smith, - -	Corporal,	–	9	
Samuel Brister, - -	"	–	10	
Edmund Parish, - -	"	–	13	
Matthew Davidson, - -	"	–	12	
Cad. W. Archer, - -	Private,	–	10	
John Allison, - -	"			
Daniel E. Allen, - -	"	–	4	
John H. Brewer, - -	"	–	7	
John H. Booth, - -	"	–	13	
Robert Brister, - -	"	–	7	
Jesse Bendall, - -	"			
John H. Brown, - -	"	–	11	
John Brown, - -	"	–	11	
William Boswell, - -	"			
Henry Chieves, - -	"	–	11	
Robert Cocke, - -	"	–	7	
Levy Carpenter, - -	"	–	10	
Jesse L. Dupuy, - -	"	–	2	
Daniel Dodson, jr. - -	"	–	9	
Lewis B. Dunn, - -	"	–	11	
John A. Ezell, - -	"	–	12	
Henry Elliott, - -	"			
James Ennis, - -	"	–	11	
Daniel Foster, - -	"	–	10	
Francis Follett, - -	"			
Christopher Ford, - -	"	–	10	
William W. Fernando, -	"	–	9	
Edmund Folks, - -	"	–	6	
Henry P. Guthrie, - -	"	–	12	
James L. Gilliam, - -	"	–	10	
Joseph Gray, - -	"	–	12	
Alexander Gordon, - -	"	–	10	
Riland Geiter, - -	"	–	11	
Samuel Hinton, - -	"	–	12	
David A. Ivy, - -	"	–	12	
Barksdale Jefferson, - -	"	–	13	
Frederick Jones, - -	"	–	12	
George H. Jones, - -	"	–	6	
John Lantrip, - -	"	–	13	
George K. Lee, - -	"	–	7	

NAMES.	RANK.	TIME OF SERVICE.		REMARKS.
		Months.	Days.	
Theodorick Lone, - -	Private,	–	5	
Robert Leath, - -	"	–	9	
Joseph H. Lee, - -	"	–	9	
Lewis Maury, - -	"	–	6	
Benjamin Mattox, - -	"	–	10	
Jones Mitchell, - -	"	–	12	
Benjamin May, - -	"	–	12	
John F. May, - -	"	–	13	
Richard May, - -	"	–	12	
Thomas Murphy, - -	"	–	13	
David Maben, - -	"	–	4	
John Owen, - -	"	–	9	
Chichester Owen, - -	"	–	5	
Williams Pace, - -	"	–	10	
Samuel Pete, - -	"	–	7	
James Prentice, - -	"	–	12	
George Roberts, - -	"	–	11	
William Smith, - -	"	–	12	
James Smith, - -	"	–	11	
Richard F. Taylor, - -	"			
Henry Tucker, - -	"	–	11	
John Tracy, - -	"	–	11	
Claiborne Vaughan, - -	"	–	9	
George Wise, - -	"	–	11	
Samuel Woodcock, -	"	–	10	
John Wright, jr. - -	"	–	12	
William Wilkinson, - -	"	–	8	
Thomas Watkins, - -	"	–	10	
John Williams, - -	"	–	7	

PAY ROLL

Of Captain Archer B. Conway's Company, of the Thirty-ninth and First Regiments, in the Service of the United States, from the 2d to the 10th July 1813, and from the 28th August to the 30th November 1814.

NAMES.	RANK.	Time of Service.		REMARKS.
		Months.	Days.	
Archer B. Conway, - -	Captain,	3	13	
John Conway, - -	Lieutenant,	3	13	
Edward Watkins, - -	"	3	13	
Jeremiah Vaughan, - -	Ensign,	3	13	
Francis Pace, - -	"	3	13	
Peter Vaughan, - -	Sergeant,	3	13	
Robert Nicholas, - -	"	3	12	
Wm. Moore, - -	"	3	4	
John Smith, - -	"	3	13	
Wm. F. Blick, - -	"	3	13	
Robert C. Ledbetter, - -	Q. M. "	3	4	
George C. Vaughan, - -	Corporal,	3	13	
James Conway, - -	"	3	4	
John E. Vaughan, - -	"	3	13	
William Mathews, - -	"	3	4	
John Conway, - -	Drummer,	3	13	
Peter Aldridge, - -	Private,	3	13	
David Aldridge, - -	"	3	13	
Jessee K. Andrews, - -	"	3	4	
Jesse Abernathy, - -	"	3	6	
Dennis Blick, - -	"	3	13	
Patrick Blick, - -	"	3	13	
Nathaniel Blick, - -	"	3	4	
Thomas Barrow, - -	"	3	3	
Richard Bayly, - -	"	3	4	Sub. for Geo. Patterson from 22d Sept. 1814.
Armistead Blankenship, -	"	3	4	
Jeremiah Conway, - -	"	3	13	
John Clemmons, - -	"	3	4	Sub. for Anthony Smith from 17th Nov. 1814.
Wyllie Chever, - -	"	3	4	Sub. for L. H. Vaughan from 5th Sept. 1814.
Robert Davis, - -	"	3	13	
Drury Dinman, - -	"	3	4	
Baker Emmons, - -	"	3	13	
William Eckle, - -	"	3	4	
Hicks Fenn, - -	"	3	13	
Edward Foulks, - -	"	3	4	
Francis Frazer, - -	"	3	4	
Daniel Griffin, - -	"	3	3	
Randolph Hawks, - -	"	3	13	
Zachariah Harrison, - -	"	3	4	Sub. for Thomas Blick from 3d Nov. 1814.
William Hall, - -	"	3	4	Sub. for Wm. Bevill from 3d Nov. 1814.
John C. Harman, - -	"	3	4	Sub. for Thomas Dunn from 4th Sept. 1814.
Thomas Jones, - -	"	3	4	
Edmond Jones, - -	"	3	3	
Philip Johnston, - -	"	3	4	Sub. for P. Philips from 20th Sept. 1814.
Littleberry B. Kirk, - -	"	3	4	
John Kirk, - -	"	3	4	
William Kid, - -	"	3	4	Sub. for Wm. H. Ghent from 29th Sept. 1814.
William Lunsford, - -	"	3	4	
Isham Lussay, - -	"	3	4	Sub. for John Wright from 1st Sept. 1814.
Thomas Lee, - -	"	3	4	
Laban Ledbetter, - -	"	3	3	

NAMES.	RANK.	Time of Service.		REMARKS.
		Months.	Days.	
Millington Moore, - -	Private,	3	4	Sub. for H. Elliott from
Asa Moore, - -	"	3	4	2d Sept. 1814.
James McCallan, - -	"	3	4	Sub. for W. B. Harwood
Richard McCullock, - -	"	3	4	from 6th Sept. 1814.
James McHenry, - -	"	3	4	
Kennon Perkinson, - -	"	3	3	
Wright Rosser, - -	"	3	4	
Raleigh Rosser, - -	"	3	4	
William Rose, - -	"	3	4	
William Ragsdale, - -	"	3	4	
John Ryland, - -	"	3	4	
Fred'k N. Robertson, -	"	1	27	
Archibald Smith, - -	"	3	4	
Ralph Stegall, - -	"	3	4	
John J. Smith, - -	"	3	3	
John Smith, - -	"	2	3	
Joseph Sturdivant, - -	"	3	3	
Anthony Tiebout, - -	"	3	4	Sub. for Jas. Williams
Henry Vaughan, - -	"	3	13	from 6th Sept. 1814.
Eaton Vaughan, - -	"	3	13	
Peterson Vaughan, - -	"	3	13	
Adam Wills, - -	"	3	4	
Pleasant Womack, - -	"	3	4	
Horrell Webb, - -	"	3	4	Sub. for H. Webb from
Edmond P. Wynn, - -	"	3	4	3d Sept. 1814.
William Whitworth, - -	"	3	4	
Rowland Whitworth, - -	"	3	4	
Charles Williams, - -	"	3	5	
Jesse Westbrook, - -	"	3	5	
Drury Wall, - -	"	3	5	
Joseph Weatherford, - -	"	3	5	
Rob. W. Washington, - -	"	3	4	
Samuel Woodcock, - -	"	2	9	
James Westbrook, - -	"	2	12	
Thornton Yancy, - -	"	3	5	

Captain Archer B. Conway's Company—Thirty-ninth Regiment.

NAMES.	RANK.	TIME OF SERVICE.		REMARKS.
		Months.	Days.	
Joseph Fenn, - -	Sergeant,	–	9	
Benjamin Black, - -	"	–	9	
David Smith, - -	Corporal,	–	9	
Thomas Archer, - -	Private,	–	9	
William Brister, - -	"	–	9	
George Blick, - -	"	–	9	
Thomas Durrow, - -	"	–	9	
Thomas F. Fenn, - -	"	–	9	
William G. James, - -	"	–	9	
Thomas Keys, - -	"	–	9	
John Michal, - -	"	–	9	
James Rideout, - -	"	–	9	
Joel Vaughan, - -	"	–	9	
Peter Vaughan, - -	"	–	9	
Lemuel Vaughan, - -	"	–	9	
Herbert L. Vaughan, -	"	–	9	

(For rest of this company, see publication of Pay Rolls.)

MUSTER ROLL

Of Captain Edward O. Goodwin's Company, from the Thirty-ninth Regiment, Virginia Militia, Dinwiddie County, commanded by Major J. G. Wilder, in the Service from the 1st to the 6th July, 1813.

NAMES.	RANK.	TIME OF SERVICE.		REMARKS.
		Months.	Days.	
Edward O. Goodwin, -	Captain,	–	6	
Littleberry Burge, - -	Lieutenant,	–	6	
Littleberry Butterworth, -	Ensign,	–	6	
Philip Shelly, - -	Sergeant,	–	6	
John W. M. Kerby, - -	"	–	6	
Henry Moody, - -	"	–	6	
Joshua Blick, - -	"	–	6	
Claiborne Seymour, - -	Corporal,	–	6	
John Todd, - -	"	–	6	
Aaron Granger, - -	"	–	6	
William Harrison, - -	"	–	6	
John Archer, - -	Private,	–	6	
James Aldridge, - -	"	–	6	
Green W. Burge, - -	"	–	6	
Stith Butterworth, - -	"	–	6	
John Butterworth, - -	"	–	6	
Solomon Day, - -	"	–	6	
Josiah Farlow, - -	"	–	6	
Peterson Haddon, - -	"	–	6	
Pleasant Haddon, - -	"	–	6	
Littleberry Haddon, - -	"			
Jordan Hargrave, - -	"	–	6	
Jessee Heath, - -	"	–	6	
Gregory Johnson, - -	"	–	6	
Uriah Jones, - -	"	–	6	
Roger A. Jones, - -	"	–	6	
John Kerby, - -	"	–	6	
John Kirkland, - -	"	–	6	
William Morriss, - -	"	–	6	
Baker Perkins, sr. - -	"	–	6	
Thomas Parkham, - -	"	–	6	
Wright Perkins, - -	"	–	6	
David Perkins, - -	"	–	6	
Baker Perkins, jr. - -	"	–	6	
Joel Rosser, - -	"	–	6	
Wiley Rosser, - -	"	–	6	
Wright Rosser, - -	"	–	6	
Francis Smith, - -	"	–	6	
John Smith, - -	"	–	6	
James Turner, - -	"	–	6	

MUSTER ROLL

Of Captain John Hart's Troop of Cavalry, from Thirty-ninth Regiment, Virginia Militia, commanded by Major General John Pegram, in the Service of the United States, from 23d to 30th March, and from 18th to 23d May, from 30th June to 12th July, and from 30th August to 13th September, 1813.

NAMES.	RANK.	TIME OF SERVICE.		REMARKS.
		Months.	Days.	
John Hart, - -	Captain,	1	1	
Christopher Jones, - -	Lieutenant,	–	17	
Benjamin Edwards, - -	"	–	17	
Benjamin Bragg, - -	Lt. and Cornet,	–	29	
John B. Bott, - -	Lt. and Surg.	–	29	
Baker Pegram, jr. - -	Sergeant,	–	17	
Dandridge Spotswood, -	"	–	29	
John Boast, - -	"	1	8	
James Boyle, - -	"	–	17	
H. F. McKenna, - -	"	–	14	
Joshua Whitcomb, - -	"	1	5	
Geo. N. Belscher, - -	"	1	5	
Richard Toser, - -	"	–	17	
William Gilmore, - -	Corporal,	–	23	
William Young, - -	"	1	2	
Robert Spotswood, - -	"	1	2	
Bartley Weeks, - -	"	1	2	
A. S. Nanstedlor, - -	"	1	2	
Emor Harland, - -	"	1	2	
Stephen G. Wells, - -	Brig. M.	–	15	
Peyton Lynch, - -	Farrier,	–	9	
Randolph Johnson, - -	Trumpeter,	1	2	Transferred to Captain Pryor's Troop, 13th September.
John Andrews, - -	Private,	–	28	" " "
Thomas Aldridge, - -	"	–	15	" " "
William Bowden, - -	"	1	2	" " "
Edmund Burchett, - -	"	1	8	" " "
Zachariah Brewer, - -	"	1	8	" " "
John Butterworth, - -	"	–	15	" " "
James Boyle, - -	"	–	15	" " "
Richard Bate, - -	"	–	15	
James G. Caldwell, - -	"	–	15	
Samuel R. Caldwell, - -	"	–	15	
John Clark, - -	"	–	17	
Benjamin Curtis, - -	"	–	23	
Samuel Crawford, - -	"	–	15	" " "
John W. Dennist, - -	"	1	2	" " "
John Dijernett, - -	"	–	8	" " "
Jessee L. Dupee, - -	"	–	15	" " "
John R. Daniel, - -	"	–	15	" " "
Henry M. Didlark, - -	"	–	15	
Benjamin Dumas, - -	"	–	13	
Robert Elam, - -	"	1	2	" " "
Allen Finn, - -	"	1	2	" " "
William Griffin, - -	"	1	2	
Thomas E. Gray, - -	"	–	26	" " "

NAMES.	RANK.	TIME OF SERVICE.		REMARKS.
		Months.	Days.	
Edmond Heath, - -	Private,	–	15	
C. F. Jones, - -	"	–	15	Transferred to Captain Pryor's Troop, 13th September.
Walker Jones, - -	"	1	2	" " "
Lyne S. Kemp, - -	"	1	2	" " "
John Kirkland, - -	"	–	15	" " "
Thomas Lewis, - -	"	1	2	" " "
William Lownes, - -	"	1	2	" " "
Thomas T. Morgan, - -	"	–	25	" " "
Arch'd Moore, - -	"	–	15	" " "
Matthew Maben, - -	"	1	2	" " "
Richard McKae, - -	"	–	15	
Hugh F. McKenna, - -	"	–	17	
Edward H. Pegram, - -	"	1	2	" " "
Frederick J. Redfield, -	"	1	2	" " "
Milton Rose, - -	"	1	2	" " "
Joseph Rowlett, - -	"	–	26	" " "
William Robertson, jr. -	"			
Edwin Ragsdale, - -	"	–	13	
Edward Stokes, - -	"	1	2	" " "
John Stiles, - -	"	1	2	" " "
L. G. Simmson, - -	"	–	15	" " "
David Smith, - -	"	–	15	" " "
Robert Snelson, - -	"	1	2	
David Shelley, - -	"	–	26	
John B. Strachan, - -	"	–	17	
Benjamin Tucker, - -	"	1	3	
Riley Tisdale, - -	"	–	4	
Thomas P. Vial, - -	"	–	17	
David Vaughan, - -	"	–	17	
Hant Wyatt, - -	"	–	4	
Henry Wilkinson, - -	"	1	4	" " "
Robert Wilkins, - -	"	–	15	" " "
Edmond Wells, - -	"	–	15	" " "
William Wallace, - -	"	–	15	" " "
John Walker, - -	"	–	15	

MUSTER ROLL

Of Captain Charles Kent's Company, of the Thirty-ninth Regiment, Virginia Militia, in the County of Dinwiddie, called into actual Service under the general orders of the 30th June, from the 30th June to the 12th July, in the year 1813.

NAMES.	RANK.	TIME OF SERVICE.		REMARKS.
		Months.	Days.	
Charles Kent, - -	Captain,	–	13	
Thomas Wallace, - -	Lieutenant,	–	13	
George W. Stainback, -	Ensign,	–	13	
Seth Heath, - -	Sergeant,	–	13	
Stephen Paer, - -	"	–	13	
Abial Camp, - -	"	–	13	
Charles Hunt, - -	"	–	13	
Thomas Wilson, - -	Corporal,	–	13	
Wauglin W. Biggers, -	"	–	13	
Major L. Drinkard, - -	Private,	–	13	
Samuel Woodfolk, - -	"	–	13	
Alexander Crosland, - -	"	–	13	
Daniel C. Townes, - -	"	–	13	
Nelson Alley, - -	"	–	13	
Richard J. Andrews, - -	"	–	13	
John C. Armistead, - -	"	–	13	
Robert Adams, - -		–	13	
Edward Atkinson, - -	"	–	13	
Charles W. Brewer, - -	"	–	13	
Daniel Brown, - -	"	–	13	
Robert Burge, - -	"	–	13	
Thomas Braner, - -	"	–	13	
Benjamin Barnes, - -	"	–	13	
Benjamin E. Cook, - -	"	–	13	
Sampson Clements, - -	"	–	13	
William Dosh, - -	"	–	13	
Nathaniel Denby, - -	"	–	13	
Augustine Ellis, - -	"	–	13	
Ephraim Eckles, - -	"	–	13	
Martin Eanes, - -	"	–	13	
William Edwards, - -	"	–	13	
Nathaniel Friend, - -	"	–	13	
Robert Firn, - -	"	–	13	
William Fennell, - -		–	13	
William P. Graham, - -	"	–	13	
Walthal Hatcher, - -	"	–	13	
Jared Hotchkiss, - -	"	–	13	
Parham Hobbs, - -	"	–	13	
Joseph Heath, - -	"	–	13	
George Irvine, - -	"	–	13	
James B. Kendall, - -	"	–	13	
Thomas Lee, - -	"	–	13	
James P. Lownes, - -	"	–	13	
M. P. Mays, - -	"	–	13	
Jeremiah McIntosh, - -	"	–	13	
William McCay, - -	"	–	13	

NAMES.	RANK.	TIME OF SERVICE.		REMARKS.
		Months.	Days.	
Peter McCulloch, - -	Private,	–	13	
John McLarren, - -	"	–	13	
Nathaniel McTaimon, - -	"	–	13	
William Matthews, - -	"	–	13	
Thomas Neilson, - -	"	–	13	
Charles O'Harra, - -	"	–	13	
Timothy R. Ryan, - -	"	–	13	
William C. Rawlings, - -	"	–	13	
Burwell Rosser, - -	"	–	13	
Thornby Schoolar, - -	"	–	13	
Thomas Stewart, - -	"	–	13	
John Stewart, - -	"	–	13	
Charles Stewart, - -	"	–	13	
Robert Stewart, - -	"	–	13	
James Smith, - -	"	–	13	
Daniel Thompson, - -	"	–	13	
Nathan Vincent, - -	"	–	13	
Nathaniel H. Whitlow, -	"	–	13	
William Wallace, - -	"	–	13	
Silas Webb, - -	"	–	13	
William Weeks, - -	"	–	13	
Leighton Wood, - -	"	–	13	
Jonas Wood, jr. - -	"	–	13	

MUSTER ROLL

Of Captain Edward Pescud's Company, of the Thirty-ninth Regiment, Virginia Militia, called into the Service under the general orders of the 30th June, 1813, from the 30th June to the 12th July, in the year 1813.

NAMES.	RANK.	TIME OF SERVICE.		REMARKS.
		Months.	Days.	
Edward Pescud, - -	Captain,	–	13	
Richard B. Batte, - -	Lieutenant,	–	13	
John Pollard, - -	Ensign,	–	13	
William Moore, - -	Sergeant,	–	13	
Stephen Townes, - -	"	–	13	
James Gibbon, - -	"	–	13	
Gideon Johnson, - -	"	–	13	
Collin Alfriend, - -	Private,	–	13	
William Allison, - -	"	–	13	
James Andrews, - -	"	–	13	
John L. Andrews, - -	"	–	13	
Samuel Boothe, - -	"	–	13	
Daniel Bass, - -	"	–	13	
Hector Brander, - -	"	–	13	
John H. Banister, - -	"	–	13	
John W. Bell, - -	"	–	13	
Stephen Barnes, - -	"	–	13	
Ezra Beal, - -	"	–	13	
James Bagley, - -	"	–	13	
George Brown, - -	"	–	13	
John Bragg, - -	"	–	13	
William Bradley, - -	"	–	13	
John Bennett, - -	"	–	13	
William Clarke, - -	"	–	13	
Samuel Christian, - -	"	–	13	
George Cooper, - -	"	–	13	
Joseph Cooper, - -	"	–	13	
Robert Cohen, - -	"	–	13	
William Cumming, - -	"	–	13	
Moses Cohen, - -	"	–	13	
George Dunn, - -	"	–	13	
John Dunlop, - -	"	–	13	
Thomas Dunn, - -	"	–	13	
Samuel Dilworth, - -	"	–	13	
Daniel Dugger, - -	"	–	13	
Henry Fernando, - -	"	–	13	
Francis Fraser, - -	"	–	13	
George Fein, - -	"	–	13	
Lawson B. Flack, - -	"	–	13	
Peter D. Gibbs, - -	"	–	13	
J. L. George, - -	"	–	13	
William B. Harwood, -	"	–	13	
Travis Harwood, - -	"	–	13	
Daniel Hanson, - -	"	–	13	
John Hardy, - -	"	–	13	
Arthur Johnson, - -	"	–	13	
William Johnson, - -	"	–	13	
James Lockhead, - -	"	–	13	
John Lemosuirer, - -	"	–	13	

NAMES.	RANK.	TIME OF SERVICE.		REMARKS.
		Months.	Days.	
Thomas Lownes, - -	Private,	–	13	
A. S. Lockhead, - -	"	–	13	
Dabney Lipscomb, - -	"	–	13	
William Laird, - -	"	–	13	
Jacob Melliman, - -	"	–	13	
Nathaniel Massenburg, -	"	–	13	
Peter McLean, - -	"	–	13	
Henry Mountcastle, - -	"	–	13	
Thomas T. Miller, - -	"	–	13	
John McDowell, - -	"	–	13	
Samuel Nargen, - -	"	–	13	
William Neal, - -	"	–	13	
Griffin Orgain, - -	"	–	13	
John Patterson, - -	"	–	12	
Samuel Pearce, - -	"	–	13	
George Read, - -	"	–	13	
Justus Smith, - -	"	–	13	
Henry Shroyer, - -	"	–	13	
Robert Simmons, - -	"	–	13	
J. M. Shaul, - -	"	–	13	
Jeremiah Sadler, - -	"	–	13	
Samuel Snow, - -	"	–	13	
Nathaniel Snelson, - -	"	–	13	
Thomas Smith, - -	"	–	13	
Lewis Timmer, - -	"	–	13	
John D. Townes, - -	"	–	13	
William Thweatt, - -	"	–	13	
William Thompson, - -	"	–	13	
Peter Tatum, - -	"	–	13	
John Taliaferro, - -	"	–	13	
John Thompson, - -	"	–	13	
Charles Wise, - -	"	–	13	
Thomas G. Warthine, -	"	–	13	
Pleasant Womack, - -	"	–	13	
John U. Wilcox, - -	"	–	13	
John Withers, - -	"	–	13	
Paskal Wells, - -	"	–	13	
Francis G. Yancey, - -	"	–	13	

PAY ROLL

Of Captain George Morris' Company, of the Fortieth Regiment, Louisa, attached to the First Regiment, First Brigade of Virginia Militia, in the Service of the United States, commanded by Col. William Trueheart, at Camp Bottom's Bridge, under the command of Brigadier-General William Chamberlayne, from 28th August to 3d December 1814.

NAMES.	RANK.	Time of Service.		REMARKS.
		Months.	Days.	
George Morris,	Captain,	3	26	
William Price,	Lieutenant,	3	26	
Ambrose Flannagan,	"	3	26	
Martin Wash,	Ensign,	3	26	
Isham Worsham,	"	3	26	
Arthur Clayton,	Sergeant,	3	26	
John S. May,	"	3	26	
William F. Toler,	"	3	26	
Nat. H. Parrish,	"	3	26	
Oswald Gibson,	"	3	26	
Zachariah Perkins,	"	3	26	
Robert Michie,	Corporal,	3	26	
Reuben Reynolds,	"	3	26	
William Armstrong,	"	3	26	
Garrett Merriwether,	"	3	26	
Thomas Poindexter,	"	3	26	
Howard Edwards,	"	3	26	
Hardin Perkins,	"	3	26	
John Walter,	"	3	26	
Anderson Simms,	Fifer,	3	26	
William Armstrong,	Private,	3	26	
David Armstrong,	"	3	26	
John Armstrong, Sr.,	"	1		
Thomas Boyd,	"	3	26	
William Butler,	"	1		
And'w C. Cutler,	"	3	26	
Rich'd Clough,	"	3	26	
Pleasant Cawley,	"	3	26	
Thomas Duke,	"	3	26	
Bennet Drumright,	"	2	20	
John Evans,	"	3	26	
Robert Flemming,	"	1	1	
Simeon Foster,	"	3	26	
William Flemming,	"	3	26	
George Gentry,	"	3	26	
William Harmon,	"	3	26	
Samuel Johnson,	"	3	26	
James Johnson,	"	3	26	
David T. Kennon,	"	3	26	
John Meeks,	"	3	26	
John Massie,	"	3	26	
Joshua Morris,	"	3	26	
William Moss,	"	3	26	
William McBride,	"	3	26	
William McGehee,	"	3	26	
Sylvanus Meeks,	"	3	26	
Carr McGehee,	"	1	1	
John Mason,	"	1	1	
William O. Morris,	"	1	1	
Simeon Milton,	"	3	26	
Joel May,	"	3	26	
Ichabod Mallory,	"	3	26	

NAMES.	RANK.	Time of Service.		REMARKS.
		Months.	Days.	
William Nuckles, - -	Private,	3	26	
Lewis Nuckles, - -	"	3	26	
Charles Nuckles, - -	"	1	1	
Stephen Nuckles, - -	"	1	1	
James Parrish, - -	"	3	26	
William Parrish, - -	"	3	26	
Parks Parrish, - -	"	3	26	
Richard Poindexter, - -	"	3	26	
William Ready, - -	"	3	26	
Nathan Ross, - -	"	3	26	
James Rowe, - -	"	3	26	
John Rowe, Jr., - -	"	3	26	
Thomas Rowe, - -	"	3	26	
John Ryan, - -	"	3	26	
David Richardson, - -	"	3	26	
Thomas Saunders, - -	"	3	26	
William I. Smith, - -	"	3	26	
James Smith, - -	"	3	26	
John Smith, (S. G.) - -	"	3	26	
Francis Smith, - -	"	3	26	
Benjamin Simms, - -	"	3	26	
Nicholas Sprouse, - -	"	3	26	
John Sergeant, - -	"	3	36	
Jasper Sergeant, - -	"	3	26	
William Sheppard, - -	"	3	26	
Philip Smith, - -	"	3	26	
Willis Seay, - -	"	1	1	
Barnett Smith, - -	"	1	1	
Rich'd W. Thompson, -	"	3	26	
Christopher J. Thomas, -	"	3	26	
Christopher Tompkins, -	"	3	26	
James Thomas, - -	"	3	26	
Foster Tranham, - -	"	3	26	
James Tranham, - -	"	3	26	
Ephraim Tinder, - -	"	2	20	
Nathaniel Tate, - -	"	3	26	
William Tate, - -	"	2	20	
David Tisdale, - -	"	3	26	
Thomas Thacker, - -	"	3	26	
Berry Thompson, - -	"	3	26	
William Thompson, - -	"	3	26	
Arch'd Thompson, - -	"	1	1	
Lipscomb B. Thompson, -	"	3	26	
James Turner, - -	"	2	4	
David Thacker, - -	"	1	1	
Thomas Waldrope, - -	"	3	26	
Thomas Woodward, - -	"	3	26	
Thomas Walker, - -	"	3	26	
William Walker, - -	"	3	26	
Francis Waldrope, - -	"	3	26	
Samuel Waldrope, - -	"	1	1	

Captain George Morris' Company—Fortieth Regiment.

NAMES.	RANK.	TIME OF SERVICE.		REMARKS.
		Months.	Days.	
Francis Anderson, - -	Private,	–	25	
Benj. Chapman, - -	"	–	26	
Joseph Coats, - -	"	–	26	
Obadiah Gordon, - -	"	–	21	Transferred to Capt. Jackson's company.
Fontaine McGehee, - -	"	3	26	Substitute for Jno. R. Cheek.
Richard Robertson, - -	"	–	21	
Nathaniel Talley, - -	"	–	16	
Nathaniel Thompson, -	"	–	27	

(For rest of this company, see publication of Pay Rolls.)

PAY ROLL

Of Captain David Watson's Company, Virginia Militia, Louisa County, stationed at Camp Holly, under the command of Major William Armistead, and then of Colonel John H. Cocke, from 19th March to August 1813.

NAMES.	RANK.	Time of Service		REMARKS.
		Months.	Days.	
David Watson, - -	Captain,	3	28	
Frederick Harris, - -	1st Lieutenant,	3	28	
Richmond Terrill, - -	2d "	3	28	
Hezekiah Dickinson, - -	Cornet,	3	28	
Garret M. Quarles, - -	Sergeant,	3	28	
Richard Loving, - -	"	3	28	
Thomas Jones, - -	"	3	28	
John Connell, - -	"	3	28	Or Carrol.
William Fortune, - -	Corporal,	3	28	
Geo. Hollins, - -	"	1		
John B. Lasley, - -	"	2		
David Thompson, - -	"	3	28	Or Thomason.
Nath. Hughson, - -	"	3	28	
William Crawford, - -	"	3	28	
Paul Ulgate, - -	Saddler,	3	28	Or Uleyate.
William Adams, - -	Private,	3	28	
Thomas Atkins, - -	"	3	28	
Peter S. Burnett, - -	"	2	-	Or Barrett.
Jos. S. Crawford, - -	"	2	28	Or Jas. S.
William Crawford, - -	"	2		
John Digges, jun. - -	"	3	28	
Ballard Dickinson, - -	"	3	28	
Ballard S. Dudley, - -	"	3	28	
Griffin Dickinson, - -	"	2	-	Or Griffith.
John Day, - -	"	3	28	
Edward Downing, - -	"	2		
Whittle Flannagan, - -	"	1	28	
Nat. Garland, - -	"	3	28	
William Goodwin, - -	"	3	28	
Pollard Gooch, - -	"	3	28	
James Gooch, - -	"	3	28	
Roland Gooch, - -	"	3	28	
Arch'd Hutchinson, - -	"	3	28	Or Hawkinson.
Thomas Harris, - -	"	3	28	
Richard Hollins, - -	"	2	28	
Thomas Johnson, - -	"	3	28	
Moses Lipscomb, - -	"	3	28	
James F. Michie, - -	"	3	28	
Salmon H. Nelson, - -	"	3	28	Or Solomon.
Hartwell Parsons, - -	"	3	28	
Joseph Perkins, - -	"	1	28	
Edmund Swift, - -	"	3	28	Or Edward.
Francis Smith, - -	"	2	28	
Jesse Trice, - -	"	3	28	
John Whitlocke, - -	"	3	28	
William Wash, jun. -	"	3	28	

Captain David Watson's Company.

NAMES.	RANK.	TIME OF SERVICE.		REMARKS.
		Months.	Days.	
William O. Dabney, -	Private,	1	28	

(For rest of this company, see publication of Pay Rolls.)

Captain James Watson's Company.

NAMES.	RANK.	TIME OF SERVICE.		REMARKS.
		Months.	Days.	
John H. Arnold, - -	Private,	–	24	
Nathan Bell, - -	"	–	17	
Charles Maddox, - -	"	1	23	
Joseph Wilson, - -	"	1	23	

(For rest of this company, see publication of Pay Rolls.)

MUSTER ROLL

Of the Sick Noncommissioned Officers and Privates belonging to a detachment of Militia, commanded by Colonel James McDowell and left at Camp Holly Spring Hospital on the 13th October 1813.

NAMES.	RANK.	TIME OF SERVICE.		REMARKS.
		Months.	Days.	
In Capt. Danl. Huffman's Company.				
John Grizsby, - -	Sergeant.			
George Hossborth, - -	Private,	–	–	Died 22d October 1813
In Capt. John Gilkerson's Co.				
Robert Stevenson, - -	Private.			
Joseph Guy, - -	"			
In Capt. Joseph Hanna's Co.				
Geo. Jourdan, - -	Private.			
Peter Franklin, - -	"			
John Johns, - -	"			
Daniel Core, - -	"			
Ferman Stevens, - -	"			
Anderson Manuel, - -	"			
Matthias Hover, - -	"			
John Newcomb, - -	"			
In Capt. James Cartmell's Co.				
James L. Turner, - -	Sergeant.			
Jacob Switzer, - -	Private.			
William Dunbar, - -	"			
Samuel Hamilton, - -	"			
John Holland, - -	"			
Jacob Bolton, - -	"			
Merit Martin, - -	"			
John Campbell, - -	"			
William Overhain, - -	"			
John M. Culley, - -	"			
Samuel Gross, - -	"			
Charles Weaver, - -	"			
John Cohon, - -	"			
Joseph Gladden, - -	"			
Geo. Fultz, - -	"			
Joshua Snyder, - -	"			
Moses Skelton, - -	"			
John Lawson, - -	"			
Josbua Tate, - -	"			
James Switzle, - -	"			

Captain James Dunington's Company—at Camp Holly.

NAMES.	RANK.	TIME OF SERVICE.		REMARKS.
		Months.	Days.	
James Dunington,	Captain,			
Peter Dudley,	1st Lieutenant,			
William B. Lynch,	2d "			
John Robinson,	Sergeant,			
Edmund B. Norrell,	"			
Samuel Garland,	"			
James Benligh,	"			
William Martin,	Corporal,			
Christopher Fowler,	"			
Robert Thurman,	"			
French S. Gray,	"			
Benjamin Crenshaw,	Drummer,	1		
John Y. Johnson,	"	4		
John F. Lamb,	Private,	1		
David Campbell,	Matross,			
John Mays,	"			
Fielding Bradford,	"			
Isham Puckett,	"			
David F. Mason,	"			
Joseph Mays,	"			
John N. Anderson,	"			
Hezakiah Ellis,	"			
Littleton Rose,	"			
Nathan B. Harmon,	"			
Aaron Williams,	"			
Spelly Lee,	"			
Daniel Young,	"			
Hugh M. Rose,	"			
Joseph E. Royall,	"			
John McAllester,	"			
Isaac Gregory,	"			
John Reed,	"			
Gideon Mitchell,	"			
John Davis,	"			
Geo. Mettart,	"			
Netherland Tait,	"			
John B. Roy,	"			
John Vaister,	"			
Harrison Robinson,	"			
Nicholas C. Horsley,	"			
Robert Gray,	"			
William Doyle,	"			
James Walferford,	"			
Pleasant Parter,	"			
James D. Askins,	"			
Harden D. Murrell,	"			
Cornelius Pierce,	"			
Peter E. Booker,	"			
John Mattox,	Driver,			
William M. Rieves,	Matross,			
John H. Norman,	"			
John Strong,	"			
James T. Wright,	"			
Edmond Watt,	"			
Charles G. Cobbs,	Matross,			
David Smith,	Driver,			
John Y. Johnson,	"			

(For rest of this company, see publication of Pay Rolls.)

Captain Lunsford Loving's Company—at Camp Holly.

NAMES.	RANK.	TIME OF SERVICE.		REMARKS.
		Months.	Days.	
Robert Hunter, - -	Corporal,	1	27	

(For rest of this company, see publication of Pay Rolls.)

Captain James Mallory's Company—At Camp Holly.

NAMES.	RANK.	TIME OF SERVICE.		REMARKS.
		Months.	Days.	
James Mallory,	Captain,	1		
William Boyan,	Lieutenant,	1		
Jessee Katspon,	Ensign,	1		Or Katsfon.
Jeremiah Sullivan,	Sergeant,	1		
Martin Tutwiler,	"	1		
John Holliday,	"	1		
Philip Holt,	"	1		
Solomon Ritchie,	Corporal,	1		
Florence Mahoney,	"	1		
Philip Parrott,	"	1		
John S. Herring,	"	1		
Jonas Hinchie,	Drummer,	1		
Burgess Grady,	Fifer,	1		
Geo. Armenstreet,	Private,	1		
Christopher Armentrout,	"	1		
John Baker,	"	1		
John Bryan,	"	1		
Jacob Bargahiser,	"	1		
John Brown,	"	1		
John Barrick,	"	1		
Philip Baker,	"	1		
James Brown,	"	1		
Daniel Bazzil,	"	1		
William Brackney,	"	1		
James Bryan,	"	1		
Michael Clinefelter,	"	1		
John Clabough,	"	1		
Valentine Dotherby,	"	1		
Michael Dever,	"	1		
Geo. Done,	"	1		
John Hin,	"	1		
John Hortinger,	"	1		
David Hughes,	"	1		
Geo. Jenkins,	"	1		
William Jenkins,	"	1		
John Kenny,	"	1		
Jacob Lawson,	"	1		
James McCulley,	"	1		
Edward Moonley,	"	1		
Timothy Mahoney,	"	1		
John Miller,	"	1		
John Ott,	"	1		
Adam Pierce,	"	1		
Massie Rush,	"	1		
Phillip Ritchie,	"	1		
Phillip Rudy,	"	1		
Henry Ritchie,	"	1		
William Spangler,	"	1		
Henry Shoemaker,	"	1		
Christian Shoemaker,	"	1		
Andrew Stoneburner,	"	1		
David Summers,	"	1		
Jacob Spraher,	"	1		
Balsor Shaver,	"	1		

NAMES.	RANK.	TIME OF SERVICE.		REMARKS.
		Months.	Days.	
Joseph Spangler, - -	Private,	1		
Sampson Tinsley, - -	"	1		
Andrew Tencke, - -	"	1		
Abraham Tishlor, - -	"	1		
David Turner, - -	"	1		
Jacob Vance, - -	"	1		
Jacob Varner, - -	"	1		
Isaac Witsell, - -	"	1		
John Weller, - -	"	1		
James Wilson, - -	"	1		

(For rest of this company, see publication of Pay Rolls.)

MUSTER ROLL

Of Captain Charles Comer's Company, of the Sixty-third Regiment, Virginia Militia, in the service of the State, from 1st July to the 10th of the same month, in the year 1813.

NAMES.	RANK.	TIME OF SERVICE.		REMARKS.
		Months.	Days.	
Charles Comer,	Captain,	–	10	
Wm. E. Rivers,	Lieutenant,	–	10	
James Young,	Ensign,	–	9	
Wm. E. Temple,	Sergeant,	–	10	
Richard H. Mare,	"	–	10	
Jesse Mustleright,	"	–	10	
John Lee,	"	–	10	
Marcus Cook,	Corporal,	–	10	
Laban Ledbetter,	"	–	10	
Epps Leath,	"	–	10	
Robert Ledbetter,	"	–	10	
William Alley,	Private,	–	10	
Reaps Ambrose,	"	–	10	
Wood Burge,	"	–	10	
Littleberry Bonner,	"	–	9	
Wm. Bishop,	"	–	10	
Edmund Bishop,	"	–	10	
Henderson Crowder,	"	–	10	
Wm. Cotton,	"	–	10	
Edward Davenport,	"	–	10	
Frederick Heath,	"	–	10	
Drury Heath,	"	–	10	
Herbert Heath,	"	–	10	
Adam Heath,	"	–	10	
Richard Harwell,	"	–	9	
Armistead Harwell,	"	–	10	
Elijah Harwell,	"	–	10	
Leath Harewell,	"	–	10	
Willis Hall,	"	–	10	
W'mson Kirkland,	"	–	10	
Littleberry Lee,	"	–	10	
Green Lee,	"	–	9	
Jonathan Perkins,	"	–	9	
Nathaniel Rains,	"	–	10	
John Shands,	"	–	10	
Joshua Temple,	"	–	10	
Charles G. Tatum,	"	–	10	
Frederick Temple,	"	–	10	
James Y. Temple,	"	–	10	
Edwin Temple,	"	–	10	
Robert Temple,	"	–	10	
Pleasant Temple,	"	–	10	
Reuben Tucker,	"	–	10	
Hartwell Tucker,	"	–	9	
Reuben Wright,	"	–	8	

MUSTER ROLL

Of a detachment from Captain Thos. Redd's Company, of Virginia Militia, from the Sixty-third Regiment, in the Service from the 30th August to 6th September, 1814.

NAMES.	RANK.	TIME OF SERVICE.		REMARKS.
		Months.	Days.	
John Stevens, - -	2d Lieutenant,	-	8	
John B. Hunt, - -	Drummer,	-	8	
William Armistead, - -	Private,	-	8	
James Armistead, - -	"	-	8	
John Conner, - -	"	-	8	
Robert Chumleigh, - -	"	-	8	
John Broadway, - -	"	-	8	
John Boatright, - -	"	-	8	
Griffin Dickerson, - -	"	-	8	
John T. Dicke, - -	"	-	8	
Joshua Davidson, - -	"	-	8	
Jennings Fowlkes, - -	"	-	8	
Pleasant Gauldin, - -	"	-	8	
John Hudson, - -	"	-	8	
William Jackson, - -	"	-	8	
William Leneve, - -	"	-	8	
James B. Medley, - -	"	-	8	
William D. Nash, - -	"	-	8	
Presley Nash, - -	"	-	8	
Thomas P. O'Brien, - -	"	-	8	
Sharp Spencer, - -	"	-	8	
Willard Uriah, - -	"	-	8	

MUSTER ROLL

Of Captain Henry Edmunds' Company of the Sixty-sixth Regiment, Virginia Militia, from the County of Brunswick, called into actual Service under the general orders of the 28th June, from the 4th to the 6th July, in the year 1813.

NAMES.	RANK.	TIME OF SERVICE.		REMARKS.
		Months.	Days.	
Henry Edmunds,	Captain,	–	3	
John Juda,	Lieutenant,	–	3	
Thomas Meredith,	Ensign,	–	3	
Benj. Jones,	Sergeant,	–	3	
Obadiah Stith,	"	–	3	
Braxton Narsome,	"	–	3	
Thomas Crook,	"	–	3	
James Smith,	"	–	3	
Josiah Nolley,	"	–	3	
Richard Morris,	Drummer,	–	3	
Anderson Johnson,	Fifer,	–	3	
Elisha Abernethy,	Private,	–	3	
John Abernethy,	"	–	3	
William Black,	"	–	3	
Nathaniel Bass,	"	–	3	
Joel Baugh,	"	–	3	
Benj. H. Bass,	"	–	3	
Veries Browne,	"	–	3	
James Brintte,	"	–	3	
Sterling Briggs,	"	–	3	
William Buckner,	"	–	3	
Benj. Bennett,	"	–	3	
George Crooke,	"	–	3	
Nicholas Daniel,	"	–	3	
James Eldridge,	"	–	3	
Matthew Edwards,	"	–	3	
Allen Floyd,	"	–	3	
Frederick Hawthorne,	"	–	3	
Wm. W. Harper,	"	–	3	
John House,	"	–	3	
Freeman Jordan,	"	–	3	
David Jackson,	"	–	3	
William Johnson,	"	–	3	
John Kirkland,	"	–	3	
Wm'son Kirkland,	"	–	3	
Micajah Lane,	"	–	3	
Jessee Matthews,	"	–	3	
James Manly,	"	–	3	
Growner Ower,	"	–	3	
John L. Penington,	"	–	3	
Wm. Redcoat,	"	–	3	
William Rainely,	"	–	3	
Benj. Rawlings,	"	–	3	
Daniel Rawlings,	"	–	3	
John Slate,	"	–	3	
Samuel Sims,	"	–	3	
Wm'son Smith,	"	–	3	
Sterling Thacker,	Private,	–	3	
Banister Tomason,	"	–	3	
Wm. Taylor,	"	–	3	
Wm. Vaughan,	"	–	3	
Robert Vaughan,	"	–	3	
John R. Williams,	"	–	3	

PAY ROLL

Of Captain James Fisher's Company, of the Sixty-sixth Regiment of Virginia Militia, in the Service of the United States, at Fort Powhatan, from July 1814 *to January* 1815.

NAMES.	RANK.	Time of Service.		REMARKS.
		Months.	Days.	
James Fisher, - -	Captain,	5	9	
Bradford Burge, - -	1st Lieutenant,	6	10	
James Seward, - -	1st "	6	10	
Ben. Ingraham, - -	1st "	2	27	
Ben. L. Rainey, - -	2d "	2	27	
Charles Boothe, - -	Q. M. Serg't,	2	27	
Kinchin Harris, - -	Sergt. Major.	2	28	
Nicholas Lanier, - -	Sergeant,	2	27	
Lewis Wright, - -	"	6	17	
Roberson Powell, - -	"	2	6	
Edwin Hobbs, - -	"	3	18	
David Jackson, - -	Corporal,	5	12	
Jones Floyd, - -	"	5	6	
Henry House, - -	"	3	5	
James S. Bass, - -	"	6	17	
James Goodwyne, - -	"	5	11	
Burwell Hill, - -	"	6	17	
Charles Chuly, - -	"	5	12	
Philip Madera, - -	"	4	17	
Lewis Mayes, - -	"	6	15	
Richard Ezell, - -	"	6	15	
James B. Adams, - -	Private,	2	29	
John Allen, - -	"	5	10	
Wm. V. Avery. - -	"	6	15	
Thomas Adams. - -	"	6	17	
Amos Archer, - -	"	6	17	
William Bracey, - -	"	6	17	
John Barnes, - -	"	6	14	
Richard Barnes, - -	"	6	17	
Samuel Bennett, - -	"	6	15	
Francis A. Burge, - -	"	2	27	
Ben. J. Buford, - -	"	6	15	
Robert Brockwell, - -	"	3	18	
Edward Branch, - -	"	1	11	
Robert Chuly, - -	"			
Charles Coleman, - -	"	6	14	
Littleberry Chappell, - -	"	5	7	
Lewis Chambliss, - -	"	6	17	
Thomas Cannon, - -	"	5	7	
Henry Colton.				
John Davis, - -	"	4	16	
Thomas Davis, - -	"	5	21	
James Davis, - -	"	6	17	
Wm. N. Davis, - -	"	6	17	
Henry Davis, - -	"	5	19	
Gresham Dunkley, - -	"	6	15	
Robert Dean, - -	"	5	23	
Josiah Fuqua, - -	"	2	24	
Edwin Fielding, - -	"	5	18	
Saml. Fuqua, - -	"	1	13	
Thomas Gibbon, - -	"	2	27	
Hartwell Gordon, - -	"	6	17	
Dudley Gunn, - -	"	5	12	

NAMES.	RANK.	Time of Service.		REMARKS.
		Months.	Days.	
Henry Gibbs, - -	Private,	4	25	
Green S. House, - -	"	3	15	
Wm. Howerton, - -	"	5	29	
William House, - -	"	5	19	
Jno. J. Hatch, - -	"	6	15	
John Hunt, - -	"	6	17	
Samuel Harris, - -	"	6	17	
Gilliam Hawkins, - -	"	4	7	
Hollin Hobbs, - -	"	1	6	
William Harden, - -	"	1	10	
Thomas Johnson, - -	"	5	14	
James Johnson, - -	"	5	23	
Philip Johnson, - -	"	6	16	
John Jones, - -	"	6	17	
Thomas Kelly, -	"	4	16	
James Kelly, -	"	2	23	
Joseph Kelly, -	"	4	19	
William Leigh, - -	"	1	6	
Hamlin Lewis, - -	"	5	5	
John Lanier, - -	"	4	23	
Sterling Lanier, - -	"	4	21	
Jesse Lucy, - -	"	6	6	
Edlar Lynch, - -	"	6	17	
Hamlin Ledbetter, - -	"	6	17	
Joseph Mitchell, - -	"	6	17	
Daniel Malone, - -	"	6	17	
John Mitchell, - -	"	6	13	
George Malone, - -	"	6	14	
Francis Moore, - -	"	5	11	
Green Morris, - -	"	6	17	
William Massey, - -	"	5	19	
Hardway Moseley, - -	"	6	17	
Cudberth Moseley, - -	"	6	14	
Nathan Minge, - -	"	3	17	
Henry Magon, - -	"	3	19	
Wyatt Morris, - -	"	3	18	
Young D. Perkins, - -	"	3	1	
Thomas Pearey, - -	"	6	15	
Robert Peebles, - -	"	2	27	Deserted.
Gilliam Parrish, - -	"	6	15	
Osborne Phenix, - -	"	6	15	
George Pollard, - -	"	5	24	
Robinson Powell, - -	"	4	11	
John Quarles, - -	"	6	17	
John Rivers, - -	"	4	15	
James Robinson, - -	"	6	15	
Charles Ross, - -	"	5	10	
John Roland, - -	"	2	29	
James Reid, - -	"	6	17	
Joseph Reese, - -	"	3	18	
Henry Swinebroad, - -	"	6	16	
Thomas Stith, - -	"	6	16	
Charles Spyers, - -	"	6	16	
Solomon Shell, - -	"	4	23	
Robert Spyers, - -	"	1	6	
James Spyers, - -	"	1	6	
Wm. Tunstall, - -	"	2	28	
Daniel Tunstall, - -	"	6	17	
Jones Taylor, - -	"	6	17	
Jordan Vaughan, - -	"	6	15	
William Vaughan, - -	"	6	15	
Wilson Vick, - -	"	6	17	
Ranson Vick, - -	"	6		
Wm. R. Wynne, - -	"	4	17	
Reuben Weeks, - -	"	6	16	

****

NAMES.	RANK.	Time of Service.		REMARKS.
		Months.	Days.	
Robert Whitby, - -	Private,	4	19	
John Williams, - -	"	6	13	
Waller Warthen, - -	"	5	15	
Walter Warthen, - -	"	2		
Francis Wray, - -	"	2	28	
Wilson Ward, - -	"	5	6	
William J. Williams, - -	"	3	10	
Walter G. Warthen, - -	"	3	3	
George C. Wright, - -	"	1	22	
Anderson Wray, - -	"	1	28	
Zachariah Williams, - -	"	3	17	

Captain James Fisher's Company—Sixty-sixth Regiment.

NAMES.	RANK.	TIME OF SERVICE.		REMARKS.
		Months.	Days.	
Kinchea Mabry, - -	Sergeant,	–	27	
Beverley B. Burge, - -	Private,	–	27	
Richard Ezell, - -	"	–	28	
John Hall, - -	"	–	27	
Henry House, - -	"	–	7	Josiah Fuqua sub.
Kindred Jackson, - -	"	–	20	
Jesse Lewis, - -	"	–	26	
Robert Lanier, - -	"	–	27	
Lewis Mays, - -	"	–	29	
Thomas Manning, - -	"	–	28	
William Noble, - -	"	–	26	
Edmund Short, - -	"	–	27	

(For rest of this company, see publication of Pay Rolls.)

MUSTER ROLL

Of Captain Isaac Medley's Company, from the Sixty-ninth Regiment, Virginia Militia, Halifax County, in the Service, from the 5th to 20th July, 1813.

NAMES.	RANK.	TIME OF SERVICE.		REMARKS.
		Months.	Days.	
Isaac Medley, - -	Captain,	–	15	
William Edmundson, - -	Lieutenant,	–	15	
William Kirby, - -	Ensign,	–	15	
William Howerton, - -	Sergeant,	–	15	
Thomas Howerton, - -	"	–	15	
Thornton Puryear, - -	"	–	15	
Jeremiah Morgan, - -	"	–	15	
William Hughes, - -	"	–	15	
Hopkins G. Jones, - -	"	–	15	
Austin Brigg, - -	"	–	15	
Samuel Edmundson, - -	"	–	15	
Elias Smith, - -	"	–	15	Or Elas.
Coleman Burton, - -	"	–	15	
Lewis Siah, - -	"	–	15	
Martin Blalock, - -	"	–	15	
Frederick Briggs, - -	"	–	15	
William Drummond, - -	"	–	15	
Joseph Clardy, - -	"	–	15	
Daniel Clark, - -	"	–	15	
Thomas Chambers, - -	"	–	15	
John Hart, - -	"	–	15	
Joel Henderson, - -	"	–	15	
Elias Washer, - -	"	–	15	Or Walker.
Quiller Carlton, - -	"	–	15	
Larbome Cooper, - -	"	–	15	
Joseph G. Griesham, - -	"	–	15	
John L. Whitland, - -	"	–	15	
John Goode, - -	"	–	15	
Powell Tuck, - -	"	–	15	
Isby Wall, - -	"	–	15	
Seth P. Pool, - -	"	–	15	
Irby Duberry, - -	"	–	15	
Alexander Cumbo, - -	"	–	15	
Thomas Watkins, - -	"	–	15	
Richard Arrington, - -	"	–	15	
John Warren, - -	"	–	15	
Samuel Hailey, - -	"	–	15	
Joseph Drumman, - -	"	–	15	
Henry Elliott, - -	"	–	15	
Joseph Lizmore, - -	"	–	15	
Thomas Duncan, - -	"	–	15	
John Turpin, - -	"	–	15	
Claiborne Rice, - -	"	–	15	
Thomas Taylor, - -	"	–	15	
John Davis, - -	"	–	15	
Edward Murphy, - -	"	–	15	
William L. Boyd, - -	"	–	15	
Thomas Poinor, - -	"	–	15	
John Bennett, - -	"	–	15	
William Stainley, - -	"	–	15	

****

NAMES.	RANK.	TIME OF SERVICE.		REMARKS.
		Months.	Days.	
John Anderson, - -	Private,		15	
Francis State, - -	"		15	
Vines Browder, - -	"		15	
Brooking C. Griffin, - -	"		15	
William Lofter, - -	"		15	
William Guthrie, - -	"		15	
William Saunders, - -	"		15	
Robert Harris, - -	"		15	
Henry McCarter, - -	"		15	
Pool White, - -	"		15	

Captain William Leigh's Company—Second Elite Corps.

NAMES.	RANK.	TIME OF SERVICE.		REMARKS.
		Months.	Days.	
Thomas Pate, - -	Sergeant,	–	18	
Stephen E. Wood, - -	Corporal,	–	–	Dead.
Alexander Asher, - -	Private,	–	12	
Vincent Birch, - -	"	–	20	Sub. for Vin. Carlton.
Edward Carlton, - -	"	–	21	" " Ambrose Hart.
William Dickey, - -	"	–	14	" " John Dickey.
Samuel Harwood, - -	"	–	20	Sub. for John Crenshaw.
Elijah Rives, - -	"	–	14	
Charles Read, - -	"	–	14	
John Simmons, - -	"			
Thomas Simmons, - -	"	–	13	Sub. for John Simmons.
Chesley Taylor, - -	"	–	13	
James Walton, - -	"	–	11	

(For rest of this company, see publication of Pay Rolls.)

MUSTER ROLL

Of Captain Joseph Sandford's Company of Cavalry, from the Sixty-ninth Regiment, Virginia Militia, in the County of Halifax, called into Service under general orders of the 27th June, 1813, *from 27th June to 19th August, in the year* 1813.

NAMES.	RANK.	TIME OF SERVICE.		REMARKS.
		Months.	Days.	
Joseph Sandford, - -	Captain,	1	23	
Benjamin Marable, - -	Lieutenant,	1	23	
Stephen Davenport, - -	"	1	23	
William Martin, - -	Cornet,	1	23	
Clement Ragland, - -	Sergeant,	1	23	
Jeremiah Moore, - -	"	1	23	
Beverley Sydnor, - -	"	1	23	
William Chambers, - -	"	1	23	
Richard Oliver, - -	Corporal,	1	23	
Pleasant Farmer, - -	"	1	23	
Edward Stubblefield, - -	"	1	23	
Samuel H. McCraw, - -	"	1	23	
Elisha Bell, - -	Private,	1	23	
Charles Brice, - -	"	1	23	
William Brance, - -	"	1	22	
Harrison Bowen, - -	"	1	23	
John Britton, - -	"	1	23	
John Claiborne, - -	"	1	23	
Paul Carrington, - -	"	1	23	
Aansy Carrington, - -	"	1	23	
George Claughton, - -	"	1	23	
William S. Craddock, -	"	1	23	
Theo. Carter, - -	"	1	23	
John B. Dodson, - -	"	1	23	
Elisha Dodson, - -	"	1	23	
Caleb Dodson, - -	"	1	23	
Thomas Dodson, - -	"	1	23	
Richard Edmonson, - -	"	1	23	
Edmund Edmundson, -	"	1	23	
Martin Ferrill, - -	"	1	23	
Richard Fling, - -	"	1	23	
James Gann, - -	"	1	23	
Thomas Gresham, - -	"	1	23	
Thomas Glascock, - -	"	1	23	
John Hobson, - -	"	1	23	
Thomas C. Hoskins, - -	"	1	23	
Edward P. Hughs, - -	"	1	23	
Daniel Irvine, - -	"	1	23	
Richard Jordan, - -	"	1	23	
Bird Janner, - -	"	1	23	
Isham Lane, - -	"	1	23	
Edward Morriss, - -	"	1	23	
Samuel Major, - -	"	1	23	
John Oliver, - -	"	1	23	
Samuel Pate, - -	"	1	23	
Roper Ribis, - -	"	1	23	
Joseph Royall, - -	"	1	23	

NAMES.	RANK.	TIME OF SERVICE.		REMARKS.
		Months.	Days.	
Dabner Ragland, - -	Private,	1	23	
Josiah Robertson, - -	"	1	23	
John W. Scott, - -	"	1	23	
Joel Tynes, - -	"	1	23	
John Talknor, - -	"	1	23	
James P. Vass, - -	"	1	23	
Philip Vass, - -	"	1	23	
Robert Williams, - -	"	1	23	
Christopher Wooding, -	"	1	23	

MUSTER ROLL

Of the Field and Staff Officers of the Seventy-fourth Regiment of Virginia Militia, commanded by Colonel William Trueheart, in the Service of the United States from 20th March to 2nd July in the year 1813.

NAMES.	RANK.	TIME OF SERVICE.		REMARKS.
		Months.	Days.	
Wm. Trueheart, - -	Lt. Colonel,	3	12	
Thom[illegible] Starke, - -	Major,	3	12	
Park[illegible] Street, - -	"	3	12	
Edmond G. Goodwin, -	Adjutant,	3	12	
William Bowe, - -	P. Master,	3	12	
John W. Ellis, - -	Q. Master,	3	12	
Charles Morris, - -	Surgeon,	3	12	
Joseph M. Sheppard, -	S. Mate,	3	12	

MUSTER ROLL

Of Captain Patrick Anderson's Company of the Seventy-fourth Regiment, Virginia Militia, commanded by Lieutenant Colonel William Trueheart, in the Service of the United States from 20th to 29th March, from 27th to 29th June, and from 1st to 2d July, in the year 1813.

NAMES.	RANK.	TIME OF SERVICE.		REMARKS.
		Months.	Days.	
Patrick Anderson,	Captain,	–	14	
James Gentry,	Lieutenant,	–	14	
Thomas G. Tinsley,	Ensign,	–	14	
Henry Langford,	Sergeant,	–	14	
Obadiah Archer,	"	–	14	
Dimack Hay,	"	–	14	
James Kirby,	"	–	14	
Bartlett Anderson,	Private,	–	14	
John Anderson,	"	–	14	
James Andrews,	"	–	13	
Obadiah Atkinson,	"	–	14	
Benjamin Brand,	"	–	13	
Overton Butler,	"	–	1	
John Brooks,	"	–	14	
Nathan Bumpass,	"	–	14	
David Clarke,	"	–	12	
Henry Curtis,	"	–	14	
James B. Clarke,	"	–	14	
David R. Clarke,	"	–	14	
Christopher Corthan,	"	–	2	
Joseph Clarke, jr.	"	–	4	
Pitman Dobson,	"	–	14	
Wm. C. Eggleston,	"	–	14	
Joseph N. Edmundson,	"	–	3	
Richard Epperson,	"	–	4	
William Gardner,	"	–	14	
Henry D. Gentry,	"	–	14	
Fleming Green,	"	–	14	
Edward B. Geddy,	"	–	14	
Jeremiah Hooper,	"	–	14	
Rice Hughes,	"	–	14	
Fleming Hughes,	"	–	1	
John Haw (or Hane,)	"	–	14	
Isaac Hay,	"	–	14	
Richard H. Johnson,	"	–	14	
John Jenkins,	"	–	14	
John Jones,	"	–	14	
Elisha Kirby,	"	–	14	
Matthew Kersey,	"	–	14	
Francis E. Kindrick,	"	–	4	
Thomas Lumpkin,	"	–	14	
Robert Lumpkin,	"	–	14	
James Littlepage,	"	–	14	
William Lyle,	"	–	14	
John K. Miller,	"	–	14	
Robert Martin,	"	–	14	
Hezekiah Mantillo,	"	–	14	

NAMES.	RANK.	TIME OF SERVICE.		REMARKS.
		Months.	Days.	
Henry W. Nicholes,	Private,	–	14	
William R. Nelson,	"	–	14	
Isaac Oliver,	"	–	14	
John Oliver,	"	–	13	
Thomas B. Puller,	"	–	14	
Robert Page,	"	–	14	
John Puller,	"	–	14	
John Patterson,	"	–	14	
Cobbett Richardson,	"	–	14	
Patrick Roane,	"	–	4	
George W. Rabinan,	"	–	10	
William Sizer,	"	–	14	
William Sansom,	"	–	14	
William Smith,	"	–	14	
Robert Sherlock, jr.	"	–	13	
Thomas Tyler,	"	–	14	
Benjamin Tyler,	"	–	12	
Thruston Thomas,	"	–	14	
Nicholas Talley,	"	–	12	
James Thomas,	"	–	14	
William Thomas,	"	–	14	
William Tombs,	"	–	14	
Lewis Trueheart,	"	–	14	
James V. Tyler,	"	–	14	
John P. Tyler,	"	–	14	
Skelton Tyler,	"	–	12	
John Talley,	"	–	14	
James Tyler,	"	–	12	
Elkanah Talley,	"	–	14	
John Talley, (son of Billey,)	"	–	14	
Billey Talley,	"	–	14	
Benjamin B. Tyler,	"	–	14	
Nathaniel Talley,	"	–	14	
Zachariah Tyler,	"	–	4	
William Via,	"	–	14	
Claiborne Wicker,	"	–	4	
Robert White,	"	–	14	
Charles Whitlock,	"	–	14	
James Whitlock,	"	–	7	
Benjamin West,	"	–	13	
Nathaniel Whitlock,	"	–	9	
David Wade,	"	–	12	
William White,	"	–	14	
Elliott Wicker,	"	–	11	

MUSTER ROLL

Of Captain Bentley Brown's Company of the Seventy-fourth Regiment, Virginia Militia, commanded by Colonel William Trueheart, in the Service of the United States at different periods in the year 1813.

NAMES.	RANK.	TIME OF SERVICE.		REMARKS.
		Months.	Days.	
Bentley Brown, - -	Captain,	–	23½	
William Smith, - -	Lieutenant,	–	23½	
William Woolfolk, - -	Ensign,	–	23½	
Thomas Taylor, - -	Sergeant,	–	23½	
James Sharp, - -	"	–	23½	
Benjamin Spicer, - -	"	–	23½	
Dabney Dickinson, - -	"	–	23½	
William Arnall, - -	Private,	–	23½	
Genet Anderson, - -	"	–	13	
John Butler, - -	"	–	23½	
John Byars, - -	"	–	23½	
Miller Brown, - -	"	–	21½	
Nelson Brooks, - -	"	–	14	
George Bumpass, - -	"	–	14	
Thomas W. Claybrook, -	"		23½	
Richard Chase, - -	"	–	23½	
John Dickinson, - -	"	–	19½	
Lewis Day, - - -	"	–	23½	
Nathaniel Dickinson, -	"	–	23½	
William D. Goodwin, .	"	–	19	
John Gunnel, - -	"	–	12	
James Hall, - -	"	–	23½	
James Harris, - -	"	–	23½	
Terry Hewlett, - -	"	–	23½	
William Hargrave, - -	"	–	19	
Francis V. Howlet, - -	"	–	23½	
John Hancock, - -	"	–	19½	
Joseph Hancock, - -	"	–	23½	
Henry J. Hall, - -	"	–	23½	
Aaron Hall, - -	"	–	23½	
Zephaniah Hall, - -	"	–	23½	
Jacob Holloway, - -	"	–	23½	
Simeon Hall, - -	"	–	23½	
James Hall, - - -	"	–	19½	
Tarlton Hancock, - -	"	–	23½	
David Hanes, - -	"	–	23½	
Garland Hall, - -	"	–	23½	
Pleasant Hinchey, - -	"	–	23½	
John Hall, - - -	"	–	21	
William Harper, - -	"	–	23½	
Benjamin Hancock, - -	"	–	23½	
William Hall, - -	"	–	23½	
William Johnson, - -	"	–	15	
Richard F. Jones, - -	"	–	23½	
John Lester, - -	"	–	23½	
Garrett Lowry, - -	"	–	23½	
William Luck, - -	"	–	23½	
William Lawrence, - -	"	–	19	

****

NAMES.	RANK.	TIME OF SERVICE.		REMARKS.
		Months.	Days.	
Robert Mallory, - -	Private,	–	23½	
Warner W. Minor, - -	"	–	23½	
John Martin, - -	"	–	19½	
John Moody, - -	"	–	19½	
Nicholas Mills, - -	"	–	23½	
Charles Mills, - -	"	–	15	
Thomas Nelson, - -	"	–	19½	
William Noel, - -	"	–	23½	
Thos. Nelson, (son of Wm.)	"	–	21	
Samuel Oldham, - -	"	–	23½	
William Philips, - -	"	–	23½	
Lewis Philips, - -	"	–	23½	
Austin Pate, - -	"	–	21	
Edward Patterson, - -	"	–	14	
James Quarles, - -	"	–	23½	
William Seay, - -	"	–	23½	
Luke A. Seay, - -	"	–	23½	
James Smith, - -	"	–	23½	
Solomon Stanley, - -	"	–	21	
John Stanley, - -	"	–	23½	
Benjamin Stanley, - -	"	–	23½	
Charles Swift, - -	"	–	23½	
Robert Sharp, - -	"	–	21	
William Swift, - -	"	–	23½	
Strangeman Stanley, -	"	–	23½	
William Stanley, (son of O.)	"	–	23½	
William Stanley, (son of J.)	"	–	21½	
Thomas Stanley, - -	"	–	23½	
William B. Syms, - -	"	–	23½	
Lewis Smith, - -	"	–	21½	
Zachariah Smith, - -	"	–	21½	
Maddox Stanley, - -	"	–	23½	
John T. Smith, - -	"	–	21½	
Edward Thacker, - -	"	–	23½	
Chesley Thacker, - -	"	–	23½	
Thomas Price, - -	"	–	23½	
James Taylor, - -	"	–	23½	
Charles Terrell, - -	"	–	23½	
Edmund Terrell, - -	"	–	21½	
John Terrell, - -	"	–	23½	
Garland Thompson, - -	"	–	19	
David Terrell, - -	"	–	21	
Francis Thompson, - -	"	–	23½	
Roger Thompson, - -	"	–	19½	
Overton Watkins, - -	"	–	23½	
Thomas Watkins, - -	"	–	19½	
Horatio G. Winston, -	"	–	23½	
William Wash, - -	"	–	13	
Richard White, - -	"	–	23½	
Joel Walton, - -	"	–	21½	
Pleasant Yeamans, - -	"	–	21½	
Austin Yeamans, - -	"	–	21½	
Charles Yeamans, - -	"	–	23½	
Preston Yeamans, - -	"	–	2	

PAY ROLL

Of Captain Nathaniel Bowe's Company, of the Seventy-fourth Regiment of Virginia Militia, Hanover County, attached to the First Battalion, commanded by Colonel John H. Cocke, at Camp Holly, from 27th June to 26th July 1813.

NAMES.	RANK.	Time of Service.		REMARKS.
		Months.	Days.	
Nathaniel Bowe, - -	Captain,			
John D. Hendrick, - -	Lieutenant,	1		
Edward N. Clough, - -	Ensign,	1		
Hugh Watt, - -	Sergeant,	1		
George Mason, - -	"	1		
William Wingfield, - -	"	1		
Henry Tyler, - -	"	1		
Archibald Richardson, - -	Corporal,	1		
Thomas Travillian, - -	"	1		
Daniel Mitchell, - -	"	1		
Turpin Kelley, - -	"	1		
John Anderson, - -	Private,	1		
Edward H. Anthony, - -	"	1		
William Bowles, - -	"	1		
Daniel Booze, - -	"	1		
Meredith Brown, - -	"	1		
William Burnett, - -	"	1		
Christopher Butler, - -	"	1		
Richard Childress, - -	"	1		
Alexander Chisholm, - -	"	-	24	Joined Captain Wingfield on the 20th June. See his pay roll.
Robert A. Dandridge, - -	"	1		
John Dickinson, - -	"	1		
A. Denton, - -	"	1		
Miles C. Eggleston, - -	"	1		
Austin Ford, - -	"	1		
John Harris, - -	"	1		
Garland Hall, - -	"	1		
John Hancocke, - -	"	1		
Pleasant Hatton, - -	"	1		
David Mallory, - -	"	1		
John F. Mallory, - -	"	1		
James Moore, - -	"	1		
Samuel Moseley, - -	"	1		
William Melton, - -	"	1		
Joseph Magee, - -	"	1		
Hezekiah Mantle, - -	"	1		
John Martin, - -	"	1		
Robert Martin, - -	"	1		
Richard Phillips, - -	"	1		
Plummer Potter, - -	"	1		
Joseph Perkins, - -	"	1		
William Powers, - -	"	1		
Landon Richardson, - -	"	1		
Julius Stephens, - -	"	1		
William Stanley, - -	"	1		
William Southworth, - -	"	1		
John Southworth, - -	"	1		
Thomas Southworth, - -	"	1		
Robert Sherlock, - -	"	1		
Nathaniel Stephens, - -	"	1		
L. Smith, - -	"	1		
Zach. Smith, - -	"	1		
John T. Smith, - -	"	1		
James Thacker, - -	"	1		

NAMES.	RANK.	Time of Service.		REMARKS.
		Months.	Days.	
William Thacker, - -	Private,	1		
Pleasant Toler, - -	"	1		
Samuel Turner, - -	"	1		
Isham Tyre, - -	"	1		
Saml. Tomlinson, - -	"	1		
A. M. Thornton, - -	"	1		
William Thomas, - -	"	1		
Joel Walton, - -	"	1		
Carter Wade, - -	"	1		
Winfree Wright, - -	"	1		
Thomas Watkins, - -	"	1		

Captain Nathaniel Bowe's Company—Seventy-fourth Regiment.

NAMES.	RANK.	TIME OF SERVICE.		REMARKS.
		Months.	Days.	
Nath'l Bowe, - -	Captain,	–	25	
James Christian, - -	Private,	1		
Jacob Christian, - -	"	1		
Francis Taylor, - -	"	–	9	Furnished a substitute.
Attached to Captain Jones' Co.				
Ch. D. Alvis, - -	"	–	10	
Henry Arnall, - -	"	–	10	
Davis Arnall, - -	"	–	10	
Rich'd Arnall, - -	"	–	10	
Thomas Bowles, - -	"	–	10	
Peter Bowles, - -	"	–	10	
Joseph Bowles, - -	"	–	10	
Ambrose Brooks, - -	"	–	10	
John Bell, - -	"			
Daniel Caker, - -	"	–	10	
Chas. Childress, - -	"	–	10	
Alex'r Chisholm, - -	"	–	24	Joined Capt. Wingfield on the 20th June.
Chris. Cawthon, - -	"	–	10	
Geo. Davis, - -	"	–	10	
John Donnolly, - -	"	–	10	
Pleasant Ford, - -	"	1		
Thomas F. Green, - -	"	–	10	
James Higgason, - -	"	–	10	
Norman Harvey, - -	"	–	10	
Ben. Harris, - -	"	–	10	
Ben. Jenkins, - -	"	–	10	
Ben. Jenkins, - -	"	–	10	
John Jude, - -	"	–	2	
Ed. Maynard, - -	"	–	10	
Joseph Patterson, - -	"	–	10	
William Pearson, - -	"	–	10	
James B. Parker, - -	"	–	10	
Neal D. McCook, - -	"	–	10	
Thomas Richardson, - -	"	–	10	
Tindall Ragland, - -	"	–	10	
Thomas Turner, - -	"	–	10	
Joseph Shelton, - -	"	–	10	

(For rest of this company, see publication of Pay Rolls.)

MUSTER ROLL

Of Captain William Hundley's Company, from the Seventy-fourth Regiment, Virginia Militia, commanded by Lieut. Col. Wm. Trueheart, in the Service of the United States, from the 20th to 29th March, from 27th to 29th June, and from 1st to 2d July, 1813.

NAMES.	RANK.	TIME OF SERVICE.		REMARKS.
		Months.	Days.	
William Hundley, - -	Captain,	–	22½	
John D. Hendrick, - -	Lieutenant,	–	14	
Nathaniel Cross, - -	Ensign,	–	22½	
John King, - -	Sergeant,	–	22½	
John England, - -	"	–	22½	
John Frazer, - -	"	–	20	
John L. England, - -	"	–	22½	
Robert B. Bowles, - -	Drummer,	–	22½	
Bowler Whipple, - -	Fifer,	–	13	
William Andrew, - -	Private,	–	22½	
Geo. W. Adams, - -	"	–	19	
Thomas Adams, - -	"	–	18	
Thomas Bowles, (P.) -	"	–	19	
Thomas Bowles, (F.) -	"	–	19	
William Bowles, - -	"	–	20½	
John Bunpass, - -	"	–	22½	
John Bowles, - -	"	–	21	
Thomas Bowles, (son of Ben,)	"	–	22½	
John Brock, - -	"	–	22½	
Joseph Bowles, - -	"	–	4	
Henry Cross, (son of John,) -	"	–	22½	
William Cameron, - -	"	–	22½	
John Cross, jr. - -	"	–	20½	
James Christian, - -	"	–	20½	
James Donnally, - -	"	–	19½	
Wyatt Davis, - -	"	–	22½	
John Donnally, - -	"	–	22½	
Thomas Davis, - -	"	–	21	
James Davis, jr. - -	"	–	22½	
David Edwards, - -	"	–	22½	
John Glazebrook, - -	"	–	22½	
Andrew Grubbs, - -	"	–	22½	
Richard Glazebrook, - -	"	–	22½	
Richard P. Green, - -	"	–	22½	
Joel Hanes, - -	"	–	22½	
James Hooper, - -	"	–	13	
Moses Harris, - -	"	–	22½	
Fleming Harris, - -	"	–	18	
Garland Harris, - -	"	–	22½	
Benjamin Jenkins, - -	"	–	18½	
William Jenkins, - -	"	–	22½	
Thomas King, - -	"	–	21	
William King, - -	"	–	22½	
Benjamin Langford, - -	"	–	22½	
James Lynn, - -	"	–	14	
Sterling Langford, - -	"	–	17	
William Norvell, - -	"	–	19	

NAMES.	RANK.	TIME OF SERVICE.		REMARKS.
		Months.	Days.	
James Parseley, - -	Private,	–	22½	
John Perkins, - -	"	–	22½	
Samuel Priddy, - -	"	–	22½	
John Priddy, - -	"	–	22½	
Samuel Patterson, - -	"	–	22½	
Fendall Ragland, - -	"	–	20	
John Starke, - -	"	–	17	
John Sims, - -	"	–	22½	
Phillip Sheppard, - -	"	–	20½	
John A. Smith, - -	"	–	6	
John Stone, - -	"	–	6	
Benjamin Snead, - -	"	–	22½	
Wyatt Tinsley, - -	"	–	22½	
William Toler, - -	"	–	22½	
Parke Tinsley, - -	"	–	8	
Walter Tucker, - -	"	–	8	
Henry R. Winston, - -	"	–	22½	
Jessee Winn, - -	"	–	22½	
John S. West, - -	"	–	20½	
Christopher Winfield, -	"	–	22½	
Palmer Whipple, - -	"	–	2	

MUSTER ROLL

Of Captain Thomas Jones' Company, of the Seventy-fourth Regiment, Virginia Militia, commanded by Colonel William Truehart, in the Service of the United States, from 20th to 29th March, from 28th to 30th June, and from 1st to 2d July, in the year 1813.

NAMES.	RANK.	TIME OF SERVICE.		REMARKS.
		Months.	Days.	
Thomas Jones, - -	Captain,	–	15	
David R. Jones, - -	Lieutenant,	–	15	
Charles K. Bowles, - -	Ensign,	–	15	
James Colley, - -	Sergeant,	–	15	
John G. Childres, - -	"	–	15	
Thomas Carter, - -	"	–	15	
Harman A. Pulliam, - -	"	–	15	
Joseph Anderson, - -	Private,	–	15	
Archibald Atkinson, - -	"	–	15	
Anderson Bowles, - -	"	–	9	
Robert Blunhall, - -	"	–	12	
Elkanah A. Brooks, - -	"	–	15	
Joseph Burnard, - -	"	–	15	
Thomas Carver, - -	"	–	15	
William Childress, - -	"	–	15	
Charles Colley, jr. - -	"	–	15	
Alex'r Chisholm, - -	"	–	15	
Pendleton R. Childress, -	"	–	15	
John S. Crutchfield, - -	"	–	15	
Richard Childress, - -	"	–	15	
Richard Childress, jr. -	"	–	15	
Daniel Couch, - -	"	–	15	
Spotswood Childress, -	"	–	9	
Theophilus Chewning, -	"	–	15	
John R. Chisholm, - -	"	–	15	
Nathaniel W. Dandridge, -	"	–	15	
Archibald B. Dandridge, -	"	–	15	
Robert A. Dandridge, -	"	–	15	
Allen Denton, - -	"	–	15	
Thomas Denton, - -	"	–	10	
James Denton, - -	"	–	12	
Richard S. Duke, - -	"	–	12	
Elisha Ellis, - -	"	–	12	
James Glenn, - -	"	–	15	
John Glenn, jr. - -	"	–	15	
William Glenn, - -	"	–	15	
John Gentry, - -	"	–	12	
Archibald Glenn, - -	"	–	15	
Chapman Gordon, - -	"	–	15	
Thomas Hunnicutt, - -	"	–	15	
Edward Hatton, - -	"	–	15	
Richard Johnson, - -	"	–	15	
John B. Jones, - -	"	–	15	
Miles B. Locknane, - -	"	–	15	
Overton Mallory, - -	"	–	15	
Thilman Mallory, - -	"	–	15	
William Moseley, - -	"	–	15	
David Mallory, - -	"	–	15	

NAMES.	RANK.	TIME OF SERVICE.		REMARKS.
		Months.	Days.	
Richard Morris, - -	Private,	–	15	
Daniel Mitchell, - -	"	–	15	
John Nuchols, - -	"	–	15	
William Nuchols, - -	"	–	15	
Nathaniel Nuchols, - -	"	–	15	
Reuben Nuchols, - -	"	–	15	
Robert Pulliam, sr. - -		–	15	
Richard Philips, - -	"	–	15	
Robert J. Pulliam, - -	"	–	15	
Samuel Pulliam, - -	"	–	15	
George S. Pulliam, - -	"	–	15	
Joseph Perkins, - -	"	–	15	
Thomas Pope, - -	"	–	15	
Thomas Richardson, - -	"	–	6	
Tolevar Ragland, - -	"	–	6	
William Royster, - -	"	–	15	
George Shields, - -	"	–	15	
William Shoemaker, -	"	–	15	
Miles Taylor, - -	"	–	15	
Edward Taylor, - -	"	–	15	
John Taylor, - -	"	–	15	
James Underwood, - -	"	–	12	
John Underwood, - -	"	–	12	
Shadrack Vaughan, - -	"	–	15	
Benjamin Vaughan, - -	"	–		
William Williams, - -	"	–	15	
Isham R. Woodson, - -	"	–	15	
William Winston, - -	"	–	2	

MUSTER ROLL

Of Captain Joseph F. Price's Company, of the Seventy-fourth Regiment, Virginia Militia, commanded by Colonel William Trueheart, called into the Service of the United States, from 28th to 29th June, and from 1st to 2nd July, in the year 1813.

NAMES.	RANK.	TIME OF SERVICE.		REMARKS.
		Months.	Days.	
Joseph F. Price,	Captain,	–	14	
William Day,	Lieutenant,	–	14	
Francis Blunt,	Ensign,	–	14	
John Goodwin,	Sergeant,	–	14	
John Chesterman,	"	–	14	
Edward Valentine,	"	–	14	
William D. Winston,	"	–	10	
Walker Taylor,	"	–	4	
Henry Arnall, sr.	Private,	–	14	
Henry Arnall, jr.	"	–	10	
Charles D. Alvis,	"	–	14	
Len. P. Anderson,	"	–	14	
Edmund M. Anderson,	"	–	14	
Richard Arnall,	"	–	14	
Lemuel Alvis,	"	–	14	
Thomas Austin,	"	–	10	
Joseph Arnall,	"	–	14	
Davis Arnall,	"	–	14	
Robert Alvis,	"	–	14	
John Blunt,	"	–	14	
Lewis Berkley,	"	–	14	
Thomas Bowles,	"	–	14	
Samuel Busick,	"	–	14	
William Byars,	"	–	14	
Michael B. Blankenbiker,	"	–	14	
Isaac Butler,	"	–	14	
James Baber,	"	–	14	
Joseph Blunt,	"	–	10	
Nelson Brooks,	"	–	10	
Thomas B. Cosby,	"	–	14	
William Dabney,	"		14	
John Darracott,	"	–	14	
Thomas Doswell,	"	–	14	
Abram W. Davis,	"	–	14	
Walter C. Day,	"	–	14	
Miles C. Eggleston,	"	–	14	
George Eggleston,	"	–	10	
James Fortson,	"	–	14	
John Grubbs,	"	–	14	
Samuel Grantland,	"	–	14	
Richard Hope,	"	–	14	
William O. Harris,	"	–	14	
William Harris,	"	–	10	
Epaphroditus Howle,	"	–	14	
Winfield Harris,	"	–	14	
Richard B. Hendrick,	"	–	14	
William Hope,	"	–	14	

****

NAMES.	RANK.	TIME OF SERVICE.		REMARKS.
		Months.	Days.	
William Haines, - -	Private,	–	10	
David Hackney, - -	"	–	10	
John Haley, - -	"	–	10	
Winston M. Hicks, - -	"	–	10	
Johnson Jones, - -	"	–	14	
Richard C. B. Jones, - -	"	–	14	
John Jones, jr. - -	"	–	14	
Edward W. Kimbrough, -	"	–	14	
James Lowry, - -	"	–	14	
Jasper Lane, - -	"	–	11	
Solomon Lowry, - -	"	–	14	
Samuel Lowry, - -	"	–	14	
Claiborne Lowry, - -	"	–	14	
William Lumay, - -	"	–	14	
Timothy P. R. Lester, -	"	–	14	
William Long, - -	"	–	10	
William Lambert, - -	"	–	4	
Claiborne Mallory, - -	"	–	10	
William Mallory, - -	"	–	14	
William Mallory, jr. - -	"	–	14	
Turner Mallory, - -	"	–	14	
Fleming Mallory, - -	"	–	14	
Stephen Mallory, - -	"	–	14	
James May, - -	"	–	14	
James M. Morriss, - -	"	–	10	
Pleasant Mathiss, - -	"	–	14	
William Norvell, - -	"	–	14	
Thomas W. Norvell, - -	"	–	14	
Mordecai Page, - -	"	–	14	
John Patterson, - -	"	–	14	
Samuel Patterson, - -	"	–	14	
Joseph Patterson, - -	"	–	14	
Edmund Patterson, - -	"	–	10	
William Pearson, - -	"	–	14	
Plummer Potter, - -	"	–	14	
Thomas R. Rootes, - -	"	–	14	
Archibald Richardson, - -	"	–	14	
Landon Richardson, - -	"	–	14	
Nathaniel Stephens, - -	"	–	14	
Julius Stephens, - -	"	–	4	
John Seddons, - -	"	–	14	
Thomas Southward, - -	"	–	14	
Simeon Souther, - -	"	–	14	
William Sheppard, - -	"	–	14	
John Southward, - -	"	–	14	
William Shirley, - -	"	–	14	
Pleasant Terrell, - -	"	–	14	
Anthony Thornton, - -	"	–	14	
William D. Taylor, - -	"	–	10	
Armistead Thornton, - -	"	–	14	
John D. Thilman, - -	"	–	14	
Thomas Trevilian, - -	"	–	14	
Walker Taylor, - -	"	–	10	
William Terrell, - -	"	–	14	
Meredith Thacker, - -	"	–	10	
George Valentine, - -	"			
William C. Williams, - -	"	–	14	
Samuel Williams, - -	"	–	14	
James Winston, - -	"	–	14	
Phil. B. Winston, - -	"	–	14	
John Williams, jr. - -	"	–	14	
Thomas Yarbrough, - -	"	–	10	
Jesse Yarbrough, - -	"	–	14	
Elisha Yarbrough, - -	"	–	14	

MUSTER ROLL

Of Captain Charles Thompson, jr.'s Company, from the Seventy-fourth Regiment, Virginia Militia, commanded by Colonel William Trueheart, in the Service of the United States, from 20th to 29th March, from 28th to 29th June, and from 1st to 2d July, in the year 1813.

NAMES.	RANK.	TIME OF SERVICE.		REMARKS.
		Months.	Days.	
Charles Thompson, jr.	Captain,	–	14	
Edmund Higgason,	Lieutenant,	–	14	
Henry H. Jones,	Ensign,	–	14	
Michael R. Jones,	Sergeant,	–	14	
John Higgason,	"	–	14	
George S. Netherland,	"	–	14	
Frederick Shoemaker,	"	–	14	
William Callis,	Private,	–	14	
William Corker,	"	–	14	
Richard Callis,	"	–	14	
Daniel Corker,	"	–	2	
William S. Dandridge,	"	–	2	
Gideon Hanes,	"	–	14	
Martin Hall,	"	–	14	
Pleasant Hanes,	"	–	14	
Garland Higgison,	"	–	14	
Richard Higgason,	"	–	14	
Christopher Hanes,	"	–	14	
Samuel R. Jones,	"	–	14	
William Mills,	"	–	14	
Wade Mills,	"	–	14	
Jackson Mills,	"	–	14	
Fleming Puryear,	"	–	14	
David Sims, jr.	"	–	14	
William Stanley,	"	–	14	
Thomas Swift,	"	–	14	
Chapman Stuard,	"	–	14	
Richmond Terrell,	"	–	14	
William A. Thompson,	"	–	14	
Thomas W. Thacker,	"	–	14	
William Walton, jr.	"	–	14	
Joseph Watson,	"	–	14	

PAY ROLL

Of Captain Hudson M. Wingfield's Company, of the Seventy-fourth Regiment of Virginia Militia, Second Battalion, of the Detachment at Camp Holly, commanded by Col. John H. Cocke, from the 27th June to 26th July 1813.

NAMES.	RANK.	Time of Service.		REMARKS.
		Months.	Days.	
Hudson M. Wingfield, -	Captain,	1		
William Cocke, - -	Lieutenant,	1		
Henry A. Timberlake, -	Ensign,	1		
William Timberlake, - -	1st Sergeant,	1		
James P. Ragland, - -	2d "	1		
Edmund Tyler, - -	3d "	1		
William Turner, - -	4th "	1		
Jno. B. Timberlake, - -	1st Corporal,	1		
Thomas Hix, - -	2d "	1		
Ben. A. Timberlake, - -	3d "	1		
Thomas Walker, - -	4th "	1		
Thomas Starke, - -	Fifer,	1		
Caleb B. Walker, - -	Drummer,	1		
Frederick Bowe, - -	Private,	1		
Absalom Browning, - -	"	1		
Jehu Browning, - -	"	1		
George Cleveland, - -	"	1		
Thomas Cross, - -	"	1		
Alex'r Chisholm, - -	"	1		
William Ford, - -	"	1		
Gilly Ford, - -	"	1		
Thomas Hobson, - -	"	1		
Claiborne Jennings, - -	"	1		
Absalom Jones, - -	"	1		
Thomas Kersey, - -	"	1		
John King, jr. - -	"	1		
Thos. W. Norvell, - -	"	1		
Elijah Priddy, - -	"	1		
Jno. P. Starke, - -	"	1		
Laney Timberlake, - -	"	1		
James Tyler, - -	"	1		
Skelton Tyler, - -	"	1		
Elisha White, - -	"	1		
Thomas Wingfield, - -	"	1		
Joseph Wingfield, - -	"	1		

MUSTER ROLL

Of Captain Hudson M. Wingfield's Company, of the Seventy-fourth Regiment, Virginia Militia, in the Service of the United States, from 20th to 29th March, 1813.

NAMES.	RANK.	TIME OF SERVICE.		REMARKS.
		Months.	Days.	
Hudson M. Wingfield,	Captain,	–	10	
William Priddy,	Lieutenant,	–	4	
William Cock,	"	–	1	
Henry A. Timberlake,	Ensign,	–	1	
William Timberlake,	Sergeant,	–	10	
Francis Starke,	"	–	10	
Elisha Jones,	"	–	10	
Frederick Bowe,	Private,	–	10	
Absalom Browning,	"	–	10	
Jehu Browning,	"	–	10	
John C. Brocke,	"	–	10	
Thomas Cross,	"	–	10	
William Cocke,	"	–	10	
Hector Davis,	"	–	10	
William Ford,	"	–	10	
Robert Hicks,	"	–	10	
Thomas Hicks,	"	–	10	
Thomas Hobson,	"	–	10	
Thomas Kersey,	"	–	10	
John King, jr.	"	–	10	
James L. Littlepage,	"	–	4	
Elijah Priddy,	"	–	10	
James P. Ragland,	"	–	10	
John P. Starke,	"	–	10	
Henry A. Timberlake,	"	–	9	
Benj'n A. Timberlake,	"	–	9	
William Turner,	"	–	9	
Thomas Walker,	"	–	9	
Thomas Wingfield,	"	–	9	
Joseph Wingfield,	"	–	9	
John Wingfield,	"	–	9	
Benjamin Wingfield,	"	–	9	

MUSTER ROLL

Of the Field and Staff Officers of the Eighty-third Regiment, Virginia Militia, in the County of Dinwiddie, commanded by Lieutenant Colonel James Scott, in the Service of the United States from 1st to 6th July in the year 1813.

NAMES.	RANK.	TIME OF SERVICE.		REMARKS.
		Months.	Days.	
James Scott,	Lieut. Col.	–	6	
Armstead Burwell,	Major,	–	6	
William Wynne,	"	–	6	
Henry Young,	Adjutant,	–	6	
Tingnal Jones,	Surgeon,	–	6	
John Manlove,	"	–	6	
John C. Pegram,	Surg. Mate,	–	6	
John C. Boisseau,	Pay Master,	–	6	
Thomas Thweatt,	Qr. Master,	–	6	
Herbert Gregory,	Qr. Serg't,	–	6	
Joseph Sturdivant,	Serg't Major,	–	6	
Calvin Hine,	Fife Major,	–	6	

MUSTER ROLL

Of Captain Thomas Bevill's Company of Virginia Militia, in the Eighty-third Regiment, Dinwiddie County, under the command of Lieutenant Colonel James Scott, in the Service from the 1st to the 6th July, 1813.

NAMES.	RANK.	TIME OF SERVICE.		REMARKS.
		Months.	Days.	
Thomas Bevill,	Captain,	–	6	
John Smith,	Lieutenant,	–	6	
Arch'd J. Bevill,	Ensign,	–	6	
William Malone,	Sergeant,	–	6	
John Malone,	"	–	6	
Williamson Knight,	"	–	6	
David Harrison,	"	–	6	
John Goodwin,	Corporal,	–	6	
George R. Watts,	"	–	6	
John C. Harman,	"	–	6	
Daniel Harman,	"	–	6	
Lewis Brown,	Drummer,	–	6	
Mason Harwell,	Fifer,	–	6	
Green Jackson,	Private,	–	6	
Thomas Pilkington,	"	–	6	
Edward Perkins,	"	–	6	
James Dugger,	"	–	6	
Christopher Daniel,	"	–	6	
Francis Daniel,	"	–	6	
Joshua Perkins,	"	–	6	
William Noble,	"	–	6	
Harper Malone,	"	–	6	
Johnson Suit,	"	–	6	
Berryman Chappell,	"	–	6	
Briggs Chappell,	"	–	6	
John Abernathy,	"	–	6	
Thomas Goodrich,	"	–	6	
Henry Heath,	"	–	6	
Benjamin Malone,	"	–	6	
Henry Tucker,	"	–	6	
William Sturdivant,	"	–	6	
Robert Malone,	"	–	6	
Benjamin H. Copeland,	"	–	6	
John Stanton,	"	–	6	
Staunton Butler,	"	–	6	
James Binford,	"	–	6	
Micajah Peebles,	"	–	6	
Howell Hines,	"	–	6	
Bernard M. Perkins,	"	–	6	
David Smith,	"	–	6	
Robert Davis,	"	–	6	
Burwell Brown,	"	–	6	
Ethiel Crowder,	"	–	6	
Augustin Suit,	"	–	6	
John H. Hall,	"	–	6	
Noah Brown,	"	–	6	Sub. for Jesse Spiers.
Charles B. Rives,	"	–	6	
Foster Tucker,	"	–	6	
James Wilbourne,	"	–	6	
William P. Smith,	Private,	–	6	
William Kerkland,	"	–	6	
Roger Daniel,	"	–	6	
Charles Mingge,	"	–	6	
John Mingge,	"	–	6	
David Chappell,	"	–	6	
James Hawkes,	"	–	6	
William C. Tucker,	"	–	6	
Elijah Scoggin,	"	–	6	
Benjamin Heath,	"	–	6	

MUSTER ROLL

Of Captain Irby Brown's Company of Virginia Militia, from the Eighty-third Regiment, commanded by Lieutenant Colonel James Scott, in the Service from the 1st to the 6th of July, 1813.

NAMES.	RANK.	TIME OF SERVICE.		REMARKS.
		Months.	Days.	
Irby Brown, - -	Captain,	–	6	
Burwell Goodwyn, - -	Lieutenant,	–	6	
Balaam Wells, - -	Ensign,	–	6	
Joseph Sturdevant, - -	Sergeant,	–	6	
Edward Young, - -	"	–	6	
Jessee Goodwin, - -	"	–	6	
Green Rivers, - -	"	–	6	
William J. Aldridge, -	Corporal,	–	6	
Barney Hawkins, - -	"	–	6	
Claiborne Wells, - -	"	–	6	
Thomas Rose, - -	"	–	6	
Philip Hawkins, - -	Private,	–	6	
John Hawks, - -	"	–	6	
Lewis Hawkins, - -	"	–	6	
Francis Gent, - -	"	–	6	
Peter Lewis, - -	"	–	6	
Joshua Young, - -	"	–	6	
Josiah Pebles, - -	"	–	6	
Abner T. Meanley, -	"	–	6	
Grief Hardaway, - -	"	–	6	
Daniel Hawkins, - -	"	–	6	
Berry Hawkins, - -	"	–	6	
Arms'd Hawkins, - -	"	–	6	
Markham Hardaway, -	"	–	6	
Mason Wells, - -	"	–	6	
Henry Jackson, - -	"	–	6	
William Davis, - -	"	–	6	
David Meanley, - -	"	–	6	
William Hawkins, - -	"	–	6	
William Waller, - -	"	–	6	
John Vaughan, - -	"	–	6	
Thomas G. Hardaway, -	"	–	6	
Norman Crawford, - -	"	–	6	
James Kidd, - -	"	–	6	
Robert Hunnicutt, - -	"	–	6	
William Thrift, - -	"	–	6	
Fras. Walthall, - -	"	–	6	
Green Hawkins, - -	"	–	6	
James Hunnicutt, - -	"	–	6	
Thomas Scott, - -	"	–	6	
William Moody, - -	"	–	6	
Thomas Coleman, - -	"	–	6	
Robert Hawkins, - -	"	–	6	
Francis Lewis, - -	"	–	6	
Lemuel Stanton, - -	"	–	6	
Thomas Firth, - -	"	–	6	
Robert Sturdivant, - -	"	–	6	

PAY ROLL

Of Captain William H. Cousins' Company, of the Eighty-third and First Regiments, in Service from the 1st to the 6th of July 1813, *and from the 28th of August to the 30th of November* 1814.

NAMES.	RANK.	Time of Service. Months.	Days.	REMARKS.
William H. Cousins,	Captain,	3	10	
William E. Goode,	Ensign,	1	11	
William Goode,	Lieutenant,	3	10	
Henry D. Hicks,	"	1		
Patrick Roney,	Ensign,	3	5	
John Reese,	Sergeant,	3	5	
William Neal,	"	3	5	
William Perry,	"	1	7	
Ira E. Smith,	"	3	5	
William P. Smith,	"	3	5	
William Kirkland,	"	3	5	
William Grigg,	Corporal,	3	10	
John Smith,	"	3	10	
George Smith,	"	3	10	
Edward Traylor,	"	3	5	
John Bowers,	Fifer,	3	5	
Baker Williams,	Drummer,	3	5	
Solomon Atkinson,	Private,	3	5	
John Abernathy,	"	3	5	
Burwell G. Andrews,	"	3	5	
Joshua Burnett,	"	3	10	
Henry Barnes,	"	3	5	
Robert Brister,	"	3	5	
Richard Bragg,	"	3	5	
Tilman Butler,	"	3	5	
Augustine B. Coleman,	"	3	5	
Braxton Coleman,	"	3	5	
Nathaniel Crowder,	"	3	10	
Thomas Conwell,	"	3	10	
Williamson Coleman,	"	3	6	
Benjamin Clardy,	"	3	5	
Charles Clay,	"	3	5	
Charner Crowder,	"	3	5	
Jacob Crowder,	"	3	5	
John Crowder,	"	2	9	
Lamma Clarke,	"	3	5	
Simon Crowder,	"	3	5	
William Clay,	"	3	5	
Braxton Davis,	"	3	5	
Francis Daniel,	"	3	3	
Griffin Demoville,	"	3	5	
Giles Davis,	"	3	5	
Robert Daniel,	"	3	5	
Stephen Davis,	"	3	5	
Daniel E. Elder,	"	3	5	
Daniel C. Elder,	"	3	5	
John Evans,	"	3	5	
Nathaniel Edwards,	"	3	10	
Paschal Eynes,	"	3	10	
Peterson Elder,	"	3	5	
William Fetherstone,	"	3	10	
John Gresham,	"	3	10	
Benjamin George,	"	3	5	
Goodwin George,	"	3	5	

NAMES.	RANK.	Time of Service.		REMARKS.
		Months.	Days.	
Joseph Grigg, - -	Private,	3	5	
Thomas Goodrich, - -	"	3	5	
Berryman Hawkins, - -	"	3	5	
Bartly Hawkins, - -	"	3	5	
William H. T. Harper, - -	"	3	5	
William Hughs, - -	"	3	5	
Joseph Hall, - -	"	2	17	
Green Hawkins, - -	"	3	5	
Pleasant Hobbs, - -	"	3	5	
William Johnson, - -	"	3	8	
Coleman Jackson, - -	"	3	5	
Cary Jones, - -	"	3	5	
David Jackson, - -	"	3	5	
John H. Jeter, - -	"	3	5	
Phillips Johnson, - -	"	3	5	
Thomas Kidd, - -	"	3	10	
Theodorick Lamb, - -	"	3	10	
James Leonard, - -	"	3	5	
William Leonard, - -	"	3	5	
Thomas Locke, - -	"	3	5	
Wyatt Leigh, - -	"	3	5	
William Lewis, - -	"	2	5	
Abraham Mayes, - -	"	3	5	
Jeremiah Merrymoon, - -	"	3	5	
Stephen McLauclin, - -	"	3	5	
Anthony North, - -	"	3	5	
Henry Nunnally, - -	"	3	5	
Jeremiah Nunnally, - -	"	3	5	
Thomas Powell, - -	"	3	5	
Bernard M. Perkins, - -	"	3	5	
Robert Philips, - -	"	3	5	
Isham Reese, - -	"	3	5	
John Robertson, - -	"	3	5	
Nicholas Roney, - -	"	3	3	
Benjamin Snead, - -	"	3	5	
Francis E. Spain, - -	"	3	5	
Grief Slaughter, - -	"	3	5	
John Stow, - -	"	3	5	
Joseph Still, - -	"	3	5	
Johnson Suit, - -	"	3	5	
Miles Smith, - -	"	3	5	
David Thomas, - -	"	3	10	
John T. Tucker, - -	"	3	10	
Alexander Wills, - -	"	3	5	
Isham Wells, - -	"	3	5	
Thomas Wells, - -	"	3	5	
William Worsham, - -	"	3	5	
William G. Waller, - -	"	3	5	
David White, - -	"	3	5	
Elliott Young, - -	"	3	5	

Captain William H. Cousins' Company—Eighty-third Regiment.

NAMES.	RANK.	TIME OF SERVICE.		REMARKS.
		Months.	Days.	
Brooke Duval, - -	Sergeant,	–	5	
Shadrack Alfriend, - -	"	–	5	
John F. Evans, - -	"	–	5	
John Murrell, - -	Corporal,	–	5	
Edward Goode, - -	"	–	5	
Francis Reese, - -	"	–	5	
Alexander G. Hall, - -	Drummer,	–	5	
William Elder, - -	Private,	–	11	
Howell Featherstone, - -	"	–	5	
William Hunnicutt, - -	"	–	5	
Peterson Harper, - -	"	–	5	
Amas S. Johnson, - -	"	–	24	
Right King, - -	"	–	–	Deserted.
Peter Lamb, - -	"	–	5	
Joseph Nunnally, - -	"	–	–	Deserted.
Clement Old, - -	"	–	5	
Patrick-H. Poythress, - -	"	–	5	
Peter Poythress, - -	"	–	5	
John Spain, - -	"	–	5	
John Williams, - -	"	–	5	
Robert West, - -	"	–	5	
Pleasant Wells, - -	"	–	27	Enlisted in U. S. Army.

(For rest of this company, see publication of Pay Rolls.)

MUSTER ROLL

Of Captain John Fraser's Company, from the Eighty-third Regiment, Virginia Militia, commanded by Lieutenant Colonel James Scott, in the Service from the 1st to the 6th July, 1813.

NAMES.	RANK.	TIME OF SERVICE.		REMARKS.
		Months.	Days.	
John Fraser, - -	Captain,	–	6	
James G. Young, - -	Lieutenant,	–	6	
Allen Thweatt, - -	Ensign,	–	6	
Lewis Meredith, - -	Sergeant,	–	6	
Thomas Lewis, - -	"	–	6	
William Reames, - -	"	–	6	
Abraham Spain, - -	"	–	6	
Peter M. Ledbetter, - -	Corporal,	–	6	
Francis Dabney, - -	"	–	6	
David Pilkington, - -	"	–	6	
Thomas Rollins, - -	"	–	6	
Henry Chandler, - -	Private,	–	6	
John Gee, - - -	"	–	6	
John Crowder, - -	"	–	6	
Edmond Grigg, - -	"	–	6	
William Chandler, - -	"	–	6	
William A. Meredith, -	"	–	6	
Robert Gee, - -	"	–	6	
Peter Elder, - -	"	–	6	
Samuel S. Wells, - -	"	–	6	
William Harper, - -	"	–	6	
Joseph B. Cornwall, -	"	–	6	
Wesley Williamson, -	"	–	6	
Richard Allen, - -	"	–	6	
John Thweat, - -	"	–	6	
Coleman Wells, - -	"	–	6	
William Wells, - -	"	–	6	
Sterling Overbey, - -	"	–	6	
Vines C. Williams, - -	"	–	6	
John Coleman, - -	"	–	6	
Daniel Elder, - -	"	–	6	
Buckner Kirkland, - -	"	–	6	
William Cox, - -	"	–	6	
Gardner Ledbetter, - -	"	–	6	
Williams Reames, sen. -	"	–	6	
John Robertson, - -	"	–	6	
Sandf'd Coleman, - -	"	–	6	
Hamilton Williamson, -	"	–	6	
Thomas Rivers, - -	"	–	6	
Gabriel Baughan, - -	"	–	6	
William Ledbetter, - -	"	–	6	
William Lewis, - -	"	–	6	
Grief Slaughter, - -	"	–	6	
Peter Vaughan, - -	"	–	6	
Edward Clay, - -	"	–	6	
John Still, - -	"	–	6	
Geo. W. Still, - -	"	–	–	On duty at Norfolk.
Jeremiah Browder, - -	"	–	–	" "
Jeremiah Still, - -	Private,	–	–	On duty at Norfolk.
Dr. John Robertson, -	"	–	–	" "
James Wallace, - -	"	–	–	" "
William McConnell, -	"	–	–	" "
John Clemonds, - -	"	–	–	" "
Thomas Grant, - -	"	–	–	" "

MUSTER ROLL

Of Captain William Ross' Company, from the Eighty-third Regiment, Virginia Militia, commanded by Lieutenant Colonel James Scott, in the Service of the United States, from the 1st to the 5th July, 1813, and from 28th August to 13th September 1814.

NAMES.	RANK.	TIME OF SERVICE.		REMARKS.
		Months.	Days.	
William Ross,	Captain,	–	22	
Edward Scott,	Lieutenant,	–	22	
Francis Scott,	"	–	22	
Thomas Rogers,	Cornet,	–	22	
Hamlin Hargrave,	Sergeant,	–	5	
Alex'r E. Bolling,	"	–	5	
Thomas A. Oliver,	"	–	22	
John C. Hambleton,	"	–	22	
Benjamin Pegram,	"	–	15	Transferred to Captain Pryor's troop 10th September.
Joel Manlove,	"	–	15	Transferred to Captain Pryor's troop 10th September.
William B. Clemans,	Corporal,	–	5	
Andrew Waugh,	"	–	5	
William E. Booth,	"	–	5	
Hartwell H. Hobbs,	"	–	17	
Hardaway T. Rives,	"	–	17	
Thomas Rose,	"	–	17	
David Westmoreland,	"	–	15	Transferred to Captain Pryor's comp'y 10th September.
John Abernathy,	Private,	–	20	Transferred to Captain Pryor's comp'y 10th September.
John Atkerson,	"	–	17	
Robert Bolling,	"	–	22	
John Bolling,	"	–	17	
Peterson Burge,	"	–	17	
Samuel P. Bolling,	"	–	17	
Alex'r E. Bolling,	"	–	15	Transferred to Captain Pryor's comp'y 10th September.
William E. Boothe,	"	–	15	Transferred to Captain Pryor's comp'y 10th September.
James Boothe,	"	–	5	
Robert Chappell, jr.	"	–	17	Substitute for John Chappell.
Benjamin H. Copeland,	"	–	6	App'ted surgeon's mate 2d September.
John Chappell,	"	–	5	
John Dabney,	"	–	22	
Griffin Demovill,	"	–	5	
Lucas Elder,	"	–	5	
John Field,	"	–	1	Appointed hospital surgeon's mate 23d August.

****

NAMES.	RANK.	TIME OF SERVICE.		REMARKS.
		Months.	Days.	
John Grubbs, - -	Private,	–	15	Substitute for Sterling Woodward, and transferred to Captain Pryor's troop.
Merewether S. Gilliam, -	"	–	22	
Benjamin Harris, - -	"	–	22	
Hartwell Hitchcock, - -	"	–	20	Transferred to Captain Pryor's troop on 10th Sept.
Burwell Hitchcock, - -	"	–	20	" " "
Alexander G. Hall, - -	"	–	15	" " "
Hartwell H. Hobbs, - -	"	–	5	
Benjamin Jackson, - -	"	–	–	Never joined.
Littleberry Jackson, - -	"	–	5	
John Lantroop, - -	"	–	15	Transferred to Captain Pryor's troop.
Peter M. Leadbetter, - -	"	–	17	" " "
Gustavus A. Muir, - -	"	–	17	
Isaac Oliver, - -	"	–	22	
William Pryor, - -	"	–	15	Transferred to Pryor's troop, 10th Sept.
Peter Pryde, - -	"	–	15	" " "
Nicholas Roney, - -	"	–	5	
Cincinatus Stith, - -	"	–	6	Appointed wagon master.
Peter Scott, - -	"	–	17	
William Stepperdson, -	"	–	20	Transferred to Captain Pryor's troop.
Anthony W. Smith, - -	"	–	15	" " "
Cary Wilkerson, - -	"	–	22	
Isaac Williamson, - -	"	–	22	
Charles Williamson, - -	"	–	17	
Vines C. Williamson, -	"	–	17	
Alexander Wells, - -	"	–	17	Substitute for Thomas Firth.
Sterling Woodward, - -	"	–	5	
John Watkins, - -	"	–	5	

MUSTER ROLL

Of Captain James W. Smith's Company, (commanded by Lieut. Pryor C. Shepperson,) from the Eighty-third Regiment, in the County of Dinwiddie, called into actual Service under the general orders of the 30th June, 1813, from 1st to 6th July, in the same year.

NAMES.	RANK.	TIME OF SERVICE.		REMARKS.
		Months.	Days.	
James W. Smith,	Captain,	–	6	
Pryor C. Shepperson,	Lieutenant,	–	6	
Jesse Abernathy,	Ensign,	–	6	
John H. Davis,	Sergeant,	–	6	
Manson Harwell,	"	–	6	
Abner Adams,	"	–	6	
John B. Brodnax,	"	–	6	
Jesse Pearce,	Corporal,	–	6	
John Bolling,	"	–	6	
Miles King,	"	–	6	
David Westmoreland,	"	–	6	
Frederica Adams,	Private,	–	6	
John Adams,	"	–	6	
William Barrow,	"	–	6	
Freeman W. Brodnax,	"	–	6	
William H. Brodnax,	"	–	6	
Burwell Cross,	"	–	6	
Richard C. Claiborne,	"	–	6	
Joseph E. Davis,	"	–	6	
David Draper,	"	–	6	
Richard Evans,	"	–	6	
John Goode,	"	–	6	
William Holloway,	"	–	6	
Robert Harwell,	"	–	6	
William Jackson,	"	–	6	
Carey Jones,	"	–	6	
Hamlin Lewis,	"	–	6	
James Lunceford,	"	–	6	
Joseph Lunceford,	"	–	6	
Christopher Manlove,	"	–	6	
Thomas B. Manlove,	"	–	6	
William Mason,	"	–	6	
Robert Manlove,	"	–	6	
Thomas Parsons,	"	–	6	
Anderson Parrish,	"	–	6	
Christopher Shepperson,	"	–	6	
John F. Sherman,	"	–	6	
John M. Vaughan,	"	–	6	
William Wells,	"	–	6	
Daniel Wall,	"	–	6	
Burwell Williams,	"	–	6	
David W. Withers,	"	–	6	
Thomas Wells,	"	–	6	
Joseph Wells,	"	–	6	
James Wilson,	"	–	6	
Hartwell Westmoreland,	"	–	6	
Thomas Wilson,	"	–	6	

****

MUSTER ROLL

Of Captain John T. Sydnor's Company of the Eighty-third Regiment, Virginia Militia, in the County of Dinwiddie, called into actual Service under the general orders of the 30th June, 1813, from 1st to 6th July in the year 1813.

NAMES.	RANK.	TIME OF SERVICE. Months.	Days.	REMARKS.
John T. Sydnor, - -	Captain,	–	6	
Isaac Dancy, - -	Lieutenant,	–	6.	
Edward H. Jones, - -	Ensign,	–	6	
Joel Stowe, - -	Sergeant,	–	6	
Enoch Rather, - -	"	–	6	
John Candle, sen. - -	"	–	6	
Arch'd Candle, - -	"	–	6	
William Parhan, - -	Corporal,	–	6	
Daniel Wells, - -	"	–	6	
Daniel Browder, - -	"	–	6	
Joshua Young, - -	"	–	6	
Epes Allen, - -	Private,	–	6	
Rich'd Browder, - -	"	–	6	
Tilman Butler, - -	"	–	6	
Geo. Browder, - -	"	–	6	
Thos. Browder, - -	"	–	6	
Henry Barnes, - -	"	–	6	
Edward Birchett, - -	"	–	6	
John Coleman, - -	"	–	6	
Charner Crowder, - -	"	–	6	
Jacob Crowder, - -	"	–	6	
John G. Dyson, - -	"	–	6	
Isham Eppes, - -	"	–	6	
Elisha Eanes, - -	"	–	6	
Wm. Elder, - -	"	–	6	
Rice Eanes, - -	"	–	6	
Wm. French, - -	"	–	6	
John Grant, - -	"	–	6	
Rich'd Goode, - -	"	–	6	
Everard Green, - -	"	–	6	
Wm. Hambleton, - -	"	–	6	
John Hughes, - -	"	–	6	
Green Moss, - -	"	–	6	
Abel T. Puckett, - -	"	–	6	
John Pandle, jr. - -	"	–	6	
Branch Perkinson, - -	"	–	6	
Jesse Reames, - -	"	–	6	
Wm. Slaughter, - -	"	–	6	
Fendal T. Sutherland, -	"	–	6	
Wm. Sandiford, - -	"	–	6	
Joshua Spain, - -	"	–	6	
Wm. Spain, - -	"	–	6	
Jno. B. Spain, - -	"	–	6	
Thompson Stewart, -	"	–	6	
Joel Wells, - -	"	–	6	
James Williams, - -	"	–	6	
Herbert Williams, - -	"	–	6	
John A. Waugh, - -	Private,	–	6	
James Young, - -	"	–	6	
Elliott Young, - -	"	–	6	
John Young, jr. - -	"	–	6	

****

MUSTER ROLL

Of Captain William B. Thompson's Company, of the Eighty-third Regiment, Virginia Militia, in the County of Dinwiddie, called into actual Service under the general orders of the 30*th June*, 1813, *from the* 1*st to the* 6*th July, in the same year.*

NAMES.	RANK.	TIME OF SERVICE.		REMARKS.
		Months.	Days.	
William B. Thompson, -	Captain,	–	6	
Stith Thompson, - -	Lieutenant,	–	6	
Anderson Harper, - -	Ensign,	–	6	
Charles W. Bristow, -	Sergeant,	–	6	
John Wainwright, - -	"	–	6	
Daniel Connolly, - -	"	–	6	
Peter Davis, - -	"	–	6	
Benjamin Rives, - -	Corporal,	–	6	
Samma Clark, - -	"	–	6	
Samuel H. Kirkes, - -	"	–	6	
Charles S. Tucker, - -	"	–	6	
John Atkinson, - -	Private,	–	6	
Daniel Algood, - -	"			
William Baily, - -	"	–	6	
Robert C. Booth, - -	"	–	6	
Laban Beames, - -	"			
William Booth, - -	"	–	6	
John Crawford, - -	"	–	6	
John B. Clarke, - -	"	–	–	On duty at Norfolk.
William Davis, - -	"	–	6	
Daniel E. Elder, - -	"	–	6	
John Evans, - -	"	–	6	
Petersen Elder, - -	"	–	6	
Alexander Fraser, - -	"	–	6	
William Ferguson, - -	"	–	6	
Thomas Gee, - -	"	–	–	" "
John Grubbs, - -	"	–	6	
William Grigg, - -	"			
Bartholomew Ingram, -	"			
Richard K. Jones, - -	"	–	6	
T. John Jott, - -	"	–	6	
Nelson Jones, - -	"	–	6	
William Locke, - -	"	–	6	
Thomas Locke, - -	"	–	6	
William Malone, - -	"	–	–	" "
William Mason, - -	"	–	6	
Gustavus A. Muir, - -	"	–	6	
Daniel Malone, - -	"	–	6	
Anthony North, - -	"	–	6	
Hardaway T. Rives, -	"	–	6	
James Sandiford, - -	"	–	6	
William N. Tucker, - -	"	–	6	
Isaac Tucker, - -	"	–	6	Jas. Eiples his sub.
David Tucker, - -	"	–	6	
George Trotter, - -	"	–	6	
Littleberry West, - -	"	–	–	On duty at Norfolk.
Burwell Whitmore, - -	"	–	–	" " "
McKie Wainwright, - -	"	–	6	
Joseph Whitmore, - -	Private,	–	6	
Thomas Whitmore, - -	"	–	6	
Samuel Wainwright, -	"	–	6	
Freeman Wainwright, -	"	–	6	

****

MUSTER ROLL

Of Captain Theodorick Walker's Company, from the Eighty-third Regiment, in the County of Dinwiddie, called into actual Service under the general orders of the 30*th June*, 1813, *from* 1*st July to the* 6*th of the same month, in the year* 1813.

NAMES.	RANK.	TIME OF SERVICE.		REMARKS.
		Months.	Days.	
Theodorick Walker,	Captain,	–	6	
Abraham Mitchell,	Lieutenant,	–	6	
Benj. Roney,	Ensign.	–	6	
Robert Roney,	Sergeant,	–	6	
Wm. G. Nunnely,	"	–	6	
Jno. T. Goodwin,	"	–	6	
Thos. Roney,	"	–	6	
Paschal Tucker,	Corporal,	–	6	
Jas. Stacy,	"	–	6	
Thomas Tucker,	"	–	6	
Pat'k R. Smith,	"	–	6	
Robert Mitchell,	Drummer,	–	6	On duty at Norfolk.
Chas. Mitchell,	Fifer,	–	6	" " "
Chas. Abernathy,	Private,	–	6	
How'd Abernathy,	"	–	6	
William Alfriend,	"	–	6	
Martin Abernathy,	"	–	6	
Harm'n Abernathy,	"	–	6	
Freeman Abernathy,	"	–	6	
Geo. Abernathy,	"	–	6	
Jeremiah Bishop,	"	–	6	
Drury Bishop,	"	–	6	
Robt. Bolling,	"	–	6	Joined the cavalry.
James Bishop, jr.	"	–	6	
John Bainey,	"	–	6	
Robert Curtis,	"	–	6	
Henry Farlow,	"	–	6	
Robt. Greenway,	"	–	6	
Laban Harrison,	"	–	6	
John Hawkins,	"	–	6	
Green B. Hamlet,	"	–	6	
Robt. Harper,	"	–	6	
Hartwell Hartwell,	"	–	6	
Gardner Hankins,	"	–	6	
Joseph H. Jackson,	"	–	6	
William Jackson,	"	–	6	
Richard Jackson,	"	–	6	
Jeremiah Miles,	"	–	6	
Jessee Medling,	"	–	6	
Joseph W. Medling,	"	–	6	
Obadiah Nunnely,	"	–	6	
Charles Nunnely,	"	–	6	
Thomas Nunnely,	"	–	6	
Thos. Parch,	"	–	6	
Cadrick P. Poole,	"	–	6	
Peterson P. Poole,	"	–	6	In the U. S. service.
Stephen P. Poole,	"	–	6	

NAMES.	RANK.	TIME OF SERVICE.		REMARKS.
		Months.	Days.	
Wiley Parsons, - -	Private,	–	6	
James Poarch, - -	"	–	6	
Jeremiah Rowland, - -	"	–	6	
David Thrift, - -	"	–	6	
John Thrift, - -	"	–	6	
Colwell Tolley, - -	"	–	6	
Wm. Wilkinson, - -	"	–	6	
John Wells, - -	"	–	6	
Hubbard Wyatt, - -	"	–	6	Bishop Wyatt his sub.
Charles Young, - -	"	–	6	
Thos. Yarborough, - -	"	–	6	

MUSTER ROLL

Of Captain Samuel Carr's Troop of Cavalry, of the Eighty-eighth Regiment, Virginia Militia, from the County of Albemarle, called into the Service of the United States by the Proclamation of the Governor of Virginia, of the 26th August, 1814, commencing the 29th day of August and ending the 20th day of September, in the year 1814.

NAMES.	RANK.	TIME OF SERVICE.		REMARKS.
		Months.	Days.	
Samuel Carr,	Captain,	–	22	
John H. Craven,	Lieutenant,	–	22	
James Ragland,	"	–	22	
Peter Minor,	Cornet,	–	22	
Pleasant Sandidge,	Q. M. Serg't,	–	22	
John Neilson,	Sergeant,	–	22	
Archbold Buckner,	"	–	22	
Achilles Broadhead,	"	–	22	
Daniel F. Carr,	"	–	22	
John Walker,	Corporal,	–	22	
James Minor,	"	–	22	
John F. Carr,	"	–	22	
William H. Coleman,	"	–	22	
Eli Alexander,	Private,	–	22	
Obadiah Austin,	"	–	22	
John Barksdale,	"	–	22	
Daniel M. Bailey,	"	–	22	
Briscoe G. Baldwin,	"	–	22	
Peter Carr,	"	–	22	
Francis Catterton,	"	–	22	
James Crawford,	"	–	22	
James O. Carr,	"	–	22	
Thompson Crutchfield,	"	–	22	
Davis Dunett,	"	–	22	
Robert Dunett,	"	–	22	
Charles M. Dickerson,	"	–	22	
William Donahue,	"	–	22	
Robert Donlbert,	"	–	22	
William Davis,	"	–	22	
William Digges,	"	–	22	
Richard Duke,	"	–	22	
William F. Garden,	"	–	22	
Francis W. Gilmer,	"	–	22	
Benjamin Gillaspy,	"	–	22	
Pleasant C. German,	"	–	22	
George Gilmer,	"	–	22	
Valentine Head,	"	–	22	
Alsatone Johnson,	"	–	22	
Larkin Kirby,	"	–	22	
William Lindsay,	"	–	22	
John Minor,	"	–	22	
James M. Macon,	"	–	22	
Conway Macon,	"	–	22	
Thomas Miller,	"	–	22	
Thomas W. Nash,	"	–	22	
Charles Penn,	"	–	22	
Harden Quinn,	"	–	22	
William Robertson,	Private,	–	22	
William Smithson,	"	–	22	
Daniel Shackleford,	"	–	22	
Hazlewood Ship,	"	–	22	
John Shiplet,	"	–	22	
Mathew Turner,	"	–	22	
Dubray Terrell,	"	–	22	
Arthur Whitehurst,	"	–	22	
William White,	"	–	22	

PAY ROLL

Of Captain John P. Gray's Company, attached from the Ninety-first and Tenth Regiments, Bedford, to the Second Regiment, at Camp Bottom's Bridge, commanded by General William Chamberlayne, in the Service of the United States, from the 31st August to the 8th December 1814.

NAMES.	RANK.	*Time of Service.*		REMARKS.
		Months.	Days.	
John P. Gray, - -	Captain,	3	25	
William B. Jones, - -	Lieutenant,	3	25	
William Hurt, - -	"	3	25	
William Feazel, - -	Ensign,	3	25	
Thomas Preston, - -	"	3	25	
Andrew B. Read, - -	Ord. Serg't,	3	16	
Rufus Thomas, - -	Q. M. Serg't,	3	25	
Orson Gray, - -	Sergeant,	3	25	
Micajah Turner, - -	"	3	25	
Wm. B. Whitten, - -	"	3	25	
Samuel H. Crenshaw, - -	"	3	25	
Nat. Parker, - -	Corporal,	3	25	
Jonathan Cundiffe, - -	"	3	25	
Joseph D. Stratton, - -	"	3	25	
Thomas Hardy, - -	"	3	25	
Ephraim Fuqua, - -	"	3	25	
Henry Stiff, - -	"	3	25	
George Parker, - -	"	3	25	
Stephen Preston, - -	"	3	25	
Thomas Walker, - -	Drummer,	3	25	
Mark Homan, - -	Fifer,	3	25	
Thomas J. Anderson, - -	Private,	3	25	
Francis Amos, - -	"	3	25	
William Boggs, - -	"	3	25	
John Brown, - -	"	3	25	
Braxton Bailey, - -	"	3	25	
Reuben Boudurant, - -	"	3	25	
Joseph Boyer, - -	"	3	25	
James T. Brown, - -	"	3	25	
Paschal Butler, - -	"	3	25	
Peter Bobbitt, - -	"	3	25	
Griffin Butler, - -	"	3	25	
John R. Brown, - -	"	3	25	
John B. Campbell, - -	"	3	25	
Samuel Clarke, - -	"	3	25	
Thomas Cottrell, - -	"	3	25	
John Coffendaffer, - -	"	3	25	
Henry Campbell, - -	"	3	25	
Thomas Cain, - -	"	3	25	
Stephen Cottrell, - -	"	3	25	
James H. Craig, - -	"	3	25	
Christopher Cundiff, - -	"	3	25	
David Crenshaw, - -	"	3	25	
Tazewell Cobbs, - -	"	3	25	
Thomas Dixon, - -	"	3	25	
Moses Dowdy, - -	"	3	25	
John Dooley, - -	"	3	25	
Thomas Dooley, - -	"	3	16	
Hezekiah Dickinson, - -	"	3	25	
Jesse Freeman, - -	"	3	25	
William Franklin, - -	"	3	25	
Henry W. Franklin, - -	"	3	25	
Henry T. Franklin, - -	"	3	25	
Tarlton Franklin, - -	"	3	25	

****

NAMES.	RANK.	Time of Service.		REMARKS.
		Months.	Days	
John Frederick, - -	Private,	3	25	
Burwell Gibbs, - -	"	3	25	
Thomas Gibbs, - -	"	3	25	
George Gray, - -	"	3	25	
James Gibbs, - -	"	3	25	
Abram Greenwood, - -	"	3	25	
Zachariah Hogan, - -	"	3	25	
Samuel Holt, - -	"	3	25	
William Holloway, - -	"	3	25	
Thomas Holloway, - -	"	3	25	
William Hanks, - -	"	3	25	
Bartholomew Holdren, - -	"	3	25	
Henry Holdren, - -	"	3	25	
Cornelius Holdren, - -	"	3	25	
James Jones, - -	"	3	25	
Ben. Irvin, - -	"	3	25	
William Jones, - -	"	3	25	
Wm. P. Jones, - -	"	3	25	
John Jordan, - -	"	3	25	
William Kerr, - -	"	3	25	
Abram King, - -	"	3	25	
Joseph Lockett, - -	"	3	25	
Richard Lockett, - -	"	3	25	
James Lockett, - -	"	3	25	
Levi Loyd, - -	"	3	25	
John Morrison, - -	"	3	25	
William Marshall, - -	"	3	25	
William Meador, -	"	3	25	
Creed Meador, - -	"	3	25	
Osborne Meador, - -	"	3	25	
Hugh McCraw, - -	"	1	8	Trans'd to Capt. Hurt.
William North, - -	"	3	25	
Caleb Newman, - -	"	1	8	" "
John Owen, - -	"	3	25	
Stephen Phillips, - -	"	3	25	
Westley Phillips, - -	"	3	25	
Edward Powell, - -	"	3	25	
Josiah Powell, - -	"	3	25	
Ezra Parker, - -	"	3	25	
James Ramsay, - -	"	3	25	
Raleigh Rather, - -	"	3	25	
Robert Reese, - -	"	3	25	
Daniel Rather, - -	"	3	25	
John B. Stiff, - -	"	3	25	
Edward Sinkler, - -	"	3	25	
William Sinkler, - -	"	3	25	
Isaac Sinkler, - -	"	3	25	
James Spradlin, - -	"	3	25	
John Spradlin, Sr., - -	"	3	25	
John Spradlin, Jr., - -	"	3	25	
Lott Slack, - -	"	3	25	
John Tyler, - -	"	3	7	
John Tracy, - -	"	1	8	" "
Charles Thomas, - -	"	3	25	
William Taylor, - -	"	3	25	
Nelson Tyler, - -	"	3	25	
Samuel C. Tyler, - -	"	3	25	
Thomas Taylor, - -	"	3	25	
John Taylor, - -	"	3	25	
Greenberry Taylor, - -	"	3	25	
Zachary Tyler, - -	"	3	25	
Isaac Thomas, - -	"	3	25	
Joseph Thompson, - -	"	3	25	
Henry Williamson, - -	"	3	5	
John Watson, - -	"	3	25	

Captain John P. Gray's Company—Ninety-first and One Hundredth Regiments.

NAMES.	RANK.	TIME OF SERVICE.		REMARKS.
		Months.	Days.	
William Calvert, - -	Private,	–	14	
Joseph Fuqua, - -	"	–	14	
William Fuqua, - -	"	–	14	
Wilson Meador, - -	"	3	2	
Jeremiah Meador, - -	"	–	15	
Rowley Reese, - -	"	–	15	

(For the rest of this company, see publication of Pay Rolls.)

MUSTER ROLL

Of Captain John F. Cocke's Company of the One Hundred and Second Regiment Virginia Militia, in the County of Powhatan, called into actual Service under the general orders of the 26th August, from the 28th August to the 16th September, in the year 1814.

NAMES.	RANK.	TIME OF SERVICE.		REMARKS.
		Months.	Days.	
John F. Cocke, - -	Captain,	–	19	
Will. J. Harris, - -	Lieutenant,	–	19	
Charles W. Lewis, - -	"	–	19	
Henry Booker, - -	Cornet,	–	19	
Edmond Saunders, - -	Sergeant,	–	19	
John H. Price, - -	"	–	19	
Thomas Jordan, - -	"	–	19	
William Nunnally, - -	"	–	19	
Isaac N. Cardozo, - -	Corporal,	–	19	
Henry Whitlocke, - -	"	–	19	
Jesse Owen, - -	"	–	19	
William Baugh, - -	"	–	19	
Richard Adams, - -	Private,	–	19	
Willi. C. Adams, - -	"	–	19	
Richard W. Atkinson, -	"	–	19	
Peter E. Bentley, - -	"	–	19	
James R. Bentley, - -	"	–	19	
Daniel Bagby, - -	"	–	19	
Jordan Ballew, - -	"	–	19	
Richard Bass, - -	"	–	19	
Jacob W. Branch, - -	"	–	19	
Joseph Brackett, - -	"	–	19	
William A. Cocke, jr. -	"	–	19	
Abraham N. Cardozo, -	"	–	19	
Rich'd Crump, - -	"	–	19	
Moses N. Cardozo, - -	"	–	19	
David N. Cardozo, - -	"	–	19	
Gater Clarke, - -	"	–	19	
Isham W. Clements, -	"	–	19	
Josiah Cosby, - -	"	–	19	
Smith Cocke, - -	"	–	15	
William F. Carter, - -	"	–	2	
John S. Deane, - -	"	–	19	
John Elam, - -	"	–	19	
Richard Elam, - -	"	–	19	
Pleasant Farley, - -	"	–	19	
James Faris, - -	"	–	19	
James Forsel, - -	"	–	19	
Robert French, - -	"	–	19	
Henry Gordon, - -	"	–	19	
William Goodman, - -	"	–	19	
John O. Gilori, - -	"	–	19	
John Gordon, - -	"	–	19	
James M Hanes, - -	"	–	19	
William M. Heth, - -	"	–	19	
John Johnson, - -	"	–	19	

NAMES.	RANK.	TIME OF SERVICE.		REMARKS.
		Months.	Days.	
William Lewis, - -	Private,	–	19	
Edw'd Moseley, - -	"	–	19	
Edw'd Munford, - -	"	–	19	
Thomas Moore, - -	"	–	19	
Claiborne Mays, - -	"	–	19	
Edw'd Mye, - -	"	–	19	
Thomas Merryman, - -	"	–	19	
William C. Netherland, -	"	–	19	
Bennett Povall, - -	"	–	19	
Robert Pleasants, - -	"	–	19	
John T. Pleasants, - -	"	–	19	
William Sublett, - -	"	–	19	
William Swann, - -	"	–	19	
George Swann, - -	"	–	19	
Samuel Swann, sr. - -	"	–	19	
Samuel Swann, jr. - -	"	–	19	
John Swann, - -	"	–	19	
Elijah Smith, - -	"	–	19	
George Stratton, - -	"	–	19	
Littleberry Stegar, - -	"	–	19	
Thomas Smith, - -	"	–	19	
Ro. H. Saunders, - -	"	–	9	
Warren M. Seay, - -	"	–	19	
Richard Snead, - -	"	–	19	
Martin Tucker, - -	"	–	19	
Peyton Tucker, - -	"	–	19	
Charles Taylor, - -	"	–	19	
J. D. Turpin, - -	"	–	19	
William Tompkins, - -	"	–	15	
William Utley, - -	"	–	19	
Joseph Woodson, - -	"	–	19	
Thomas Wilkinson, - -	"	–	19	
William Wellburn, - -	"	–	19	
John Whitlocke, - -	"	–	19	
Stephen D. Watkins, -	"	–	19	

Captain Samuel Marshall's Company.

NAMES.	RANK.	TIME OF SERVICE.		REMARKS.
		Months.	Days.	
Samuel Marshall, - -	Captain,	1	8	
Samuel Davis, - -	"	–	23	
Richard Moseley, - -	Ensign,	1	8	
Nelson Cary, - -	Sergeant,	1	8	
Benjamin T. Davis, - -	"	1	8	
Lendrey J. Mann, - -	"	–	15	
Thomas Cheatham, - -	"	–	23	
Woodson Winfree, - -	"	–	23	
Jonathan Powell, - -	"	–	23	
Joseph Sublett, - -	Corporal,	1	8	
Mark Taylor, - - -	"	1	8	
William Gill, - - -	"	–	23	
Thomas Maxey, - -	"	–	23	
Jessee Taylor, - -	Drummer,	–	23	
William Gates, - -	Fifer,	–	23	
Creed Aminette, - -	Private,	–	23	
Henry Bowles, - -	"	–	23	
William Bowles, - -	"	–	23	
William Bransford, - -	"	–	23	
Pleasant S. Bowler, - -	"	–	23	
Henry Bowman, -	"	–	23	
James Blankenship, - -	"	–	23	
Litty Boatwright, - -	"	–	15	
David Battray, - -	"	–	15	
Matt. Baker, - - -	"	–	15	
James Criddle, - -	"	–	23	
Walthall Davis, - -	"	–	23	
Chesley Davis, - -	"	–	23	
Berkley Farley, - -	"	–	23	
Daniel Farley, - -	"	1	8	
Soammi Frost, - -	"	–	23	
Alexander Farley, - -	"	–	15	
Fielding Gardner, - -	"	–	15	
Joel Gathwright, - -	"	–	15	
David Hall, - - -	"	–	23	
Willey Jackson, - -	"	1	8	
Benjamin Jennings, - -	"	–	23	
Elias Jackson, - -	"	–	15	
John Jessee, - - -	"	–	15	
Jacob Ingram, - -	"	–	23	
Rolling M. Langden, - -	"	–	15	
David Lacy, - - -	"	–	23	
Elijah Maxey, - - -	"	1	8	
Eli Moore, - - -	"	1	8	
James Moore, - - -	"	–	15	
John Mosby - - -	"	–	23	
Linsey J. Mann, - -	"	–	23	
John Miller, - - -	"	–	23	
George Mosby, - -	"	–	15	
Robert McLaurin, - -	"	–	15	
Elijah Nunnally, - -	"	–	15	
William B. Pemberton, -	"	–	23	
William Smith, - -	"	–	23	
Thomas Stratton, - -	"	–	23	

NAMES.	RANK.	TIME OF SERVICE.		REMARKS.
		Months.	Days.	
Michal Squiggins, - -	Private.	–	15	
James Syms, - -	"	–	15	
John A. Smith, - -	"	–	15	
Jeff. Swann, - -	"	–	15	
Richard A. Swann, - -	"	–	15	
John H. Steger, - -	"	–	15	
Jessee Tillottson, - -	"	–	23	
Major Tinsley, - -	"	–	23	
Lapole Tencer, - -	"	–	23	
James Taylor, - -	"	–	23	
Anderson Traylor, - -	"	–	15	
Satterwhite Tyre, - -	"	–	15	
James R. Vaughan, - -	"	–	23	
Woodson Winfrey, - -	"	–	15	

(For rest of this company, see publication of Pay Rolls.)

MUSTER ROLL

Of Captain John Fariss' Company of the One Hundred and Seventeenth Regiment, Virginia Militia, Campbell County, in the Service from 30th August to the 15th September, 1814.

NAMES.	RANK.	TIME OF SERVICE. Months.	Days.	REMARKS.
John Fariss,	Captain,	–	16	
Richard Clark,	Lieutenant,	–	16	
Samuel Weaver,	Ensign,	–	16	
Ben. W. S. Cabell,	"	–	6	
William Thompson,	Qr. M. Serg't,	–	6	
Edmund W. Walker,	Sergeant,	–	16	
William Weaver,	"	–	6	
John Stratton,	"	–	6	Robt. Hunter sub.
Daniel Evans,	"	–	6	
Sampson Woodall,	Drummer,	–	16	
William Arrington,	Private,	–	6	R. Hunter sub.
Francis Armistead,	"	–	6	
Alexander Asher,	"	–	6	
John Brooks,	"	–	16	
Zachariah Brooks,	"	–	16	
William L. Burks,	"	–	6	Sub. for Thomas Burnett.
Thomas Burnett,	"	–	10	
Charles Burnett,	"	–	10	
William Carville,	"	–	16	Or Carwiles.
Zack. Carville,	"	–	10	Or Carwiles.
Absalom Dudley,	"	–	16	
Robert Elliott,	"	–	6	
William Fariss,	"	–	16	
Francis Fariss,	"	–	16	
Francis Grinstone,	"	–	6	
Elijah Garrett,	"	–	16	
Elijah Garvine,	"	–	6	
Thomas Holt,	"	–	6	
John Hazelwood,	"	–	16	
Edmund Haley,	"	–	16	
William Hamersley,	"	–	16	Sub. for John Stratton.
Archibald Jennings,	"	–	6	
Thomas Kitchen,	"	–	6	
John McCormick,	"	–	16	
William Mayberry,	"	–	16	
William G. Moore,	"	–	6	
Willis Martin,	"	–	6	
Benjamin Martin,	"	–	6	
William Mann,	"	–	6	
Samuel Martin,	"	–	6	
Robert D. Nash,	"	–	16	
David Perdew,	"	–	6	
David Patterson,	"	–	6	Chas. Burnett sub. for D. Patterson.
Martin O. Harrow,	"	–	6	
John Ray,	"	–	6	
John Reynolds,	"	–	16	
Archibald Robertson,	Private,	–	6	
Joseph Scott,	"	–	6	
John Still,	"	–	16	
James Shearer,	"	–	6	
Walter Taylor,	"	–	16	
David Terrence,	"	–	6	
Chesley Taylor,	"	–	6	
James Taylor,	"	–	6	
Robert Wright,	"	–	10	

PAY ROLL

Of Capt. Haley Coles' Company, of the Second Regiment of Virginia Militia, Chesterfield County, commanded by Col. John Ambler, from 28th August to 8th October 1814.

NAMES.	RANK.	Time of Service.		REMARKS.
		Months.	Days.	
Haley Cole, - -	Captain,	1	5	
Geo. W. Cole, - -	Lieutenant,	–	5	Promoted to Adj't.
John Ware, - -	Ensign,	1	5	
John H. Cole, - -	Sergeant,	1	5	
Pleasant Cole, - -	"	1	5	
Daniel Cheatham, - -	"	1	5	
Isham Cheatham, - -	"	1	5	
Jabez Rucks, - -	"	1	5	
Joseph Cole, - -	"	1	5	
Josiah Conway, - -	Corporal,	1	5	
Mark F. Flournoy, - -	"	1	5	
Edward Worsham, - -	"	1	5	
Zacheus Cheatham, - -	"	1	5	
Edward Hill, - -	"	1	5	
Henry Roberts, - -	"	1	5	
James H. Spears, - -	"	1	5	
James Lockett, - -	"	1	5	
Jesse Taylor, - -	Drummer,	1	5	
Silas Powell, - -	Fifer,	1	5	
Peter Archer, - -	Private,	1	5	
Arch'd Bass, - -	"	1	5	
Young Beazely, - -	"	1	5	
Thomas Barnes, - -	"	1	5	
Henry Bridgewater, - -	"	1	5	
Rich'd Beasely, - -	"	1	5	
Robert Baugh, - -	"	1	5	
Henry Beazely, - -	"	1	5	
William Beasley, - -	"	1	5	
Fleming Bowles, - -	"	1	5	
William Bragg, - -	"	1	5	
Arch'd Bridgewater, - -	"	1	5	
George Blankinship, - -	"	1	5	
Henry Baily, - -	"	1	5	
William Blankinship, - -	"	1	5	
Thomas Cheatham, Jr., -	"	1	5	
Henry Cheatham, - -	"	1	5	
Fountain Cheatham, - -	"	1	5	
Jackson Cashon, - -	"	1	5	
Henry Cox, - -	"	1	5	
Elam Cheatham, - -	"	1	5	
Francis Cheatham, - -	"	1	5	
Francis Cashon, - -	"	1	5	
Samuel Cashon, - -	"	1	5	
Thomas Cheatham, Sr., -	"	1	5	
Johua Condry, - -	"	1	5	
Joel Cashon, - -	"	1	5	
Jeremiah Clarke, - -	"	1	5	
James Clibourne, - -	"	1	5	
Hatcher Clarke, - -	"	1	5	
John Foulkes, - -	"	1	5	
King Fowler, - -	"	1	5	
Joel Foulkes, - -	"	1	5	
Seth W. Flournoy, - -	"	1	5	
Thomas Flournoy, - -	"	1	5	

NAMES.	RANK.	Time of Service.		REMARKS.
		Months.	Days.	
James Foulkes, - -	Private,	1	5	
John Gates, - -	"	1	5	
William Gates, - -	"	1	5	
John Hill, - -	"	1	5	
William Hill, - -	"	1	5	
Wolcoat Lacy, - -	"	1	5	
Joshua Lacy, - -	"	1	5	
Averett Moore, - -	"	1	5	
Haley Moore, - -	"	1	5	
Alexander Moore, - -	"	1	5	
Daniel Nunnally, - -	"	1	5	
Francis Patram, - -	"	1	5	
John Pringle, - -	"	1	5	
John Purdie, - -	"	1	5	
Lewis Puckett, - -	"	1	5	
Elijah Rudd, - -	"	1	5	
John A. Rudd, - -	"	1	5	
John Rudd, - -	"	1	5	
Leonard Rudd, - -	"	1	5	
Robert Rudd, - -	"	1	5	
Arch'd Rudd, - -	"	1	5	
Hezekiah Rudd, - -	"	1	5	
Frederick Rudd, - -	"	1	5	
John Robertson, - -	"	1	5	
Austin Spears, - -	"	1	5	
Richard Sizer, - -	"	1	5	
Joseph R. Simms, - -	"	1	5	
Mack Wilkinson, - -	"	1	5	
Peter Wilkinson, - -	"	1	5	
John Wilkinson, - -	"	1	5	

PAY ROLL

Of Captain Alexander Gibbs's Company, of the Second Regiment of Virginia Militia, Chesterfield County, in the Service of the United States, commanded by Col. John Ambler, from the 28th August to the 30th November 1814.

NAMES	RANK.	Time of Service.		REMARKS.
		Months.	Days.	
Alexander Gibbs,	Captain,	3	6	
James Martin,	Lieutenant,	3	6	
Leroy Branch,	O. Sergeant,	2	22	
Isaac R. Cansfield,	O. Sergeant,	3	6	
Edm'd A. May,	Sergeant,	2	29	
Vaiden Moore,	"	2	21	
Thomas Rowlett,	"	3	6	
Nelson Farmer,	"	3	6	
Isham Vaiden,	"	3	6	
William Dance,	Corporal,	3	6	
Drury Moore,	"	3	6	
Samuel Bowles,	"	3	6	
William Gary,	"	3	6	
William Jackson,	"	3	6	
Henry Roberts,	"	1	25	
John Chalkley,	"	3	6	
Robert McClellan,	"	3	6	
Joel Andrews,	Private,	3	6	
Benja. Andrews,	"	3	6	
Mark Andrews,	"	3	6	
Thomas Brittain,	"	3	6	
Edmund Belcher,	"	3	6	
George Blankinship,	"	1	25	
Daniel P. Berry,	"	3	6	
John Birch,	"	3	6	
Elias Brooks,	"	2	21	
William Blankinship,	"	1	25	
David I. Butler,	"	2	9	
Henry Bailee,	"	1	25	
Bartley Chalkley,	"	3	6	
Obed. Chalkley,	"	3	6	
Josiah Chalkley,	"	3	6	
Archer Chalkley,	"	3	6	
David Chalkley,	"	3	6	
Jeremiah Clarke,	"	1	25	
James Clibourne,	"	1	15	
Hatcher Clarke,	"	1	25	
Thomas Dance,	"	3	6	
John Dance,	"	3	6	
Josiah Dunnavant,	"	3	6	
Daniel Dishman,	"	2	21	
William Dunnavant,	"	2	22	
John Evans,	"	1	25	Dead.
Peyton Fuqua,	"	3	6	
Thomas Flournoy,	"	1	25	
Daniel Gill,	"	3	6	
Robert Gill,	"	1		
William Gill,	"	3	6	
Goode Gill,	"	3	6	
Ben. Gates,	"	3	6	
Edmund Gary,	"	3	6	
John Gates,	"	3	6	
William Gates,	"	3	6	
Ben. Goodman,	"	2	7	

NAMES.	RANK.	Time of Service.		REMARKS.
		Months.	Days.	
George Greenhow, - -	Private,	1	27	
Joshua Lacy, - -	"	1	25	
John Mann, - -	"	3	6	
Jeremiah Mall, - -	"	3	6	
Alexander Moore, - -	"	1	25	
Henry McClannon, - -	"	3	6	
William Newby, - -	"	3	6	
Daniel Nobles, - -	"	3	6	
Archer W. Perkinson, - -	"	3	6	
Worsham Perkinson, - -	"	3	6	
Dennis Parten, - -	"	2	21	
John Purdie, - -	"	1	25	
Silas Powell, - -	"	1	25	
Henry Roberts, - -	"	1	10	
Frederick Rudd, - -	"	1	10	
Richard Spain, - -	"	3	6	
Thomas Totty, - -	"	3	6	
John Truman, - -	"	1	10	
George Vaiden, - -	"	3	6	
John Whiteford, - -	"	3	6	
Lodowick Wilson, - -	"	3	6	
Dickerson Wells, - -	"	3	6	

PAY ROLL

Of Captain Ben. Goode's Company, Second Regiment of Virginia Militia, First Brigade, commanded by Col. John Ambler, in the Service of the United States, Chesterfield County, from 28th August to 30th November 1814.

NAMES.	RANK.	Time of Service.		REMARKS.
		Months.	Days.	
Ben. Goode, - -	Captain,	3	6	
Samuel Clay, - -	Lieutenant,	1	29	
Samuel Hancock, - -	"	3	6	
Thomas Graves, - -	Ensign,	3	6	
Spencer Wooldridge, - -	Sergeant,	1	14	
John Robertson, - -	"	3	6	
Major Horner, - -	"	3	6	
Felix Fergusson, - -	"	3	6	
Edm'd Lockett, - -	"	3	6	
George Beckley, - -	"	2	21	
Abner Baugh, - -	"	3	6	
Rowlett Covington, - -	"	3	6	
John Hix, - -	Corporal,	2	21	
John Varner, - -	"	3	6	
William Wilson, - -	"	3	6	
Robert Hawkins, - -	"	3	6	
John Goode, - -	"	3	6	
Ben. V. Jackson, - -	"	3	6	
Milton Cary, - -	"	3	6	
Jeremiah Ashbrooke, - -	Private,	3	6	
Wiley Andrews, - -	"	3	6	
William Atkins, - -	"	3	6	
Erasmus Andrews, - -	"	2	21	C. Blankinship sub.
George Baily, - -	"	2	21	Thomas Barnes sub.
John Burton, - -	"	3	6	
William Baily, - -	"	3	6	
William Baugh, - -	"	3	6	
Daniel Brodie, - -	"	3	6	
Jeremiah Baugh, - -	"	2	21	
John Brooks, - -	"	1	29	
Thomas Belcher, - -	"	3	6	
Laban Blankenship, - -	"	3	6	
Chastain Blankinship, - -	"	–	15	See E. Andrews.
Thomas Beazley, - -	"	–	15	See Jno. A. Pride.
John Bowman, - -	"	–	15	See Jesse Snellings.
Thomas Barnes, - -	"	–	15	See George Baily.
Jesse Cashion, - -	"	3	6	
William Couts, - -	"	3	6	
Hickerson Cox, - -	"	3	6	
Francis Covington, - -	"	3	6	
John Covington, - -	"	3	6	
Gardner Clarke, - -	"	3	6	
Charles Clarke, - -	"	3	6	
Peter Clarke, - -	"	3	6	
John Crump, - -	"	3	6	
Fountain Cheatham, - -	"	–	15	See Isham Graves.
Andrew Costly, - -	"	–	15	See Daniel.
Henry Dillion, - -	"	2	21	
Ezekiel Davis, - -	"	3	6	
Haley Dunnavant, - -	"	3	6	
John Deaton, - -	"	3	6	
Thomas Dyer, - -	"	–	15	See Nelson Flournoy.
Thomas Dean, - -	"	–	15	See Jeremiah Hancock.
Robert Elam, - -	"	3	6	

NAMES.	RANK.	Time of Service. Months.	Days.	REMARKS.
Joshua Elam,	Private,	3	6	
Ammon Elam,	"	1	4	
Jonathan Eastham,	"	2	21	
Boling or Roland Elam,	"	–	15	See John Wilkerson.
Nelson Flournoy,	"	2	21	Thos. Dyer sub.
Jeremiah Fowler,	"	3	6	
Gardner Fowler,	"	3	6	
Samuel Fuqua,	"	2	21	Ro. Stokes sub.
Mark Farmer,	"	3	6	
Bernard Farmer,	"	–	15	
William Fergusson,	"	–	15	See Henry Dillion.
John Foulkes,	"	–	15	See John Purdie.
Isham Graves,	"	2	21	Fount. Cheatham sub.
Edward Goode,	"	2	21	
Francis Gordon,	"	–	15	
John Hopkins,	"	3	6	
Spencer Hancock,	"	2	20	
James Hall,	"	3	6	
Ben. Hatcher,	"	2	21	Wiley Jackson sub.
Jeremiah Hancock,	"	2	21	Thomas Deane sub.
William Hix,	"	3	6	
Daniel Johnson,	"	3	6	
David Johnson,	"	3	6	
Watson Johnson,	"	3	6	
John Ironmonger,	"	–	15	
Wiley Jackson,	"	–	15	
John Labarreaire,	"	3	6	
Rich'd Loving,	"	3	6	
William Martin,	"	3	6	
James Moles,	"	3	6	
Micajah Mason,	"	3	6	
John Merinder,	"	3	6	
Joseph G. Mann,	"	3	6	
Christian Mann,	"	3	6	Or Chastain.
Cain Mann,	"	3	6	
John Newby,	"	3	6	
Zachariah Puckett,	"	3	6	
Joshua Powell,	"	3	6	
John A. Pride,	"	2	21	Thos. Beasley sub.
John Purdue,	"	2	21	Or Purdie, J. Foulkes sub.
Thomas Purdue,	"	3	6	Or Purdie.
Daniel Patram,	"	2	21	And'w Cortly sub.
John Parker,	"	–	15	See Edw'd Watkins
Robert Royall,	"	2	21	Bernard Turner sub.
Dan'l Rowlett,	"	3	6	
William Rowlett,	"	3	6	
Gabriel Rowlett,	"	3	6	
James Robertson,	"	–	15	See Henry Tatum.
Jesse Snellings,	"	2	21	Jno. Bowman sub.
John Sorrel,	"	3	6	
Alex'r Smith,	"	3	6	
Thomas Smith,	"	2	21	
Isham Smith,	"	3	6	
John Smith,	"	3	6	
Granville Smith,	"	3	6	
Wm. B. Smith,	"	3	6	
James Stuart,	"	–	15	See John Walthall.
Henry Tatum,	"	2	21	John Robertson sub.
Henry Turpin,	"	3	6	
Stephen Turner,	"	3	6	
John Tarrant,	"	3	6	
Solomon Vaiden,	"	1	4	
John Wilkinson,	"	2	21	Roland Elam sub.
Sam'l Wilkinson,	"	3	6	

NAMES.	RANK.	Time of Service.		REMARKS.
		Months.	Days.	
Edw'd Watkins, - -	Private,	2	21	Jno. Parker sub.
Henry Williams, - -	"	3	6	
Rich'd Womack, - -	"	3	6	
Joseph Whitefield, - -	"	3	6	
Francis Walthall, - -	"	3	6	
John Walthall, - -	"	2	21	James Stuart sub.
Green Wood, - -	"	3	6	
Henry Woodcock, - -	"	3	6	
Littleton Wilson, - -	"	3	6	
Thos. Wilson, - -	"	3	6	
Creed Wilson, - -	"	3	6	

PAY ROLL

Of Captain John Hewett's Company, Second Regiment of Virginia Militia, in the Service of the United States, commanded by Colonel John Ambler, Chesterfield County, from the 1st September to the 8th December 1814.

NAMES.	RANK.	Time of Service.		REMARKS.
		Months.	Days.	
John Hewett, - -	Captain,	2	17	
Thomas E. Everett, - -	Lieutenant,	1	8	
William Tinsley, - -	"	1	2	
John W. Holt, - -	Ensign,	3	9	
Richard Davis, - -	"	3	9	
John Robinson, - -	Ord. Serg't,	3	9	
T. W. W. Davies, - -	Q. M. Serg't,	1	25	David Thomas sub.
George Williams, - -	"	3	9	
Joseph R. Carter, - -	Sergeant,	3	9	
Peyton Foster, - -	"	3	9	
John B. Witt, - -	"	3	9	
Samuel Mitchell, - -	Corporal,	3	9	
Richard Bagwell, - -	"	3	9	
Charles Bayne, - -	"	3	9	
John Hewett, - -	"	3	9	
John M. Eubank, - -	"	3	9	
Edmond Burton, - -	"	3	9	
Roderick Waugh, - -	"	3	9	
James L. Cobbs, - -	"	3	9	
Howell Robinson, - -	Drummer,	1	16	
Jabez Beard, - -	Fifer,	3	9	
Thomas Atkinson, - -	Private,	3	17	
Jesse Adams, - -	"	3	17	
Adam Beard, - -	"	3	9	
Thomas Bondurant, - -	"	3	9	
Nat. Butler, - -	"	3	9	
Waddy Bocock, - -	"	3	9	
Charles Baker, - -	"	1	10	Or Baber, sub. for W. O. Hurt.
John Crumpecker, - -	"	3	9	
Cornelius Cobbs, - -	"	3	9	
Pleasant Canaday, - -	"	3	9	
Claiborne Dowdy, - -	"	3	9	
John Dearing, - -	"	3	9	
Amos Elliott, - -	"	3	9	
William Elliott, - -	"	3	9	
George Ellis, - -	"	3	9	
Jesse Edens, - -	"	3	9	
Alexander Edens, - -	"	3	9	
Abram Fuqua, - -	"	3	9	
Booker Foster, - -	"	3	9	
Richard Foster, - -	"	3	9	
Thomas Floyd, - -	"	3	9	
William Foster, - -	"	3	9	
Robert Gay, - -	"	3	9	
Robert Gibbs, - -	"	2	17	Drury Hicks sub.
Josiah Garrett, - -	"	3	9	
Peterson Hawkins, - -	"	3	9	
Pleasant Howard, - -	"	3	9	
Robert Howard, - -	"	3	9	
William O. Hurt, - -	"	1	19	Charles Baber sub.
Mesheck Haile, - -	"	3	9	
Stephen Hix, - -	"	3	9	
George Hurt, - -	"	3	9	
Drury Hicks, - -	"	2	17	See Robert Gibbs.

NAMES.	RANK.	*Time of Service.* Months.	Days.	REMARKS.
William Hatcher, - -	Private,	3	9	
Edward Hatcher, - -	"	3	9	
Arch'd Hatcher, - -	"	3	9	
Sandford Holley. - -	"	1	10	
Julius W. Hatcher, - -	"	3	9	
Bobinson Hilton, - -	"	3	9	
James Harris, - -	"	3	9	
William Humphrey, - -	"	3	9	
John Hunter, - -	"	3	9	
Willis Hunter, - -	"	3	9	
John Hughes, - -	"	3	9	Sub. for Justin Wills.
Ambrose Jones, - -	"	3	9	
Joseph Krantz, - -	"	3	9	
David Lockett, - -	"	3	9	
Richard Lee, - -	"	3	9	
James H. Mitchell, - -	"	3	9	
Robert Mitchell, - -	"	3	9	
Joseph Mitchell, - -	"	3	9	
Jesse Mitchell, - -	"	3	9	
Charles McGehee, - -	"	3	9	
Samuel Mead, - -	"	3	9	
Hugh McCraw, - -	"	1	8	
Owen Milnor, - -	"	3	9	
Robert Milnor, - -	"	3	9	
Ben. Milam, - -	"	3	9	
Charles Milam, - -	"	3	9	
Paschal Nance, - -	"	3	9	
Paschal W. Nance, - -	"	3	9	
George Nowell, - -	"	3	9	
Joel Nance, - -	"	3	9	
Caleb Newman, - -	"	3	9	
Thomas Overacre, - -	"	3	9	
Jesse Roberts, - -	"	3	9	
Thomas Roberts, - -	"	3	9	
John Robinson, - -	"	3	9	
Caleb Reynolds, - -	"	3	9	
William Rucker, - -	"	3	9	
Ben. Roberts, - -	"	3	9	
Philip Roberts. - -	"	3	9	
John Rice, - -	"	3	9	
Lewis Saunders, - -	"	3	9	
John Setty, - -	"	3	9	
Ben. Sheppard, - -	"	3	9	
Nat. Stewart, - -	"	3	9	
Fleming Thomason, - -	"	3	9	
William Trent, - -	"	3	9	
Wesley Tracey, - -	"	3	9	
Joshua Thomas, - -	"	3	9	
John Tracey, - -	"	3	9	
Edw'd M. Tracey, - -	"	3	9	
John Terry, - -	"	3	9	Sub. for John Trusty.
Creed Tucker, - -	"	3	9	
David Thomas, - -	"	1	14	Substitute for J. W. W.
Woodson Wills, - -	"	3	9	Davies.
Ignatius Wills, - -	"	2	9	Silas Wood substitute.
Justin Wills, - -	"	1	24	John Hughes sub.
Jesse White, - -	"	3	9	
George White, - -	"	3	9	
John Wigginton, - -	"	3	9	
John Witt, - -	"	3	9	
Uriah White, - -		2	17	
George Wigginton, - -	"	3	9	
Alexander Waugh, - -	"	3	9	
William Wright, - -	"	3	9	
Joseph Whilton, - -	"	3	9	
Nicholas Waugh, - -	"	3	9	
Silas Wood, - -	"	1	-	See Ignatius Wills.

PAY ROLL

Of Captain Edward Johnson's Company, of the Second Regiment of Virginia Militia, Chesterfield County, in the Service of the United States, commanded by Gen. Wm. Chamberlayne, from 28th August to 30th November 1814.

NAMES.	RANK.	Time of Service.		REMARKS.
		Months.	Days.	
Edward Johnson,	Captain,	2	27	
William Goff,	Lieutenant,	3	6	
Isaac Davis,	"	3	6	
John Lord,	Ensign,	3	6	
Young Pankey,	"	3	6	
James Fore,	Sergeant,	3	6	
Jacob Lord,	"	3	6	
Thomas Drake,	"	3	6	
Jno. W. Dandridge,	"	3	6	
Henry Branch,	"	3	6	
Wilson Layne,	"	1	2	
James Gray,	"	1	16	Hugh Bragg sub.
Alex'r Brooking,	"	–	15	
Frederick Kuhn,	Corporal,	3	6	
Austin Porter,	"	3	6	
John Weisiger,	"	3	6	
William Simpson,	"	3	6	
William Giles,	"	3	6	
David Luckadoe,	"	3	6	
John Fowler,	"	3	6	
Bennett Goode,	"	–	24	Linsey J. Mann.
William Lang,	"	2	1	
Rich'd W. Crouch,	–	–	15	
Ro. H. Adams,	Private,	3	6	
Jos. C. Adkins,	"	3	6	
James Adkins,	"	3	6	
Rich'd Atkinson,	"	2	6	Thomas Waller sub.
And'w Atkins,	"	3	6	
James Ames,	"	1	23	W. S. Winfree sub.
Watkins Anderson,	"	1	25	John Porter sub.
James Armstrong,	"	2	21	
John Brooks,	"	3	6	
Geo. W. Branch,	"	3	6	
Levin H. Bowles,	"	3	6	
Charles Bricken,	"	3	6	
William Brightwell,	"	3	6	
John Boston,	"	3	6	Or Booton.
John G. Brown,	"	3	6	
William Brown,	"	3	6	
James Burnett.				
Thomas Bass,	"	1	10	Archer Bass sub.
John Brimmall,	"	3	6	
John Burton,	"	3	6	
Blair Burwell,	"	1	10	Wm. Hill sub.
Thos. A. Brooking,	"	2	21	
Rich'd Beasley,	"	1	6	Sub. Jno. Cardwell.
Archer Bass,	"	1	26	" Thos. Bass.
Hugh Bragg,	"	1	20	" Jas. Gray.
William Bragg,	"	2	3	" Ben. Watkins
Anderson Bowles,	"	2	19	" Royal Martin
Henry Beasley,	"	1	25	" Henry Moody
William Butcher,	"	1	22	" Archer Parter
Martin Chalkley,	"	3	6	
John Caskie,	"	1	15	R. W. Crouch his sub.

NAMES.	RANK.	Time of Service.		REMARKS.
		Months.	Days.	
John Cardwell,	Private,	2	–	Rich'd Beasley sub.
Asa Chapman,	"	1	21	John Hill.
Francis Cheatham,	"	2	21	
Rich'd W. Crouch,	"	1	6	See John Caskie.
Fred'k Cheatham,	"	–	15	
Jacob A. Flournoy,	"	3	6	
Wells Floyd,	"	3	6	
William Fuqua,	"	1	20	New. Newby his sub.
David Farmer,	"	3	6	
Daniel Fergusson,	"	1	25	Sub. J. B. Sheppard.
Bartho. Fernier,	"	1	6	" Ro. Vaughan.
William Goode,	"	3	6	
Thomas Gibbs,	"	3	6	
Pleasant Gordon,	"	3	6	
Charles Graves,	"	3	6	
Fielding Gardner,	"	2	20	Sub. Rich'd Michiaux.
Francis Girard,	"	2	23	" Jno. Rozell.
Ben. Horner,	"	3	6	
Rich'd C. Hudson,	"	3	6	
William Hunley,	"	3	6	
Thomas Holt,	"	3	6	
William Hill,	"	1	26	Sub. Blair Burwell.
John Hill,	"	1	15	" Asa Chapman.
Neal C. Kelley,	"	3	6	
Elisha Keen,	"	3	6	
William P. Lancaster,	"	3	6	
Drury L. Luckadoe,	"	3	6	
Thomas E. Lacy,	"	3	6	
John McCollum,	"	2	–	Sub. by Jno. A. Rudd.
James Mills,	"	3	6	
Riley Moore,	"	3	6	
David Morrissett,	"	3	6	
Royal Martin,	"	–	17	Sub. by And. Bowles.
Rich'd Micheaux,	"	–	16	" by Field. Gardner.
Elisha Meredith,	"	3	6	
Henry Moody,	"	1	11	" by Henry Beasley.
Linsey J. Mann,	"	1	27	" by Bennett Goode.
Rich'd Moxley,	"	2	28	" by Sam'l Winfree.
Matthew Newby,	"	3	6	
Daniel Nunnally,	"	3	6	
Newman Newby,	"	1	1	Sub. Wm. Fuqua.
Josiah R. Olds,	"	3	6	
Francis Patram,	"	3	6	
Martin Phillips,	"	3	6	
Nelson Phillips,	"	3	6	
James Perdue,	"	3	6	
Arch'd Parten,	"	1	14	" by Wm. Butcher.
John Porter,	"	2	1	" W. Anderson.
John Rozell,	"	–	13	" Francis Girard.
Wm. Radford,	"	3	6	
Jno. A. Rudd,	"	1	6	" Jno. McCollom.
John Simpson,	"	3	6	
Turner Sharp,	"	3	6	
James Short,	"	3	6	
William Short,	"	3	6	
Wm. Stephenson,	"	3	6	
Spencer Smith,	"	3	6	
Jesse B. Sheppard,	"	1	11	" by Dan'l Ferguson.
George Sallie,	"	2	21	
Josiah Taylor,	"	3	6	
William Turpin,	"	3	6	
Robert Vaughan,	"	2	–	" by B. Fernier.
James Willett,	"	3	6	
Thomas Waller,	"	1	–	" by R. Atkinson.
Sam'l Winfree,	"	–	8	" by R. Moxley.

NAMES.	RANK.	Time of Service.		REMARKS.
		Months.	Days.	
Francis O. Watkins, - -	Private,	3	6	
John Walden, - -	"	3	6	
Ben. Watkins, - -	"	1	3	Sub. by Wm. Bragg.
Walter S. Winfree, - -	"	1	13	" " Jas. Ames.
Edward Wright, - -	"	3	6	
Abner Winfree, - -	"	3	6	
Miles Watkins, - -	"	1	7	

-A-

www.ingramcontent.com/pod-product-compliance
Lightning Source LLC
LaVergne TN
LVHW061237100826
845148LV00008B/976
* 9 7 8 0 7 8 8 4 7 7 7 4 4 *